Praise for "John Guillermin"

Hopefully, *John Guillermin: The Man, The Myth, The Movies* will prompt many a film student to re-view and reassess the man and his contributions, without which the film industry would not be what it is today. At the least, this volume fills a major gap in film history literature and should be included in serious film biography or history holdings as a foundation work.

—*Diane Donovan,*
Senior Reviewer, Midwest Book Review

John Guillermin: The Man, The Myth, The Movies . . . pays overdue serious critical attention to what was by any measure a remarkable body of work. Guillermin started in British B pictures in the late 1940s, and within a decade established himself as one of the leading directors in England. . . . There's no work about a film director quite like it, at least none that I've read. . . . It's an unusual, idiosyncratic, fascinating book about a neglected artist of immense talent; it's also a love story.

—*Stephen Vagg, FilmInk.com*

This is a fascinating look at the life and career of the director. . . . It's a brilliant read, insightful, educational and passionate . . . . Thoughtfully written and exceptionally presented, . . . it is a fascinating book loaded with anecdotes and trivia about an enigmatic man and a tremendous array of films. The book is filled with great imagery, alongside reproductions of handwritten notes from Guillermin himself. It's a book that will have you reaching back to watch the John Guillermin films you love, as well as seeking out those you never knew existed.

—*Niall Browne, Movies in Focus*

John Guillermin

JOHN GUILLERMIN

THE MAN
THE MYTH
THE MOVIES

EDITED BY MARY GUILLERMIN

PRECOCITY PRESS

Copyright © 2020 by Mary Guillermin. All rights reserved.

Published by Precocity Press, Los Angeles, CA
Editorial Direction and Editor: Susan Peters
Creative Director and Designer: Susan Shankin
Cover Designer: Barbara Garibay

No part of this book may be reproduced or transmitted in any form or by any means, electronic or mechanical, including photocopying, recording, or by an information storage and retrieval system—except by a reviewer who may quote brief passages in a review to be printed in a magazine, newspaper, or on the web—without permission in writing from the publisher. For permission requests, email the publisher at: susan@precocitypress.com

ISBN: 978-1-7362174-0-5

DEDICATION

John Guillermin was, even in his 80s, an irrepressible life-force, funny, cantankerous, profane, sophisticated, urbane.

A gentleman of the old school, a pilot in the RAF during WWII, and later an eloquent filmmaker of taste and judgment—his movies speak for themselves, and also for him—for he is there, living inside them, his personality tumbling out in every reel.

Farewell, sir, you were one of a kind—and your like will not ever come again. John Guillermin, 1925–2015.

—Nick Redman
Founder of Twilight Time

CONTENTS

Preface	ix
Poem and Introduction | Mary Guillermin	xiii

PART ONE — 1

1. The Early Films 1950 to 1966 | Mary Guillermin	3
2. Deo Profundis | John Guillermin	13
3. Early Days with Adelphi Films | Vic Pratt and Kate Lees	25
4. Irascible Iconoclast | Neil Sinyard	55
5. A Lover of Femininity in All its Fullness | Mary Guillermin	75
6. Double Header: Two Children's Films | Neil Sinyard and Mary Guillermin	97

PART TWO — 105

7. The Heart of the Matter 1965 | Mary Guillermin	107
8. Girl on the Edge: *Rapture* | Melanie Williams	111
9. Filming *Rapture* | Brian Hoyle	127
10. Rapture in the #MeToo Era | Mary Guillermin	155
11. Interlude: Savage Spectacles | Olaf Möller	169

PART THREE	**177**
12. The American Years 1968 to 1988	Mary Guillermin	179
13. *The Towering Inferno:* Saved by a Fiery Visionary	Brett A. Hart	187
14. How John Guillermin Inspired and Influenced Me	Brett A. Hart	203
15. The Big One: *King Kong*	Ray Morton	209
16. A Gorgeous Panoply: *Death on the Nile*	Sarah Street	245
Epilogue. Life After Directing 1998 to 2015	267
Appendix A. Films That Never Got Made and Other Complaints	271
Appendix B. From Crazy to Sane: Or Am I?: The Marriage Section	275
Appendix C. Love Poems from John to Mary	281
Notes	289
Bibliography	293
Acknowledgments	295
Biographies	297

PREFACE

THIS IS THE FIRST BOOK to be published about the life and career of John Guillermin, a prodigiously gifted but critically neglected filmmaker. The contributors come from a wide range of backgrounds, enabling the book to reach out to an audience of both film scholars and film fans, an aspiration of which John would have undoubtedly approved, as he was justly proud of the enjoyment his films have given to millions of people worldwide. It also contains a never-before-published autobiographical essay by the director which throws new light on the man and the films. Permeating the whole text is the vision and wisdom of his widow, Mary, whose sympathetic and expert guidance to all connected with the project could be said to illuminate the text from within.

An initial spur to the compilation of this volume came, ironically, from a negative source. In the "Hall of Fame" section of the 2016 Oscars ceremony, in which the audience is invited to remember distinguished film personnel who had died the previous year, the name of John Guillermin was omitted from the parade of celebrities commemorated. This was an unpardonable oversight as well as poor film history. He had, after all, directed some of Hollywood's most popular big-screen extravaganzas: e.g. the war epic, *The Blue Max*, the disaster movie, *The Towering Inferno*, the large-scale remake of *King Kong*. British cineastes would have equally fond memories of movies he made in the UK before his move to Hollywood, films as varied and diverse as *Town on Trial, I Was*

Monty's Double, Never Let Go, The Waltz of the Toreadors, and *Guns at Batasi.* Perhaps this variety of output was the reason behind the critical underestimation. He seemed capable of turning his hands to anything; he was a difficult director to pigeonhole; and auteurist critics have always struggled with the idea of versatility. Not that his films were impersonal, as the accounts in this book will make clear and fellow professionals recognized. Charlton Heston, who had worked with giants like Welles, Wyler and Stevens, prized Guillermin highly; and, as early as 1961, a cinematic master like Joseph Losey, whose films have some affinities with Guillermin's, was citing him as one of the British directors who had what he called "a signature," a recognizable style which, in Losey's view, put him in the class of Carol Reed, Alexander Mackendrick, Lindsay Anderson and Seth Holt. Why, then, the neglect, and the necessity for revaluation and a restoration of justice?

"Early on I realized I had some cinematic talent," Guillermin said, but he recognized that it is one thing possessing ability and potential; it is quite another finding the material and being given the opportunity to express it. Like many a director before and since, in order to make a living, he was dependent on what was on offer. "*Rapture* is the nearest I've ever got to shaping a film my way," he said. It is not surprising that this extraordinary, daring and compassionate film, emanating from a big Hollywood studio but which nevertheless looks like vintage French New Wave, looms large in our reappraisal. Ignored on its first release, its reputation has climbed over the years; and for many who were encountering it for the first time on its Blu-ray release in 2014 (UK; 2011 US), it must have come as a revelation.

If *Rapture* is the film that raises the whole profile of Guillermin's career and particularly signals the necessity for reassessment, it would be fair to say that what lifts this book onto another plane is the input of his widow, Mary Guillermin, whose passion has been its driving force. Her intimacy with the subject inevitably gives an additional dimension to the films, even to the way he used the camera, and her assessment of his personality and how it carried into his work has a unique authority. It was sometimes said of him that he might have gone further in the profession if he had got on better with the producers or studio heads he dealt with. He had a reputation for volatility and found interaction difficult with people in authority, for which his autobiographical essay offers some explanation (insubordination is something of a recurrent sub-text in his films). Mary brings a wife's perspective to that aspect of his personality, just as her experience as a psychotherapist is shown in her sensitivity to his understanding of the theme of women in peril, which he directs with such urgency. The whole project has been enriched by the bravery of her self-revelations and how these have fed into her appreciation of her husband's work; by her devotion to his memory and her unwavering conviction of his talent, and by her determination to bring it at last to public and critical attention. Very few critical studies of film directors are also a love story. This one is.

—NEIL SINYARD
Emeritus Professor of Film Studies at the University of Hull, UK

TO JOHN,
MY BELOVED, TWO YEARS DEAD.

The landscape we once drove over is
stained with your name, your scent, your shape.

You hover over me and draw me into the arms
of my memories of flat, crisp Essex fields,
and the pheasant I plucked from the road,
freshly dead, and dripping.

This was a land of contrasts, the sweet joy of new presence,
of sharing, of calling your name, and the baleful howls
of too much whisky, the heavy steel of your grim depression.

But I knew the same land, not the whisky shouts,
but the jubilant highs, the steep valley lows,
and so I made my home against your side, nestled against
the warm love you gave that throbbed in your heart
like a beating, visible vein in your neck.

No regrets. Not ever. Few have been loved
as you loved me, and I, you,
no matter the days of darkness and despair
we weathered each for, and with, the other.

Those who have loved, and have been loved,
so deep in the veins of the heart, are wise
to forbear some few imperfections.

—MARY GUILLERMIN

October 6, 2017, driving to Stansted Airport, Essex, England

INTRODUCTION

My Husband Was Many Things

MARY GUILLERMIN

My husband was an artist. I am a psychotherapist, not a film critic, but I can the see the innovation in his framing of shots, his imaginative angles and his use of sound and hand-held cameras to conjure up emotional states that overpower the character (and the audience) and I know them to be unusual in the world of 1950s and '60s British cinema. Neil Sinyard, one of the contributors herein, wrote about Joseph Losey, "The characteristic that most distinguishes [his] early films from other English films of their time is the energy of his style ... British cinema of this time seemed mostly devoid of film stylists: form tended to be subordinate to content." He could have written that about my husband. John himself considered *Rapture* (1965) to be the only film he directed that wholly satisfied his vision as an artist.

My husband was a difficult man. He told me so himself: "Don't marry me. I'm impossible." Dino de Laurentiis nicknamed him "The Wild Man." He fought with management his whole career. He yelled at the crew when things didn't match his vision. Charlton Heston said of him that he "was an imaginative and skillful director with an irascible streak."

My husband was a passionate man. Born to French parents under the steely-grey skies of London town, and a sensitive, feeling child set amongst stolid English schoolboys, we know from his own words in the opening essay of this book how he suffered for his Frenchness. To the end of his life, he played pool with shouts of glee, loudly stamping his cue on the floor when he potted the ball, and he often mimed playing an imaginary saxophone or clarinet with absolute intensity to every jazz number that moved him. While listening to the slow movements of Mozart's piano concertos, he would turn to me and ask, with a hint of suspiciousness, whether I was crying too.

My husband was a lover of femininity. He understood and respected women. His early female characters give voice to thoughts and sentiments not commonly (if ever?) seen in 1950s films, and it is my belief that his childhood experiences of school bullying and oppression were transmuted into understanding how women feel when threatened by male power. These understandings are explored in my essay focusing on his attitudes to the portrayal of women and femininity.

The other contributors to this book include Kate Lees, owner of Adelphi Films (and granddaughter of Arthur Dent, the founder of the independent Adelphi Studios which gave the young director early support and backing), who writes with Vic Pratt of the British Film Institute (commonly referred to as BFI) about John's early work with Adelphi in particular and the background of film making and distribution in 1950s Britain in general. Neil Sinyard, with many books on film to his name, writes about John's talent for bringing out powerful performances from his actors — a talent that served him well when he made blockbusters in the 1970s with huge casts. Sinyard focuses on Peter Sellers in particular. Sinyard and I independently examine the two films John directed for children.

These chapters make up the opening part of the book focused on some of the films in John's early career.

The middle part of the book — the heart of it, in fact — examines *Rapture* (1965) from three different viewpoints. John considered *Rapture* to be his best film and the only one that showed what he was really capable of. Indeed, when it was rereleased in 2011 (US) and 2014 (UK), the consensus of online reviewers was that it was a "lost masterpiece." Melanie Williams writes "Girl on the Edge," an overview and assessment of the whole film; Brian Hoyle focuses on John's extraordinary camerawork; and I contribute a chapter entitled, "*Rapture* in the #MeToo Era."

Before moving onto a look at John's 1970s blockbusters, there is an interlude with a reprint of an article from the magazine *Film Comment* by the international film critic, Olaf Möller. (January/February 2014). Möller takes a retrospective look at John's career, which prompted John to comment on first reading it, almost with a tone of wonder, "This guy really gets my work."

The third and last part of the book examines John's triumvirate of blockbusters from the 1970s: *The Towering Inferno* (1974), *King Kong* (1976), and *Death on the Nile* (1978). Brett Hart, who tells us how as a child he was directly inspired by John's work to become a director, writes about *The Towering Inferno*, Sarah Street examines *Death on the Nile* and Ray Morton, also a psychotherapist and an author with a passion for the huge ape, writes about *King Kong*.

The book closes with my personal reflections on my husband's changing attitudes towards his own body of work during the last seventeen years of his life. As a wife I look at how a man of huge passion with thirty-four films to his name adjusts to a retirement he didn't seek. And as a psychotherapist, I reflect in my contributions about John's view of women and my take on *Rapture* on how his formative experiences echoed not only through his work but also his daily life in his twilight years.

Take it away, John!

PART ONE

*I was born a Frenchman, but I had
the misfortune to be brought up in England.*
—JOHN GUILLERMIN

John directing his first feature—only 24 years old and his own director's chair

CHAPTER 1

THE EARLY FILMS 1950 TO 1966

MARY GUILLERMIN

As a child, John felt very loved by his mother though his father was always rather remote, but in a practical way he felt very unsupported by his parents, especially about his school life and painful experiences there with his mother only speaking French and staying disengaged. John writes about his difficult life as a schoolboy in the opening chapter of this book. He got into fights — having learnt to box as a teenager to protect himself — and once had his nose broken. He told me he hated the minor public school he was evacuated to so much that he bicycled home 60 miles every weekend, hitching a ride by hanging onto the back of lorries.

John lied about his age — he was only 17 — and enlisted to fight as World War II neared its end. (My father who was ten months older than John went to India on National Service and did not see the war). He told his mother he was going to be a rear gunner. Rear gunners had a life expectancy of only six weeks so vulnerable were they at the back of the aircraft. His mother panicked, but she knew some Francophiles high up in the RAF and after an interview John was allowed to train as a pilot, whose life expectancy was higher. In fact, after a six-month stint at Cambridge University as part of officer training, John's service was given during the winding down of the war when surrender was expected. He and his crew flew missions over the English Channel; their orders being to sink any German submarines they spotted. John told me he ignored the only submarine they ever saw, ordering the plane to turn around and return to base, and telling his crew he was going to leave "the poor bastards alone so they can go back to their wives and families." Back on the ground, John, always a good spinner of yarns, lied his way out of an interrogation by his superior officer sticking to his story that they had seen nothing. His crew, who always respected him, backed him up and stayed silent.

John felt the war saved him; he would say, "It made a man of me." His lifelong habit of drinking scotch before meals began, he told me, in the mess where all the pilots drank heavily, so terrified were they of being killed the next time they went up. Being chosen for officer training

How many 22-year-olds could convince their CO they would make it in films?

and having a team of men under him had given him self-confidence and a sense of himself as a leader of men. Before being de-mobbed himself, he was ordered to be a Careers Counselor for soldiers returning to civilian life, a position he enjoyed.

At eighteen years of age, he had to choose between being a French citizen or a British subject. He chose the latter, and ever after said, "I was born a Frenchman, but I had the misfortune to be brought up in England." After the war, he went over to France and did some documentary work, some of which was for the perfume company his father worked for. John didn't talk much about these early years of trying to get into the film industry. Dylan Cave in the program notes to the BFI's release of *The Crowded Day* (1954) states, "An immediate postwar spell in France was followed by a trip to LA where he observed the Classical Hollywood system in action." He began his own production company, Advent Films, with friend and collaborator, Robert Jordan Hill, with the support of Arthur Dent of Adelphi Films, and directed his first feature, *Torment* (1950) in collaboration with Adelphi. John directed several films with Adelphi culminating with *The Crowded Day* in 1954. He went on to make many films and television episodes. Throughout his career, he always took whatever work was offered to him, especially once he had a family to support. Part of the reason for the lack of recognition for his work is that he became known as someone who could deliver on various types of films, and was seen as a "journeyman" director — a description that is a vast understatement of his talent and achievements.

Throughout the war and in the initial postwar period, American money flooded into the British Film Industry but in the years after the war, the money began drying up. By the mid-Sixties, John was concerned about being able to make a living in Britain, and in 1968 he moved with his family to Los Angeles and continued his career overseas with the active support of George Peppard, who had really liked working with John on *The Blue Max* (1966), the year after his masterpiece *Rapture* (1965) was released.

Filmography 1950 to 1966

1950
TORMENT (PAPER GALLOWS)

1951
SMART ALEC

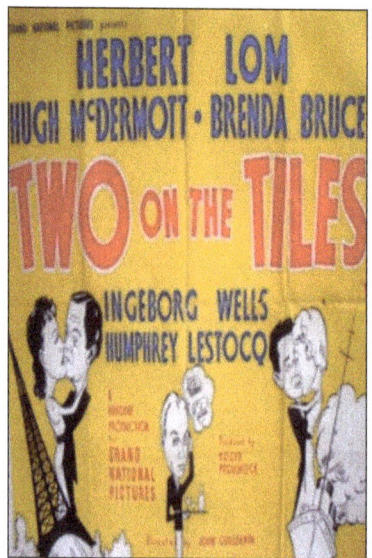

1951
TWO ON THE TILES

1951
FOUR DAYS

1952
SONG OF PARIS
(BACHELOR IN PARIS)

1952
MISS ROBIN HOOD

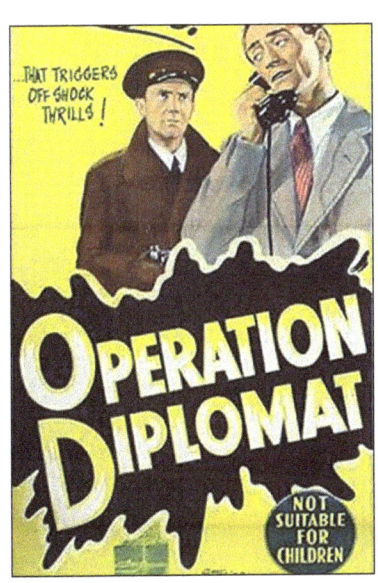

1953
OPERATION DIPLOMAT

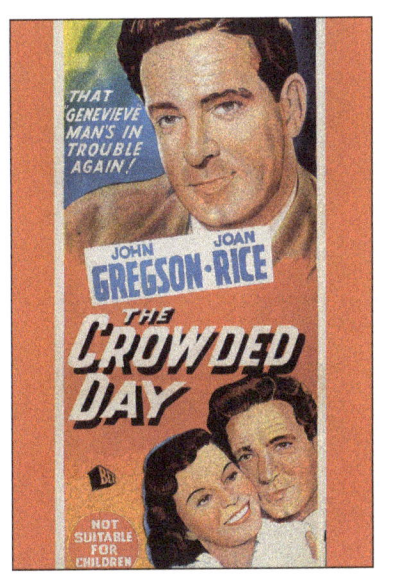

1954
THE CROWDED DAY
(SHOP SPOILED)

THE EARLY FILMS 1950 TO 1966

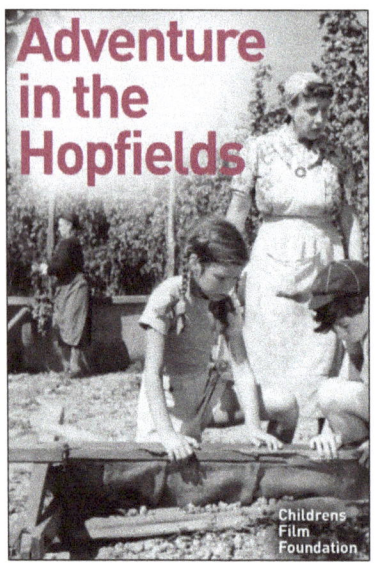

1954
ADVENTURE IN THE HOPFIELDS

1956
THUNDERSTORM

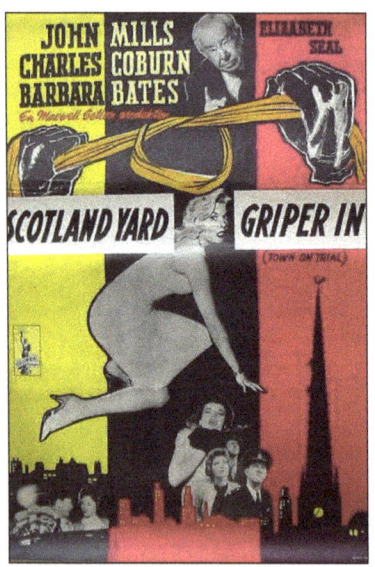

1957
TOWN ON TRIAL

1958
THE WHOLE TRUTH

1958
I WAS MONTY'S DOUBLE
(HELL, HEAVEN OR
HOBOKEN)

1959
TARZAN'S GREATEST
ADVENTURE

1960
THE DAY THEY ROBBED
THE BANK OF ENGLAND

1960
NEVER LET GO

1962
WALTZ OF THE TOREADORS

1962
TARZAN GOES TO INDIA

1964
GUNS AT BATASI

1965
RAPTURE

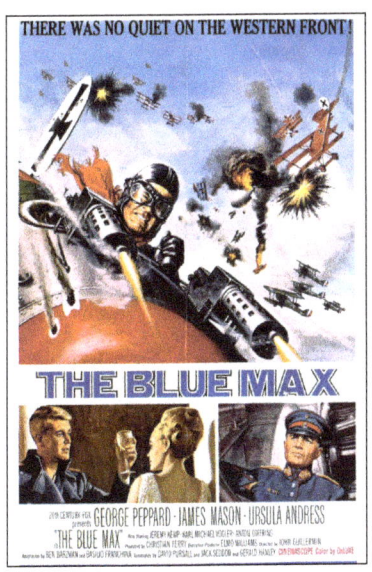

**1966
THE BLUE MAX**

CHAPTER 2

DEO PROFUNDIS

JOHN GUILLERMIN
WRITTEN IN 1990

I CAME OUT OF St. John's hospital in Santa Monica about three weeks ago, and sat on a wooden bench in the quiet street outside the hospital courtyard. Fred, who had kindly come to collect me, went to fetch his car.

My moments on that bench linger in my mind. The bench had trees growing near it. That morning there was no smog and the fragrance from them was exquisite. I had never before felt so at peace. I attributed this feeling, wrongly as it turned out, to a profound sense of relief. I was free of the air-conditioned purgatory of the hospital. I was alive. I had survived a ruptured appendix at the age of sixty-four years and eleven months.

The day after my operation I walked to the bathroom. Walking was encouraged, as soon as I could move, by my surgeon and the hospital staff. I was concerned about splitting myself open again, but I was told that was preferable to remaining bed-bound. The emaciated image I saw in the bathroom mirror did not disturb me. The morphine I was being fed took the edge off both pain and shock. I had lost twenty pounds in two days. I had a stubbly growth of beard and my eyes were dim and slotted. From my nose protruded an obscene tube which had been pushed up my nostrils and down into my stomach like a threaded worm in readiness for feeding. My I.V. stand, to which I was umbilically bound, was on wheels and the transparent bags of assorted antibiotics hung from its metal cross-trees and dripped into my veins through needles held in place by lengths of tape.

I set out from my room pushing my cross-on-wheels in front of me and proceeded uncertainly along the gloomy corridors. My bloated belly bulged with the noxious fumes of my infection. The doctors and nurses I passed either looked away or smiled at me as if to imply a normalcy to my appearance. No one put out a hand to help me, for which I am grateful. I had never been in hospital before except as a visitor to see family or friends.

Three weeks later, I experienced the tender delight of coming home. My wife had been unable to pick me up because two days earlier she had fractured her big toe. She was waiting for me at the top of the stairs, which led to our front door. She was radiant. She held me gently and took me inside.

Later, Fred and I played a game of pool. Connell's eyes were shining as she watched — her old man was going to be O.K. Connell is my wife's maiden name and for various reasons it has stuck. We have been married for thirty-four years. I have been in turn, fractious, difficult, depressive and suicidal, with savage mood swings in between.

She has been constant, warm and supportive. If it were not for Connell, my life would have been over long ago.

Several weeks before my hospitalization, Connell had talked to me about an article written by William Styron, which dealt with depression. She said that she thought it might help me, but she couldn't remember the magazine in which it had been published. Two days after I came home, I happened to see a review of *Darkness Visible: A Memoir of Madness* by William Styron. I went out and bought a copy of the book. Three hours later I had read this mini-masterpiece. Styron's educated guess at what he knew to be the basic cause of nearly all depression blew my mind by its utter simplicity. I had heard the reason quoted often before, but because he was able to present it, not from the polar regions of the intellect, but instead through the warm guts of our emotions, it carried a message to me (and to many others, I am sure) that is reverberating still, as I write these lines.

In an attempt to cure a lifelong depression that has severely incapacitated me, a string of psychiatrists over the years (because I could afford them) have made me acutely aware of nearly everything that has ever happened to me. But in the case of Styron's book, this was the first time that the mind of a powerful writer had taken me down the labyrinth of his own anguish and illuminated the way for me to try and trace my own pain. That same day — the day I bought and read the book — for the first time in my life I saw dimly into my own darkness. I sensed that what had happened to me in St. John's went far beyond a skirmish with death and the automatic response of deep relief at having come through the ordeal. Something far more frightening than death had invaded my sick bed.

Sixty-four years ago, when I was lying in my cradle on the balcony outside our home in a suburb of London, England, in the month of March 1926, (my mother told me I was four months old at the time) the neighbor's big black cat had come to sit comfortably on my warm, swaddled body. In the process, the cat smothered my face and was slowly choking me to death. I clearly remember the smell of the cat, the terrifying feel of the black fur, the nick-of-time arrival of my mother, the cat's throaty snarl of rage at being disturbed, and the feel of my mother's cheek as she hugged me against her for dear life.

In St. John's hospital, four weeks ago, one of the nurses left the blood pressure pad on my pillow against my cheek. The rough black material brought back to me the smell of that cat. My utter helplessness in those first post-operative days reduced me to a reliance on others quite as utter as when I was four months old. And although I had those memories many times during the course of my life, I had never recalled them at a moment when my emotional age and response were almost identical to the time when I first experienced the events in question. Today, still, several weeks later, I have only just begun to absorb their massive traumatic implications. I am daily being invaded by more memories — they constitute the very spine of who I am.

I certainly don't remember being born, but I remember the awful size of my distended belly as I lay on my hospital bed, or lurched down those long corridors, during what seemed to me a hopeless wait for the noxious gasses, trapped in my abdomen, to find their natural way out through my intestines and colon and thereby grant me blessed relief from what I imagined would be death by explosion. I remember that I felt trapped in the throes of a monstrous pregnancy. And that if I didn't give birth to myself soon, I would die! I remember also, in the deep gloomy caves where the morphine sent me to wander, that Margie, my surgeon, had suddenly sat at my bedside and said I might have an obstruction in my intestines and that she would have to operate again. I was appalled. I think I said I couldn't go through another one. I remember asking her where she would make the incision — she had already split me open from scrotum to belly button. She told me not to worry, that her next incision would follow the exact line of the first one and that my flesh would not part or disintegrate along its edges as I kept mumbling to her would be the case. Luckily for me, the barium they inserted by gastric tube into my stomach found its tortuous way to my colon three days later (on the eleventh day of my hospitalization) and I was pronounced obstruction-free! And the next day I passed gas, I passed blessed, noxious gas. I farted loud and long as Geoffrey Chaucer would have it, and I was saved. But during my ordeal, inside the labyrinth of that waking, eleven-day nightmare, I felt as though I had experienced my own birth as a fetus in my mother's womb.

At the age of five, I met Hope. Hope was the school bully who terrorized me during my sequestration at St. Anne's School for Boys in Purley, South London in the early nineteen-thirties. Mr. Leathley, the headmaster of St. Anne's, enjoyed caning me hard across my outstretched palm for minor infractions of the school rules. This treatment had reduced me to a quiet but abjectly terrorized runt, and Hope finished the job. I had noticed that Mr. Leathley kept his left hand plunged deep into his trouser pocket while he chastised me and that he was obviously playing with himself, his predator's eyes glazed with enjoyment. His love of inflicting pain, and Hope's pig eyes, which matched Mr. Leathley's, were signposts in my young life that the world around me was extremely hostile.

Perhaps some of the difficulties I encountered were aggravated by the fact that my mother, who is French, refused to set foot in my school, or anywhere else for that matter, outside the home. My father was distant and disinterested, occasionally choleric, but generally detached. My mother said she spoke English with a heavy French accent (which was true) and if she went outside her home, would be ridiculed by her neighbors. There had been much soft love between my mother and me. She had poured affection over me like soothing cream. But every day, I had to leave home without her at my side and face Hope and the others, alone. It felt as though I was continuously being betrayed. I hated her, and I loved her so much!

Hope punched me many times, hurting me once quite seriously. My mother had to reluctantly consult a neighbor about whether I should be taken to hospital. Hope had cornered me near the garbage pit. He said he would push me into the pit and make sure I never came out. I started to scream. This took place in a narrow suburban-country road in Purley, South London. Michael Stillyard came to my rescue. Michael was shorter and smaller than I was, half the size of Hope, but Michael beat Hope with his fists and finally gave him the bloodiest nose in St. Anne's history and punched him to his knees until Hope begged for mercy. How I wished at that moment I had been born Michael Stillyard. Fifteen years later, in 1940, Michael, a fighter pilot, lost his life in the Battle of Britain.

Michael Stillyard had the same first name as my son, Michael, who six years ago was killed in a car crash at the age of twenty-one, on the road from Tahoe to Truckee, California. My depression became acute from that time on. One black-dog-day afternoon, I started to write an ode to my son. I repeat it here because I am proud of him, and proud of the effort I made in those dark moments. By way of explanation of the following lines, Mike was killed alongside his two best friends, Bill and Rocky. All three were sitting in the front of Mike's pick-up truck. It is not certain which of them was driving.

Oh Mike

Truckee bound

On your way

Across the night

To the summit edge

The three of you

Shouts of delight

On the winding road

To Truckee....

At this time, I was directing a movie in Kenya. I had flown back to Los Angeles for Mike's funeral, then returned to Kenya to complete the movie. My impending divorce (by now Connell had had more than she could stand) drove me into the deepest pit that I had yet known. There seemed to be no way out.

In 1936, when I was eleven years old, I was "sent to Coventry" at St. John Fisher's Secondary School for Boys, which I was attending. I had grown into a thin, introverted boy, shy and subdued, who had no friends. Being "sent to Coventry" was a serious business in those days. It meant that none of my classmates were allowed to talk to me, they must totally ignore me. This sentence was imposed upon me by the class captain. He accused me of not owning up to talking in class. The whole of our class had been kept in during play period, that is, with the exception of me.

After nine weeks of being "sent to Coventry" by my classmates, I went to Father McCarthy and confessed that I too had been talking in class (although this was a blatant lie, I had been patently mute during the offending period). Father McCarthy immediately sent me to see Mr. Harrington. Mr. Harrington was a lay teacher who kept a thick strap on a chair in the small book-lined punishment room. When I was bending over the chair I started to blabber incoherently and Mr. Harrington sternly told me to behave like a man. He said that my conduct was so appalling that he would give me the strap "on the bare" instead of across my trousers. So I had to undo my belt and let my trousers drop to my ankles. Mr. Harrington's specialty was aiming the strap so that its end would whip in between the cheeks. He performed well that day and my screams, I am certain, could but be dimly heard through those thick book-lined walls, and in any event, who was there to listen? Who was there to care?

In England of the '20s and '30s, corporal punishment was very much in vogue. For me, at the time, it constituted the ultimate terror. We have all heard about the psychology of the beaters and the beaten, the psycho-pathology of sado-masochism. Long words that mean little to me. My memories are of the flesh, my flesh, and I know the harm it did me.

More beating, this time at the City of London School at the beginning of World War II. I was now fourteen, and progressing without redemption down my dark road. For three years, at this school, I was alone, friendless, and had found my ultimate tormentor, Tadpole Reed, a prefect who had the authority to inflict up to six strokes of the cane. Suffice to say, I was cruelly flogged by Tadpole Reed, who also (memories of Mr. Leathley at St. Anne's) while he lacerated my behind, kept his left hand deeply thrust into his trouser pocket.

In 1942 (I was now seventeen) I was accepted for pilot training in the Royal Air Force. With this came the automatic benefit (I say this with some reservations) of becoming a British citizen. I had hitherto held French nationality, like my parents. In 1943 I went to Flight School in the United States, at Falcon Field in Mesa, Arizona. In those days Mesa was only cactus desert, and my instructors were American civilian pilots. My first glimpse of the riches of America was in the PX at Camp Kilmer where, soon after landing, we were served milk, butter, eggs, etc., (all rationed in postwar Europe) a dazzling sight for the grey, bedraggled group of English cadets who had not long left the sad harbor of Southampton on the other side of the Atlantic.

The war basically saved me. It got me away from my mother. It allowed me to garner a vestige of self-esteem. At the end of the war when I was "de-mobbed" I pursued my lifelong dream of becoming a film director — an ambition I had harbored ever since I saw *Treasure Island* with Wallace Beery at the Astoria Cinema in Purley, at the age of seven. The persona I created as a director had nothing in common with my true, depressive personality. When I directed I became authoritarian and dictatorial. I felt confident, sure of myself, I made choices quickly, actors relied on me, crews hated me for my impatience, and I achieved *some* good work. When whatever film I was working on was completed, and the hundred-and-fifty-odd participants in its making disappeared as if into thin air (to their next assignments), I was left high and dry, with a desperate sense of let-down, of anti-climax, of being deserted — shades of my mother's abandonment of me, when I had to leave the safety of her warmth and face the outside world alone. I was no longer the strong leader, the director, and I reverted back to the frightened little schoolboy and crawled homewards to the bosom of my family as I had to my mother's skirts. I was not as bad a father to my children (Connell and I had a daughter, Michelle, our first born, and Mike, our son) as all this might make me out to have been. Nor, possibly, as bad a husband. The war had put some lead in my pencil, so I wavered on the brink of the pit, sometimes falling in and experiencing months on end of black depression, sometimes heaving myself out and breathing a bit of fresh air for a while. But as time progressed, my worsening depressive states began to invade the arena of my work. As I became physically exhausted during the long spells of directing large-scale, big-budget movies, my persona of the all-powerful director began to crumble while I was still "on stage" and I would become quieter and quieter, and more introverted as the shooting continued, until I was in the grip of a black depression, which naturally I tried to hide from cast and crew. They must have often wondered what strange mechanism caused these profound mood changes in me.

Mike my son was killed, but Michelle my daughter is alive, and bless her, has given me so much love in addition to the intense satisfaction of seeing her grow and develop into an attractive, successful woman. This, together with Connell's help, has enabled me to exert some equilibrium into the savage swings of my pendulum of depression.

To come to the heart of the matter, when I first read William Styron's book just after I had left the hospital, he showed me emotionally that *loss* is the basic cause of depression. But what loss had *I* ever suffered? No one in my family had died during my childhood. My elder brother had a serious operation at the age of sixteen, but he had come out of it alive. And then it came to me. I began to comprehend the loss that I had suffered all these years. It was the loss of myself, of my wholeness, of being a whole person, the loss of not feeling good about myself, the loss of not feeling equal to others, the loss of a core to my being, the loss of joy, of a sense of participation, of being able to share, the loss of *being* — the loss of being a tiny part of Albert Einstein's marvelous equation $E = mc^2$ which Stephen Hawking, the English physicist, so brilliantly explains in his treatise *A Brief History of Time*. More about that, in a moment.

In addition to these fundamental discoveries about myself, I have also begun to understand the false foundation on which I had tried to build my adulthood — the world of the child is utterly ruthless. But the world of the adult is not so. It may be fraught with moral weakness and a lust for power, but it contains compassion and above all is ruled by a rule of law (however corrupt). For adults there exists some sort of redress, some sort of justice, even if it takes, in my case, sixty years to be realized. During most of my adult life, I knew that the other adults surrounding me could no longer hurt me at will, especially when I was hiding behind my created persona of the all-powerful film director. But emotionally I found it impossible to accept this. My crucial first years on this earth had indoctrinated me to the fact that I could be destroyed at the whim of others.

The two weeks of my hospitalization have been my salvation. Conclusively, within that time, and in that place, I have learnt once and for all, during a period when I was once again totally helpless, that no one wanted to hurt or kill me. I learnt that there is compassion. There is mercy. There is callousness, but also caring, there exists a world that seeks not to hurt or crimp or beat or subdue, there is a decency that often prevails, there is what I hesitate to call normalcy, too. There is also, side by side, a very dark world. But enough of that world.

I know I shall never again enter the pit. Finally, finally the penny has dropped. It has sent a blinding reflection from its spinning edge. From within my skull the viscous poisons have been sent spiraling upwards towards the open air and the sun, which mercifully will burn them to a cinder. My life, from now on, is going to be different, with some hope, some joy. The penny has finally dropped.

At the age of fifteen, when I finally threw the Catholic catechism out of the window in a blind rage, ever since then I had not found anything to fulfill my yearnings for a credo. I read a great deal about and by the prophets, went through the philosophers, extended into physics but couldn't understand Einstein (thoroughly) — until Stephen Hawking came along with his layman's explanation of the mysteries of our lives. To Stephen Hawking, whom I have never had the privilege of meeting, I give the reverence that I wasted as a child on the Catholic priests who tried to instill religion into me with a scourge. To Stephen Hawking I dedicate whatever might be left of my faith, of my belief in Godot. Hawking's wonderful analysis, equating the infinitely small to the mind-blowing vastness of our expanding universe, and his explanation of eternity, will stay with me for good — our times bear no relation to other times, other times may be repeated endlessly in either past or future, but they carry no connection to *this* time, our time. And for whoever wants to ask the simplistic, "But what happened before *that?*" Hawking answers that *before* that could be *after* that, or *in-between* that, or split into tiny segments and shrinking to infinite smallness (when volume has ceased to exist) and when *that* will have disappeared altogether.

CHAPTER 3

EARLY DAYS WITH ADELPHI FILMS

VIC PRATT AND KATE LEES

PRACTICAL, PRAGMATIC AND PROFESSIONAL, John Guillermin was a forward-looking filmmaker, never much inclined to reminisce upon days gone by. While he always appreciated what he described as the "great opportunity" he was given in the late 1940s by veteran film executive Arthur Dent and sons, producer David Dent and finance director Stanley Dent, Guillermin remained close-lipped about his formative years at Adelphi, the Dents' small family-run independent film-making concern, where he shot his earliest British features. But despite affecting a characteristic aura of self-deprecating disdain for his postwar work at Adelphi — indeed, he cheerfully chose to describe his first fully-fledged effort as a feature director, the crime thriller *Torment*, as "a lemon" — the Dents played a crucial part in his career. For it was at Adelphi that Guillermin would learn the art and economics of feature film making. Writing, directing and producing, here he established himself as a reliable and proficient film-craftsman for hire, and began to define his methodical modus operandi as a director.

Employed on a diverse string of quota-fulfilling British features — running the gamut from modestly budgeted "B" pictures to main feature

"A" Pictures — with the Dents he learnt his craft. His earliest efforts ranged from cheerful comedies such as *Bless 'Em All,* via his directorial feature debut *Torment,* an atmospheric suspense picture, on to his most ambitious work of this formative period, a logistically-complex female-led human-interest drama, *The Crowded Day*. This varied Adelphi output — especially this last project — provided Guillermin with the opportunity both to develop directorial skills and also to establish an expertise in handling large and unwieldy casts — a talent that would still be serving him well two decades further along the line, on such star-studded blockbusters as *The Towering Inferno*.

Guillermin began his filmmaking career with Arthur and David Dent following his war-time tenure as a Flight Sergeant in the Royal Air Force, from 1942 to 1946. Sometime during his period of active service, he may well have met another member of the Dent clan: David and Stanley's brother, Harry. Harry, however, did not return home after the war to make films: a pilot, he was killed in the conflict.

Guillermin was a keen cineaste, with a passion for quality cinema. After demob (discharge) from the RAF, he worked in France on various small film projects, before returning to England with an ambition to shoot his own features. To this end, Guillermin set up two tiny production companies: Advent Films and Discovery Films, both established in the late 1940s with a friend and business partner: film director and producer Robert Jordan Hill.

Adelphi, like Guillermin's Advent, was one of many independent film production companies that proliferated in the postwar years. Adelphi, though, had hefty industry experience behind it. It was established by Arthur Dent — a jovial, indomitable, cigar-smoking film executive, who, having entered the movie business in its earliest days before the First World War, had worked his way up the corporate ladder to become Sales Director for the prestigious Associated British Picture Corporation (ABPC). In 1940, he finally struck out on his own, setting up Adelphi (and various other film-production related concerns, including Adelphi's sister company, Advance Films), employing son David as producer, and son Stanley as the money man. Adelphi would eventually produce, or end up owning 40 films, both features and shorts, and distributed many more. Like every little fish in the big pond of British film production, Arthur's outfit chased bookings in British cinemas. Notably, though, Adelphi was often in conflict with cinema circuit bosses who had no time for outspoken Arthur's emphatic articulation of the problems of the independent little men of British cinema. Driven and determined, and still fretting about bookings and box office on the very day of his death, it was only his passing that finally brought his company's film production to a close, in the mid-1950s. Adelphi still continues as a going concern to this day, currently under the control of Arthur's granddaughter, Kate Lees, who works with the BFI to make this unique "lost" collection available to the public once again.

Back in 1948, compared to the major movers and shakers of British filmmaking, Adelphi was small; but next to Advent and Discovery, it was a large and thriving concern. Boasting as many as sixteen full-time employees at one point near the end of the decade, it was in the enviable position of being able to bankroll smaller outfits to produce films for them. In a labyrinthine bit of money management, Adelphi would buy up those very same companies and swallow up their assets — including any new film productions they had just made. Discovery did not finish any films, but Advent did. These were bought out by the Dents for Adelphi. Thus it came to pass that the Dents ended up releasing the three earliest feature films Guillermin worked on: *Bless 'Em All* (1948) — a bona fide Adelphi/Advance Production — plus the bought-out Advent films *Melody in the Dark* (1949) and *High Jinks in Society* (1949). Having established a rapport, Guillermin remained with the Dents to direct the more ambitious Advance/Adelphi production *Torment* (1950), the Vandyke/Adelphi production *Song of Paris* (1952) and the Advance/Adelphi production *The Crowded Day* (1954), before moving on to new pastures.

Arthur Dent, a canny and perceptive businessman, always had an eye for new and emerging talent — and early on, it would seem, he shrewdly spotted Guillermin as a future incumbent of the director's chair. Immediately setting out to harness the young cineaste's blossoming talents to everybody's most lucrative advantage, the Dents befriended the young film-lover. Many decades later, in a 2010 email to Kate Lees, John Guillermin recalled David Dent with affection, noting, "I was fond of ironic David, and his lovely wife José." John and David were indeed close in those early years. Mr. and Mrs. Guillermin spent at least one holiday abroad with David Dent and his wife, on which they took with them a 16mm camera, used to shoot an evocative holiday home movie, documenting their sunny seaside exploits.

The first feature film project Guillermin was involved with for the Dents was a light-hearted venture described by the *Monthly Film Bulletin* as "a skit on the old army life." Entitled *Bless 'Em All*, it was a nostalgic musical variety comedy designed to warm the cockles of every old comrade in khaki who had recently served in the forces. Following in the modestly-budgeted footsteps of similarly themed patriotic American army-based call-up comedies such as Laurel and Hardy's wartime effort *Great Guns* (1941) and Abbott and Costello's postwar *Buck Privates Come Home* (1947), this quintessentially British-style parade-ground mirth-riot tracked the proud progress of a daft trio of likely lads — Skimpy (Hal Monty), Tommy (Max Bygraves) and Jock (Jack Milroy) — from call-up papers to conflict, marching with them from basic training at home into battle abroad, climaxing with them doing their bit in the liberation of France at the end of the war. "Made to measure for every ex-service man and woman in your town — and their families — shout you've got it!" saluted the marvelously militaristic press release, in no uncertain terms.

Bless 'Em All was the first of two Adelphi features to star stage and radio comic Hal Monty as silly serviceman Skimpy. Though almost entirely forgotten now, Hal Monty was a hugely popular and well-known live performer in his day. He played many theatres in Southern England, such as the Chiswick Empire, where, so legend has it, the youngsters fell about with laughter at his antics. Hal's credentials were certainly impressive. More than a decade before his first Adelphi feature, he had trod the boards in a variety double act with no less a figure than show business mogul-to-be Bernard Delfont. *Bless 'Em All* also marked the screen debut of genial singer and light entertainer Max Bygraves. Boyish Bygraves participates gamely in the straightforward slapstick on the parade ground, but he's noticeably more comfortable singing schmaltzy songs. Luckily, he's given ample opportunity to do this. The trailer (for many years all that was known to exist of this forgotten feature, which was only recently recovered from an archive overseas) foregrounds an abundantly coiffured, baby-faced Max, smoothly delivering the melodious lines, "I'm afraid to love you . . . afraid I might like it," in fulsome, theatrical fashion, while he toothily tickles the ivories of a pub piano.

The war years had taken their toll on the Dent clan, and *Bless 'Em All* was a project close to Arthur Dent's heart. He involved himself closely with the production, co-conceiving the original story with Aileen Burke and Leone Stewart, while star Hal added his own distinctive comic material to the mix. Robert Jordan Hill directed, while John Guillermin, marching smartly up to take his very first Adelphi credit, was listed as associate producer.

An amiable but uneven combination of what must even then have been vintage variety routines, music, songs, and drill-square silliness — enhanced by the impressive, blood-vessel-busting presence of Monty's regular stage foil Les Ritchie, as Skimpy's long suffering sergeant major — *Bless 'Em All* received trade show screenings in March 1949. An unusually hefty 80 minute running time may perhaps have limited its bookings (it couldn't really play support slots at such an extended length). However, it got some good reviews nonetheless from film industry journals. The *Daily Film Renter* decided, " . . . the laughs come fast and furious... a robust rib-tickler for populars," while *Kine Weekly* noted, "... wildly incoherent but cheery low comedy musical extravaganza... a trifle long but funny for the most part, it's a reliable rib tickler for the industrial masses." Despite being a "reliable rib tickler" it failed to score major circuit bookings; but still managed to perform well with the "industrial masses" of London, as it repeatedly played at independent cinemas in and around the capital, whose owners, according to newspaper *The Star*, "... were astonished by its popularity... but it is only fair to say that people were laughing their heads off." It was a profitable film for the Dents. Notable successes included three runs at the Empire Cinema, Walthamstow, beginning May 1949, with yet another entirely separate run at the nearby Granada Cinema the very next month. No matter what the circuit bosses thought about it all, it is clear that Walthamstow film fans just couldn't get enough of dear old Skimpy.

"By heck—what a neck!" Ben Wrigley in High Jinks in Society

Assuredly a stand-out player in the team that brought *Bless 'Em All* so successfully to the screen, Guillermin was soon to become more visible within the Adelphi hierarchy. By the time of *Melody in the Dark*, another light-hearted effort directed by his friend Hill, Guillermin had assumed increased responsibilities. This time, he was credited both as co-producer and co-writer on this old gothic dark house mystery comedy, filled — according to the Press book — with "eerie music and spooky bedrooms and corridors [which] give [star] Ben Wrigley and the girls [notably including future Bond girl Eunice Gayson] full opportunity for some of the funniest comedy-thriller situations ever screened."

Whether this opportunity was taken, and if the film actually yielded the funniest comedy-thriller situations ever screened, remains open to debate. Certainly, the promotional materials did their best to suggest they did, and made the most of the film's star, the now-obscure variety comic Ben Wrigley. His unique selling point was his odd physique. "By heck — what a neck!" screamed the publicity, "Look out — here's the 'New Look' comedian with the rubber neck!" This was referring to Wrigley's disquieting penchant for pushing this part of his body in and out turkey-like above his collars, whilst he delivered the funnies. However, behind all this neck fun, there was controversy. Aspects of Wrigley's act were apparently suspiciously similar to that of better-remembered comedian Nat Jackley; who, according to showbiz legend, threatened to sue Wrigley for stealing his routines. It would seem, however, that Jackley didn't hold a personal grudge against the Dents, for he later signed up with them himself — to star in their last musical comedy extravaganza, and the only colour Adelphi film, *Stars in Your Eyes* (1956).

Though Guillermin received a welcome co-writing credit for the screenplay of *Melody in the Dark*, he surely had little chance for the kind of cinematic innovation he was keen on with this particular script. For as a musical comedy based in an old dark house mystery setting, this was exceedingly familiar terrain — as featured in a plethora of other productions, such as the Bob Hope comedies *The Cat and the Canary* (1939) and *The Ghost Breakers* (1940). This Adelphi production also riffed teasingly on the name of a slightly more recent addition to the crowded mystery-comedy canon: *Whistling in the Dark* (1941) starring Red Skelton. Furthermore, it had the look of a low-budget variety revue: *Melody in the Dark* provided a showcase for a succession of cheaply-booked stage performers, including Alan Dean and the Keynotes, the Stardusters Dance Orchestra, and the luscious but little-known London Lovelies. Modest though it all was, Guillermin and Hill both seem to have immersed themselves fully in the project. Hill even went as far as composing songs for the production. Their extra efforts paid off, it would seem — the film, released in the summer of 1949, was warmly reviewed — albeit with a few reservations — by the trade papers. "One or two rather too obvious jokes do not spoil the generally happy atmosphere of the film and the enthusiasm and talent of the performers," smiled *The Daily Film Renter* generously, concluding that "laugh producing sequences . . . are slickly put over," before perceptively proclaiming Eunice Gayson "a charming heroine."

A follow-up Advent musical-variety-comedy appeared at the end of the following year. *High Jinks in Society* (1950), on which Guillermin served as producer, with Hill as director once more, was another lively vehicle for nimble-necked Mr. Wrigley, this time cast as a waggish window cleaner unexpectedly hired to guard a rich lady's valuables. Amidst this further merry mélange of variety, comedy, neck-stretching, music, and mystery, most notable perhaps was the presence in the cast of one of comic genius Will Hay's sidekicks: toothless old-timer *par excellence,* the marvelous Moore Marriott. Doing a solo turn at Advent/Adelphi (Hay's other silly satellite, fabulous fat boy Graham Moffatt, appears not to have been available), Marriott was still playing the idiotic ancient duffer role that had served him so well in Hay's classic string of late '30s comedies. *High Jinks in Society* was certainly buoyed by his involvement. The reviews were again impressive, with *Today's Cinema* describing it as, " . . . adroitly designed for the delight of the masses who will react joyfully to the Wrigley gags and sallies and respond audibly to the engaging inanities of Moore Marriott." The *Daily Film Renter* also celebrated its simplicity, pronouncing it, "... unsophisticated fun fare [which] includes hearty frolics and popular musical numbers ... a real cinch for provincial and industrial patrons. Unsophisticated entertainment designed on a robust popular plane with plenty of gags, old and new, bright music and a couple of good popular numbers."

Two out of three — John as producer of High Jinks *& director of* Torment

EARLY DAYS WITH ADELPHI FILMS

Perhaps more to Guillermin's personal taste as a filmmaker was his directorial feature debut, the crime mystery *Torment,* shot in June 1949, and released in the early months of 1950. For here, for the first time at Adelphi, the young filmmaker was given his head. He made the most of it — writing, directing and producing a modest but impressively brooding tale of murder and mystery.

A suspense thriller set in an isolated country house, *Torment* (released overseas as *Paper Gallows)* had a suitably sinister subject matter. It starred Dermot Walsh and John Bentley as brothers Cliff and Jim Brandon, a successful crime-writing duo specializing in murder mysteries, and both in love with their long-suffering secretary, Joan (Rona Anderson). But while brother Jim is a fine upstanding gentlemanly sort, brother Cliff is a moody, neurotic psychopath. Research for a new novel prompts Cliff to commit a murder; and when Joan rejects his advances, he decides to murder her too — niftily preparing a noose for his evil purpose.

Thriving on an opportunity to direct from his own script, it was with *Torment* that Guillermin's talent for clear, compact, efficient direction became evident: his tautly-shot thriller remains the strongest crime drama in the Adelphi catalogue. It would seem that the Dents were keen to reward the young director for his sterling efforts: Adelphi records reveal that while Robert Jordan Hill was paid £1,250 for directing *High Jinks in Society,* John Guillermin received the far heftier sum of £3,250 for *Torment.*

Guillermin's good work did not go unnoticed outside Adelphi either. Shortly after production commenced, *Film Industry* magazine, filing a report from tiny Southall Studios, in North West London, where *Torment* was being produced, had already drawn attention to the speed and skill of the young director, noting,

> "... nearly five minutes has been sent into the can every day and the first day's shot on the first day's shooting — a difficult

3 minute take — involved 13 different camera positions. There was 6 minutes screen time locked away after the first day's work. Nor has this speed prejudiced the production value and creative quality of the picture. First assistant Basil Keys commended the co-operation from the star players playing in conditions more crowded than usual, and Rona Anderson's work on the film has been of a splendid standard."

Following release, *Torment* was also the recipient of more macabre publicity. In an era when the media increasingly played upon public postwar anxieties and professed fears about the dangerous effect of imported American entertainments, both on the British public, and on domestic filmmaking, *Torment* became briefly entangled in controversy, when newspapers reported that a man killed himself immediately after seeing the film.

Cliff making preparations to hang Joan

A brief scene in *Torment* shows mad mystery writer Cliff making preparations to hang that unresponsive object of his obscene affections, Joan, the secretary. According to press reports, after witnessing this shocking scene onscreen, Somerset man Stanley Williams promptly went home and hanged himself — after decking himself out in a woman's "old-fashioned nightdress." Stanley's father decided that *Torment* was entirely to blame for the suicide, and asked the coroner to write to the BBFC to demand that the film be banned. The BBFC wrote back:

> "I need hardly say that we received the news of this tragic occurrence with great distress. We exercise the greatest care in our examination of this type of film. At the same time, you will I am sure appreciate that neither we nor any censorship board can be absolutely certain of the effect which every single incident in a film may have on each individual who sees it. You will I know be interested to learn that the scene in question was heavily cut by the Board before it was passed and reduced to the barest dimensions necessary to the development of the story. In the certificated version the scene only occupies a few seconds of screen time."

Peculiar and morbid as it was, this brief flash of bizarre publicity couldn't have hurt the film's prospects. The reviews, however, could — and were not as positive as they might have been. While the *Daily Film Renter* acknowledged that *Torment* had an "... interesting theme, well-acted and well photographed," and *Kine Weekly* described the film as "... a good British thriller," *Monthly Film Bulletin* derided its "cliché ridden script" and "overplayed characters." It did draw useful attention, however, to Guillermin's ambition behind the camera; perceptively suggesting, at least, that there was "a feeling once or twice that the director had some elusive Higher Thing in mind."

More worryingly than the reviews, for the Dents, who wanted to recoup on their bold investment in Guillermin's talents, *Torment* was rejected out of hand by the principal British cinema circuits. In desperation, Arthur Dent took an unprecedented step: he appealed to the Board of Trade in an attempt to reverse the decision. The Selection Committee of the Board of Trade had been established under section 5 of the Cinematograph Act 1948, to arbitrate in booking disputes between independent production companies and the big circuits. To this end, the Committee was empowered to compel the major circuits to exhibit any British film which it considered to be suitable "by reason of its entertainment value." It all sounded very grand, even-handed and above board. However, the Committee itself was of course hardly impartial — many of its members worked for, or closely with, those very same major circuits it was meant to control. Unsurprisingly, these big chains were biased in favour of showing the British-made productions of the major studios, with which they were often connected, as well as the dominant American product. This inevitably meant that independent productions were often squeezed out. Additionally, as we have noted, Arthur Dent had not made his company popular with the chains, or the Board of Trade. He had always been unusually vocal in his passionate defense of the rights of independent producers, exhibiting a commendable — if decidedly dangerous — willingness to stand up for the little men against British cinema's major players.

Watching from the wings as this unlikely David-and-Goliath-style power play unfolded, but disinclined to believe that his directorial debut could be so bewilderingly barred from the cinema circuits, Guillermin decided to take steps to try and sell the film himself. He soon realised, though, that the Dents had not been exaggerating in their accounts of the difficulties they faced. Reluctantly, he left them to sort out the matter as best they could.

Despite these by-now familiar problems for the Dents, *Torment* remained a useful calling card for the young filmmaker. Away from

Brothers Cliff and Jim struggle at the top of the stairs

Adelphi, Guillermin now began to become renowned within the industry as a robust and reliable director, as the trade journal *Film Industry* had reported, "Director John Guillermin is graduating swiftly to a record proficiency in fast original camerawork and the first rate unit working with him are confident about his ultimate recognition as a brilliant technician." Sensibly putting the disappointment of *Torment* behind him, Guillermin knocked out a palate-cleansing fast-paced string of features for other British production companies. For Grand National, he directed Quota murder mysteries *Smart Alec* (1951) and *Four Days* (1951), as well as romantic drama *Two on the Tiles* (1951); while for Group 3, he helmed the Margaret Rutherford comedy-vehicle *Miss Robin Hood* (1952). Press cuttings suggest that, on excursions abroad, between 1953 and 1955, he would also work further in France. Assuredly, by the time he returned to Adelphi to work on *Song of Paris* (1952), he was considerably more experienced as a director.

A frothy comedy feature with impressive aspirations towards "A" Picture feature status, *Song of Paris* was designed with characteristic Dent optimism for a full-circuit release and with the lucrative international market in mind. With much of the action supposedly set in the French capital, this was assuredly going to be an exceptionally ambitious undertaking, both for investors Adelphi, and for the sibling producers on board alongside the Dents, Roger and Nigel Proudlock. While the Proudlocks had previously produced only the shortest of "B" pictures, they were no strangers to the rough and tumble of filmmaking. They always got the job done, no matter what fate threw at them. Shooting an earlier effort, *Death in the Hand* (1947), they had been hampered by a postwar fuel crisis, which meant they had been left with no electric power to complete the film. So the brothers had ingeniously hired some fairground vans, with built-in generators, to keep things going. These had "made an awful noise," said a *Song of Paris* press release; but, being "sons of a dogged Yorkshireman," the Proudlocks had finished the film regardless, though "many complaints poured in from local residents; [and] sometimes an irate neighbour would burst in and spoil a shot."

Produced under the Proudlock brothers' Vandyke Picture Corporation banner, and released by the Dents' Adelphi, *Song of Paris* was certainly a lavish production by comparison with the Yorkshire lads' earlier effort. But there was no budget for overseas shooting. As a result, the continental comedy was played out against the distinctly un-Gallic backdrop of Nettlefold Studios in leafy Walton-on-Thames, Surrey. It did, however, boast a quality cast, with a genuinely international flavour. This included suave Englishman Dennis Price, recently seen in Frank Launder's *Lady Godiva Rides Again* (1951); pretty Parisian actress Anne Vernon, fresh from the success of relationship comedy *Edouard et Caroline* (1951); and prolific Russian-born American actor Mischa Auer, signed up here for his first role in a British film.

Adapted from a story by William Rose, who penned screenplays for such enduring classics as *Genevieve* (1953) and *The Ladykillers* (1955), Allan MacKinnon's script was spiced up with some lively additional material by Frank Muir and Denis Norden, the gifted writing partnership behind the popular BBC radio comedy series *Take it From Here*. With all this talent on board, the choice of director was crucial for this prestigious new project. Arthur and David Dent — and Roger and Nigel Proudlock, too, according to the *Song of Paris* press release — had been highly impressed with John Guillermin's direction of *Torment*. Welcomed back to the fold, bilingual Francophile Guillermin was offered another

A frothy comedy by Britain's youngest film director

Describing him as "Britain's Youngest Film Director," the press release for the production focused on Guillermin's fierce and unswerving passion for filmmaking. "He has only one interest: the cinema," it declared. "He reads Eisenstein as some people read their bibles.... Since the age of seven when he saw his first film Guillermin had never wavered in his determination to make a career for himself in the film industry and his sojourn in America (during WWII) was a happy period for it gave him an opportunity of meeting film producers and directors." It was an effusive and enthusiastic build-up for the young cineaste.

More than half a century later, in an email to Kate Lees, Guillermin categorized the film without effusion as "a piece of nonsense." But he recalled fondly the enduring friendship he had forged on set with Dennis Price. "I got on with Dennis famously," he wrote. "He was the very epitome of the English gentleman and able to portray that character in so many different ways on the screen, including the most villainous, and all with great talent." He also noted, "I haven't seen the picture since I made it and would like to confirm my memories of it." He finally did just that when he looked back on the production in a brief essay he wrote to accompany the 2010 BFI DVD release of the film.

"*Song of Paris* was mostly fun to make," he decided. "I met Anne Vernon, the French actress who played the lead, in Montfour Lamoury, sixty miles west of Paris. She and Claude Dauphin, the well-known stage actor, owned a delightful French miniature chateau not far from Jean Anouilh's home (whom I later met when I did *Waltz of the Toreadors.*) Anne and I got on right away — luckily I was fluent in French having been born in England of French parents — but when Claude Dauphin came down the staircase a few minutes later, apparently in a hurry, before Anne could introduce us he asked me what films of mine he might have seen. When I replied that I doubted there were any, he muttered an apology and rapidly departed. Anne explained that he was always like that, leading the way to the drawing room where we drank some excellent pre-luncheon sherry.

Dennis Price being his suave, charming self in a scene from Song of Paris

"Dennis Price played opposite Anne. He was a delightful actor with a wonderful command of what was then known as the King's English. Dennis took me to dinner at the local pub in Shepperton, The Ship, on many a happy occasion. He had a mannerism of lifting his right forearm and stretching out the fingers, simulating a faint resemblance to an ostrich's head which he used for pointing at whatever he was alluding to. After dinner, usually rather late and while still sitting at the table, he would point towards the bar where Len the barman and Maître D' would be patiently waiting, and, in beautifully modulated tones, deliver one of his favorite lines: 'Len . . . two more large ports . . . .'

Mischa Auer, the lanky Russian comedian, was always utterly professional and word perfect in his dialogue scenes. While we were shooting, his wife was blessed with the birth of a bonny baby son, and Mischa turned up at the studio somewhat the worse for wear. In fact, he was unable to stand up straight, or remain standing for more than a few seconds. I quickly decided to cut out all his moves in the scene so that his position remained static throughout. We then rehearsed with the other actors and I asked Mischa not to mind if he delivered his lines from one position. He was delighted. Two able props held him firmly round the waist to a standing position. The operator framed the shot just above their hands, and we rolled the camera. The other actors moved around Mischa, while he followed them with his eyes in a perfectly natural way, delivering his dialogue right on cue — and word perfect!"

While modern viewers are unlikely to be outraged by the innocuous humour of this quaintly coy comic curio, it was a different story back in the day, when *Song of Paris* was considered racy, risqué and daring. *The News of the World* loved it. "Pretty blondes suddenly lose their skirts and pompous aristocrats are deprived of their pants. Such fun! But meanwhile when no lingerie or trousers are involved.... The film slips over some slick and deliciously funny dialogue." *The Daily Film Renter*, meanwhile, cast a similarly appreciative, but rather more sober eye over the production. "Lively development with helpings of fun bordering on the slapstick, witty dialogue, sentimental melody and sophisticated backgrounds... bright British comedy... sophisticated style, lively continental scenes in Paris... story goes at a good pace. A laugh provoking climax... winds up a breezy comedy that is well sustained by its three principals... popular entertainment appeal." Furthermore, on this occasion even the hard to please *Monthly Film*

Song of Paris *was considered racy, risqué and daring*

Bulletin managed to force out a few words of praise. "Characters and presentation have life... the centre of charm lies in Anne Vernon, while Dennis Price has found a sympathetic role at last."

In terms of ticket sales, *Song of Paris* delivered — that is to say it certainly did far better than *Torment*. The Dents had their first Guillermin-directed money-spinner on their hands. They had invested £17,490 of a £24,000 budget, but as early as January 1953 the film had taken over £30,000 at the British box office (additionally, they later acquired the producer's rights when Vandyke went into liquidation). Foreign sales were excellent. *Song of Paris* did very well indeed in France, the Benelux territories, Spain and Norway, and was screened as far afield as the USA, Hong Kong, Australia, Israel, Egypt, Indonesia, Sierra Leone and Gambia. Guillermin's undeniable talent was beginning to turn a profit.

Away from Adelphi that year, Guillermin remained busy, directing a diverse variety of British material. For Butcher's Film Services, at Nettlefold Studios, he lensed *Operation Diplomat* (1953), an adaptation of a Francis Durbridge kidnap thriller. For Vandyke, and sharing screen credit with Don Chaffey, he worked once again with producer Roger Proudlock, directing one of the two curious tales, *The Strange Mr. Bartleby* and *The Strange Journey*, which were contained in *Strange Stories* (1953). Featuring Valentine Dyall and John Slater as two men exchanging stories en route to a train station, this eerie oddity saw release as a single portmanteau "B" picture in UK cinemas, but was split into two separate dramas for its broadcast on American television. In many ways, this minor work pointed the way forward for the domestic film industry. Upcoming years would see Guillermin — and various other British directors and actors — either upping sticks to seek employment abroad, or dividing their time between features and television work, as the new stay-at-home entertainment medium increasingly eroded the position of the cinema supporting feature.

Guillermin returned to work at Adelphi in 1954, to undertake what was arguably his most ambitious directorial venture yet: a female-led, multi-faceted shop floor melodrama, combining multiple intertwining narratives, to be played out by a large and unwieldy cast. Based on an original concept by David Dent, this film reflected John and David's lifelong interest in the position of women in society — in the world of work as well as romance. Entitled *The Crowded Day*, this challenging melodrama was an audacious, expensive attempt by the family film business to make a fully-fledged "A" Picture and take on the big boys of British film-making at their own game. Arthur Dent was determined that, despite budgetary limitations and the fact that Adelphi lacked its own studio space, this latest film should have "production values comparable with any film produced in British studios."

Richard Wattis has trouble getting a mannequin dressed

He was also keen, despite his unending troubles with the major cinema chains, to try once again to persuade market-leaders Rank and ABC to book the film across their circuits, not at sporadic locations, nor as a supporting feature, but at the top of the bill. To attempt to ensure a warm reception, he and David pulled out all the stops to ensure that *The Crowded Day* was a top-drawer product. Two well-known stars with recent hits under their belt were sub-contracted, from Rank, to play the leads — at considerable expense. These were Joan Rice, who had recently

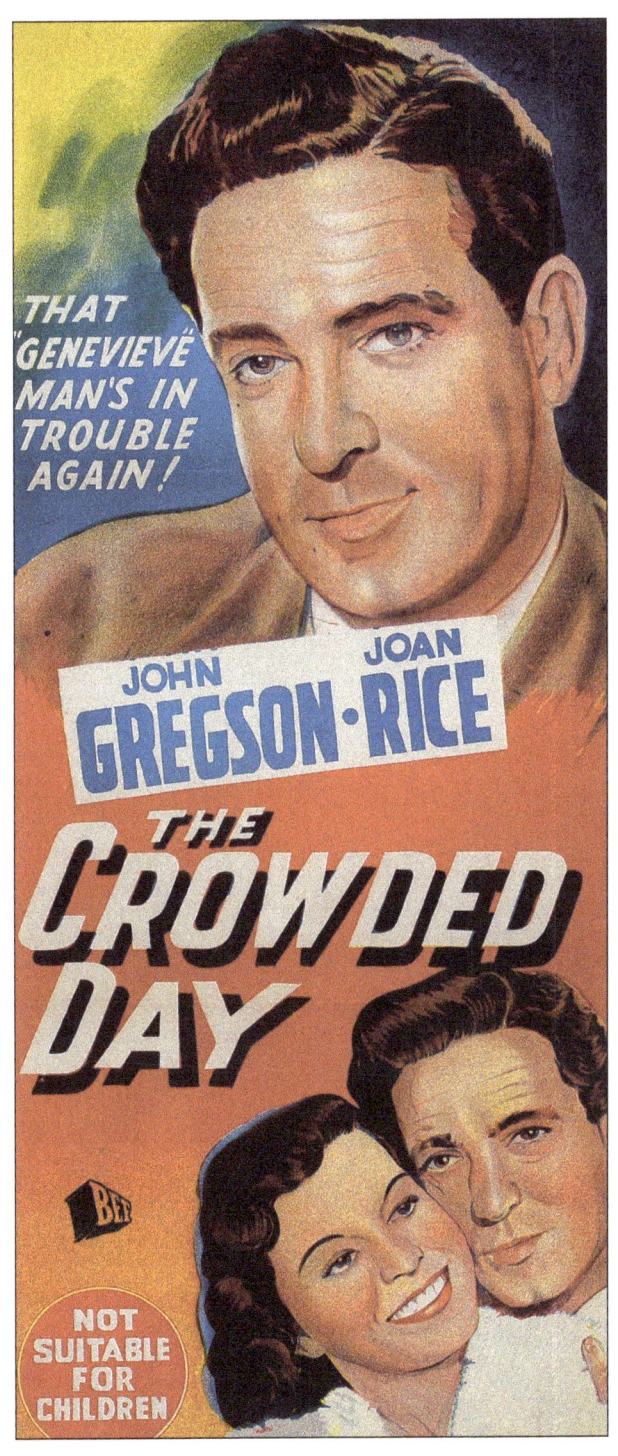

A sophisticated compendium drama telling five "one day in the life of" stories.

starred opposite Burt Lancaster in the British-American co-production *His Majesty O'Keefe* (1953), and John Gregson, still riding high on the success of vintage car comedy *Genevieve* (1953). Furthermore, the role he was to play in the new production, as automobile-obsessed owner of beloved old banger Bessie, was specially crafted to capitalize on his earlier assignment.

Taking no chances, David Dent made sure to secure an excellent supporting cast too, bustling both with familiar faces and new talent. It included the delightful Vera Day, Rachel Roberts, Dandy Nichols, Edward Chapman, Richard Wattis, Thora Hird, Dora Bryan, Prunella Scales, Sydney Tafler and Sidney James. Furthermore, Dent commissioned a tight, juicy script (originally entitled *Shop-Soiled*) from Talbot Rothwell (Rothwell had recently adapted the bedroom farce *Is Your Honeymoon Really Necessary* as an Adelphi vehicle for Diana Dors and was later to crack out various *Carry On* films), and, of course, multi-tasker supreme Guillermin was back on board to hold things together from the director's chair. He and David Dent worked hard to sharpen up the screen play still further, both making uncredited contributions to the shooting script.

Production began in February 1954, with the bulk of the shooting taking place at Nettlefold Studios, Walton-on-Thames. But David Dent also managed to secure one day's shooting at Bourne and Hollingsworth, the famous department store on Oxford Street, at no charge — in return for the publicity provided to the store. This was quite a coup. Though the shop became Bunting and Hobbs for the purposes of the drama, the real name of the shop can be clearly seen in the location-shot opening title sequence. The imposing frontage and impressive interiors lent an added air of authenticity to the drama; filming went smoothly, and by July, the film was complete.

The finished film was a sophisticated piece of urban melodrama that skillfully and engagingly reflected the emergent aspirations of five postwar women in London, their lives linked by the department store in which they worked. Touching on a variety of contemporary topics — including the then-contentious issue of unmarried mothers, and shifts in female aspiration in the postwar period — some of the numerous narrative strands were more light-hearted than others, but all were slickly conceived and intelligently, evocatively played out against the lively backdrop of a large, busy shop in the midst of a frantic Christmas rush.

A dynamic dramatic piece, *The Crowded Day* focused predominantly on the position of women in society in the 1950s, presaging patterns of life and work for women that would develop in the decades to come. It was released in 1954 — a time when Britain was still recovering from the agonies and austerities of six long years of conflict. It was already nine years since World War II had ended; yet there were still severe shortages and restrictions. It would not be until the end of the decade that the politicians would decide Britain had "never had it so good."

During World War I, women had enthusiastically undertaken what were then considered exclusively "male" occupations. They had laboured in the coal industry, worked as Land Girls, sold tickets as bus conductors, and assembled bombs in munitions factories; but at the end of the war they were banished back to their "proper" place: the home. They'd done their bit again in the Second World War, and, after that, had been similarly dismissed; but, this time, despite predictably patriarchal pressures upon the ladies to stay at home, the world of work started to open up — with a slow increase in both aspirations and employment opportunities for women. The money that women earned contributed towards paying for luxuries that were just starting to become available: foreign travel, household appliances such as washing machines and vacuum cleaners, and glamorous clothes — which had been hard to come by during the war. The coronation of Queen Elizabeth in 1953, broadcast live on television, had brought yet another new luxury item, the television set, into the home, and the popular new monarch was a vivacious role model for women across the country. After years of austerity and "making do," fashion was once more becoming flamboyant, stylish and fun, as well as relatively cheap and accessible.

Vera Day wants to challenge the dominant status quo of her boss poaching her sales

These social developments were reflected in the multiple storylines of *The Crowded Day*. Men still firmly dominated the workplace management, but — the film gently hints — there were plenty of young and ambitious women who, before long, would come to challenge the dominant status quo. Along with this narrative undercurrent of optimism for a fairer future, the film also considers the pressures and problems commensurate with being a woman in the workplace. One story strand sees a woman, married to a man who has become disabled fighting in the war overseas, pretending to be single: if she revealed she was married, the narrative suggests, she might be fired. Another plotline concerns a woman who finds herself pregnant, unmarried, and consequently suffering bitter humiliation at the hands of her errant boyfriend's snobbish mother. When her pregnancy is accidentally revealed to her employers, after she faints on the shop floor, she is interviewed by the Head of Personnel. This friendly fellow suggests that she leave work, then have the baby adopted; but he kindly offers to keep her job open for her so she can come back afterwards and "it will be as if it never happened." Despairing, the unfortunate woman ends up sadly trudging the wintry streets, considering suicide. Startling snapshots of a distant time, such scenes still resonate now: concisely reflecting the casual sexism of the workplace and of the time — albeit clad in the guise of a caring, patriarchal liberalism — that would be increasingly challenged in the decades ahead.

Guillermin recalled his time making *The Crowded Day* for an essay that accompanied the BFI DVD release of the film.

> "*Crowded Day* was a great opportunity for me in my early directing days afforded me by Arthur Dent, and his son David, of Adelphi Films. Gordon Dines was the cameraman: a tall, witty, sad looking man who worked mostly for Mickey Balcon at Ealing, and one of my favorites of all time. He used Bourne and Hollingsworth's existing lighting, adding just a few of his own units to achieve a realistic result. Furthermore, whenever I asked, 'How much longer do you think, Gordon?' his answer was always, 'Shoot it!'
>
> "I vividly remember Joan Rice, one of the leads, introducing me on set to an ageing gentleman, Harry Green the stage comedian: 'John, meet Harry Green — Harry, this is John my director.' Green stared up at me from his chair and suddenly stood up, thrusting his face forward, smashing his fist down on the small table next to him, exclaiming in a loud voice: 'I'm the greatest stage comedian that's ever lived!' I was startled and looked to Joan for guidance. She was grinning broadly, enjoying the moment which she obviously had been expecting."

Writing for the same release, actress Vera Day, who played sassy shop girl Suzy, recalled enjoying her time on the set of *The Crowded Day*, and provided some candid behind-the-scenes insights into the exasperating challenges that faced the sometimes fiery young director on set.

"I was very excited to land such a major role so early in my career. I went into it full of enthusiasm and naiveté, enabling me to give a totally natural performance. It was thrilling to work with the likes of Sidney James and so many other great artistes, too.

"Rachel Roberts, who played my mate, was a delightful lady, full of fun and always ready for a laugh. She had a feisty side to her nature and was afraid of no one. I well remember an incident which involved budgerigars. They were used in a scene which was quite dramatic and somehow they managed to escape from their cage. The result was chaos. Filming came to a grinding halt as various methods were used to try and recapture them. John Guillermin, the lovely man directing the film, alas did not find it funny at all; in fact, he was tearing his hair out trying to get them back in the cage. However, they were more than happy to spread their wings and fly about all over the studio, squeaking and squawking. Lots of time and money were wasted. Rachel and I were rather like naughty schoolgirls and John got angrier by the minute. Finally, in desperation he ordered that someone should obtain a gun and shoot them. Thankfully, the birds were captured by the crew members, calm was restored and shooting (of the film variety) continued. No wonder they say that British film crews are the best. Lots of memories, fabulous people, loads of fun. It was a privilege to work on *The Crowded Day*."

Trade screenings were well received, and the reviews were generally good, with *What's on in London* succinctly expressing what was probably the Adelphi team's dearest wish — that the film would "make producer David Dent's pockets jingle."

Vera Day enjoys the Christmas Dance with her boyfriend

But despite the lavishness of this new effort, and the previous box-office popularity of Guillermin's *Song of Paris*, which should surely have assured *The Crowded Day* a decent circuit release, there was to be no jingling. Relations between the big cinema chains and the feisty team at Adelphi remained fraught with difficulty. Despite strenuous efforts, it was only through the customary dogged Dent determination that a release was finally secured at all, in the midst of a particularly bleak winter, at a smattering of cinemas in the Odeon chain, in November 1954. Few braved the winter winds to see it.

But the fact remained that this was no bargain-basement "B" picture. Rothwell's witty, richly textured script ably combined laughter and tears; and Guillermin's fluid direction flitted moodily between light and dark, slickly alternating between smoky, film-noirish drama and coy comedy in a matter of moments. This was a film that deserved an audience — but didn't get it. Without the benefit of a full circuit release, it could not recoup its costs; but it deserved better.

John Guillermin was pleased when *The Crowded Day* received the belated beginnings of a reappraisal, following its DVD release and a special 2010 screening at BFI Southbank in London. He wrote enthusiastically at the time to Kate Lees: "It's so surprising to me that a small commercial film of that era can still elicit enough interest from serious lovers and students of the great classical cinema. Well done Adelphi Films! And my deep respect for the BFI and the relevant people involved in the enormous task of weeding out, from what must be a great deal of film, some acceptable material." As usual, there was modesty and an air of light-hearted self-deprecation in Guillermin's message; for *The Crowded Day* was certainly far more than acceptable — and despite its failure to deliver a financial return, it was undeniably one of the very strongest Adelphi productions of all. Certainly, it provided a splendid showcase for Guillermin's growing directorial talents.

These talents were, after this last and most significant project for the Dents, to be utilized elsewhere: *The Crowded Day* was Guillermin's last film for Adelphi. But with a wide range of technically-impressive and directorially demanding accomplishments now securely under his belt, and having by now become something of an experienced and reliable hand on-set, behind the typewriter, and behind the camera, he could now confidently venture on to still more ambitious projects. And perhaps John Guillermin drew upon the lessons in craftsmanship and commerce he had learned in his early years at Adelphi in the productive decades of filmmaking that lay ahead. Arthur, David and Stanley Dent were surely not at all surprised when Guillermin — like other emergent talents their family film business nurtured — went on to enjoy enduring success, both at home and across the Atlantic.

CHAPTER 4

IRASCIBLE ICONOCLAST

Reflections on the films of John Guillermin, with particular reference to Never Let Go *and* Waltz of the Toreadors

NEIL SINYARD

LOOKING BACK ON his experience on the film *Skyjacked* (1972), its star Charlton Heston was particularly complimentary about the director, John Guillermin, whom he described as, "... imaginative and skilful ... very strong on the use of his cameras."[1] Given that Heston had worked with some of the greatest filmmakers in the history of Hollywood (William Wyler, Orson Welles, George Stevens, and Anthony Mann, to name a few), this was a considerable tribute. Heston added that Guillermin had "an irascible streak."[2] Considering the fact that, despite his qualities as a director, there had at that time been no critical book on his work, barely any articles on his career, and for that matter, scarcely an extended critical appreciation of a single film of his, one might conclude that he had every reason to be irascible. After the colossal success of *The Towering Inferno* (1974), he could have expected that someone then would have taken the trouble to re-evaluate his career; but after asserting there had been no sign of progress in Guillermin's work since his early

"B" pictures, David Thompson, in the first edition of his hugely influential, overly revered *Biographical Dictionary of the Cinema* (1975), merely observed, "It speaks for the unease of modern cinema that so plain a director... should handle the most successful disaster [movie] ever."[3] I could think of several adjectives to characterise Guillermin's style as a director; "plain" would never be one of them.

Heston made another acute perception on Guillermin in his journals. "He seems," he wrote, "to have a good eye for casting."[4] This is an understatement. Guillermin's eye for new or emerging talent on screen rivalled that of Fred Zinnemann and Elia Kazan. Think of the actors who made their first big impression in a Guillermin film: Sean Connery in *Tarzan's Greatest Adventure* (1959), probably the most striking of his pre-Bond performances; Carol White in *Never Let Go* (1960), one of the sexiest performances in British cinema; Mia Farrow in *Guns at Batasi* (1964), which won her a Golden Globe award as Most Promising Newcomer; Jessica Lange in *King Kong* (1976), whose screen debut as the feisty feminist in Kong's grasp led to star roles in the following decade. Perhaps most striking was a cameo in *The Day They Robbed the Bank of England* (1960) of a young Peter O'Toole, a performance that came to the attention of David Lean when he was looking for someone to play Lawrence of Arabia.[5] The rest, as they say, is history.

As remarkable as Guillermin's ability for discovering or encouraging new talent in his films was his capacity for stretching the range of already established actors and in unexpected directions. The transformation of Peter Sellers from comic to character actor in *Never Let Go* and *Waltz of the Toreadors* (1962) is a particularly striking example; but one should also mention Sellers' co-star in *Never Let Go*, Richard Todd, unexpectedly vulnerable and moving as the ineffectual cosmetics salesman for whom the retrieval of his stolen car will be essential towards a recovery of his self-respect. "I loved doing it," he said, "because it was a character part for me"[6] and quite different from the roles of unruffled integrity he was usually assigned. No one since Hitchcock on *Stage Fright* (1950) had made better use of what Hitchcock called Todd's "expressive eyes," even if, at the end of *Never let Go* one of them is closed after the battering it has taken.

Richard Todd's expressive eyes

Although he surprisingly makes no reference to it in his autobiography, *Up in the Clouds, Gentlemen Please,* John Mills' performance as the truculent, class-conscious, chip-on-his-shoulder policeman in *Town on Trial* (1957) was a turning-point for him, paving the way for the tortured characterisations to come in *Ice Cold in Alex* (1958) and *Tunes of Glory* (1960), which are the pinnacles of his screen career. As Gill Plain put it in her fine study of Mills' screen persona in the context of popular British cinema: "In *Town on Trial*, Guillermin extracts from Mills a performance that disrupts the parameters of his customary Englishness."[7] Equally out-of-the-ordinary is Richard Attenborough's British Academy Award-winning performance as Sgt. Major Lauderdale in *Guns at Batasi,* a moustachioed, anachronistic RSM bristling with indignation at the new order of things and with a bull-in-a-china-shop approach to the nuances of nationalist sensitivities and political diplomacy. *Films and Filming* called it "adventurous casting that comes off;"[8] and Guillermin, along with Attenborough, deserves credit for making it come off.

Heston's salute to Guillermin's use of the camera also warrants closer scrutiny. Far from being "plain," Guillermin's camera style is more often restless and edgy. The camera is soon on the move in most of his films in a way that seems to suggest an inquisitive personality behind it and with a dynamism that underlines intensity of mood, augmented by insistent close-ups and extrovert stylistic display, like, for example, the zip-pans that precede the chief murder suspects to the dance in *Town on Trial.* Even when the camera is still, this seems more like bravado than placidity. In the opening of *Town on Trial,* it refuses to budge even when a police car is being driven towards it at high speed, and braking with seemingly only inches to spare; the jolt to the vehicle is felt with similar force by a film audience. The memorable introduction to Attenborough's Sgt. Major in *Guns at Batasi* shows him first in long shot as he marches towards the camera across the parade ground, and the camera then holds its position unflinchingly until his stamping boots are in close-up and he barks out a reprimand to an apprehensive African soldier. A more emphatic introduction to a main character can hardly be imagined.

There is also a strong erotic energy to his films. If '50s British cinema is usually noted for its sexual restraint and even repression, the message seems not to have got through to Guillermin. His heroines often exert a powerful presence, and the men in *Thunderstorm, Town on Trial, Never Let Go* and even *Waltz of the Toreadors* can be brought to a mesmerised standstill by the allure of strong women who are aware of their seductive effect and resisting victimisation even when placed in subservient situations.

Richard Attenborough won a BAFTA Award for his Sgt. Major performance

The great Hollywood maverick Robert Aldrich once said that not even his worst enemies ever accused him of understatement, and one feels the same is true of Guillermin. As in Aldrich's films, anger seems often to be bubbling above or below the surface; and running through his work is a strong streak of insubordination, where authority figures are invariably viewed with a cynical eye as men whose sense of self-importance exceeds their actual competence. Accordingly, his films do not always play by the rules, particularly when the context is military. If Aldrich has his iconoclastic war movies like *Attack!*, *The Dirty Dozen* and *Too Late the Hero*, Guillermin's are also offbeat and idiosyncratic, viewing military muddle from an unconventional angle (e.g. the post-imperial British posturing in *Guns at Batasi*, the post-World War One German perspective of *The Blue Max*) and where the films' sympathies are sometimes hard to decipher. In *I Was Monty's Double* (1958), it seems somehow characteristic of the director's subversive slyness that the main character is a fake who is only pretending to be a military legend but who exposes the credulity of the British and Americans as well as hoodwinking the Germans. *Variety* criticised *The Bridge at Remagen* for its confusion over the exact purpose of American and Nazi military thinking, but that was clearly the point. I have seldom seen a film in which military "orders" (the very word becomes an obsessive leitmotif presaging chaos) are so often undermined, ignored, or obeyed with catastrophic consequences. A palpable air of disenchantment hangs over the destruction, implicating both sides; as Judith Crist noted at the time, if you had not known beforehand, you would be hard pressed to guess from this film who won the war. If, as Geoff Mayer has claimed, Guillermin "... was most comfortable working within familiar genre conventions"[9] (although the decidedly unconventional nature of his masterpiece *Rapture* might challenge that), this could be because it gave him a framework against which to rebel or at least have fun with. *Death on the Nile* (1978) is one of the most entertaining of the Agatha Christie whodunits, partly because of the mischievous way he sends up the formula. At one stage he even demonstrates how each of the main suspects could have committed the crime with equal opportunity and (im)plausibility, in so doing implying that the solution to the puzzle is more or less arbitrary and dependent on the author's whim rather than any deductive skills of the audience. Even the world's most celebrated (and conceited) detective, Hercule Poirot (Peter Ustinov), is treated by the film with a certain amount of cheerful disdain and irreverence. Characters persist in referring to him as French rather than Belgian; and Angela Lansbury's writer insists on calling him "Monsieur Porridge." For all the supposed superiority of his little grey cells, by the time he has solved the first murder four more have been committed. In a Guillermin film, characters are very rarely given a chance to rest on their laurels or even relax. And his endings are more often equivocal than affirmative; pyrrhic victories at best.

Car Trouble:
Never Let Go (1960)

Like a number of Guillermin's films, *Never Let Go* has suffered over the years not only from being underrated but also from being misrepresented. The description of the film in *Time Out* as "stolid"[10] (whose OED definition is "lacking or concealing emotion... not easily excited or moved") defies belief. Even one of the most stimulating of all commentators on British cinema, Raymond Durgnat inaccurately attacked the film for suggesting that "...alas, the hero lost his nerve due to war-time shell-shock" rather than "peacetime weakness of character" which, he wrote, "would have been more interesting."[11] The film does no such thing and indeed Elizabeth Sellars' wife makes it clear that it is precisely her husband's "peacetime weakness of character" that is at the root of his dilemma. Durgnat then proceeds to fantasise a preferred, alternative narrative far inferior to the one the film has come up with. The cover for the film's DVD release is so misleading as to deserve some sort of prize for misinformation. Granting the release a "PG" rating (on first release in the UK, the film was given an "X" certificate), the DVD company explains its classification in the following way: under "Sex" it says "None" (in fact, there are three bedroom scenes in the film and it would take an exceptional lack of perception to miss the abuse and depravity at the heart of the villain's dominating relationship with his teenage mistress); under "Violence" it says "Mild, Infrequent," whereas the violence in the film is fairly constant and, even by modern standards, extreme. The hero is savagely beaten up twice; Adam Faith's young thief has his hand deliberately trapped under a gramophone lid; both Faith and Todd's family are menaced by Sellers' villain with a broken bottle; and the film concludes with a fight between Sellers and Todd in which practically the entire contents of a garage are deployed as malevolent

Todd's family are menaced by Peter Sellers' villain with a broken bottle

weapons. Even a pet terrapin is drawn into the general mayhem, being deliberately trampled on by Sellers and an act of brutality that prompts Mervyn Johns' distraught newspaper seller to commit suicide. At the other extreme is the view expressed at the time in the *Monthly Film Bulletin* (June 1960), which recognised the film's deliberately heightened style but thought "the obtrusive shock cutting, exaggerated camera angles, and a self-consciously strident use of 'adult' language all serve to accentuate the essential falsity of the characterisations."[12] This is misrepresentation of a different kind, seeming to expect the subdued social realism of a director like Basil Dearden when it is much closer in manner to the expressionist stylisation of Jules Dassin in *Night and the City* mode. "Adult language" is surely what one might expect in the criminal underworld the film is exploring. Shock cutting and exaggerated camera angles are entirely justified if what is being dramatized is the anguish of an ordinary man who finds himself suddenly in unfamiliar and dangerous territory and living a waking nightmare.

Never Let Go is a first-class British film noir. It sets up the basic situation and the main characters in an opening three minutes of classic narrative exposition without a word being said, and thereafter never lets go. Sparks fly out at the camera in the opening shot, anticipating the dramatic sparks to follow, as the operation of a stolen cars racket is shown in action (number plates being removed, cars being re-sprayed, money and information being exchanged) and its headquarters located at the garage of an ostensibly respectable businessman, Lionel Meadows (Peter Sellers). The credits are shown over a shot of a Ford Anglia, owned by John Cummings (Richard Todd) and which, so to speak, will be the engine of the entire plot. Over the soundtrack, Adam Faith sings a pop version of "When Johnny Comes Marching Home," which at first might seem incongruous but which is actually a mocking reference to the hero, called "Johnny" by his wife, who will come staggering, not marching, home and will be given anything but a hearty welcome, neither by his wife nor by Police Inspector Thomas (Noel Willman), who accuses him of jeopardising his investigations. The innovative jazz score by a young John Barry is plainly influenced by Elmer Bernstein's jazz-inflected scores which emphasised the sleazy ambience of *The Man with the Golden Arm* (1955) and *Sweet Smell of Success* (1957); and, along with Johnny Dankworth's jazz score for Joseph Losey's *The Criminal* of the same year, brought a new sound into British film scoring. The moody, nocturnal photography by that master cameraman, Christopher Challis, plunges a spectator into a world of dark shadow and murky motivation. Based on a story by Guillermin and the film's producer, Peter de Sarigny, the screenplay by an unsung master of the film and TV crime thriller, Alun Falconer, is so finely constructed that there is not a single superfluous character or scene. A gallery of infallible British supporting actors (including Nigel Stock, David Lodge, John Le Mesurier, Peter Jones) add to the film's sense of conviction and professionalism. The film also economically — and sometimes brutally — evokes a country emerging

Peter Sellers' only straight-man role, as an intimidating gangster

from an era of austerity into one of prosperity, in the process sloughing off decent people like John Cummings who have not kept pace with change. Cummings might cite the Harold McMillan slogan for the era and claim, "I've never had it so good," but the quizzical look from his younger colleague, Spink (Charles Houston) seems to suggest that his confidence is misplaced. His boss, Alec Berger (Peter Jones) will tell him that, in the new world of commerce, "we can't afford any of us to stand still." Ironically, the film's villain, Meadows, will say more or less the same thing to one of his workers, Regan (Nigel Stock), when he seems to be lagging behind in the alterations he is making to the stolen cars.

As is the case in Vittorio De Sica's neo-realist masterpiece, *Bicycle Thieves* (1948), the theft of the hero's vehicle does not simply threaten his livelihood; it accelerates a loss of self-esteem. It is worth remembering that car ownership was still a comparative rarity in postwar Britain and a symbol of status and social mobility: recall the way Laurence Harvey's ambitious hero ogles the boyfriend's car even before he ogles the tycoon's daughter as the ultimate object of his desire in *Room at the Top* (1959). Cummings' frustration is compounded by the fact that he can quickly trace the theft to Meadows, but proving it to the police is another matter; indeed the police operation seems intent on putting obstacles in his way. Inspector Thomas is mainly interested in getting to the bottom of Meadows' racket and says he could not give a damn about Cummings' stolen vehicle, which puts him at cross purposes with Cummings, whose priorities are the opposite. As a consequence, Cummings is driven to act outside the law to seek justice for himself. By now his investigations have taken on the character of a personal quest, to the detriment of his performance at work. The more obsessed he becomes, the more he comes to resemble his adversary, not only in his infringements of the law but in his abrupt mood swings and his lurches into violence. His sudden outburst of rudeness towards a client after she has complained of his lateness will lead to a demotion; and the supercilious attitude of his replacement prompts Cummings to throw some boxes at him, an action which he knows will lead to his dismissal. The closer his behaviour comes to that of Meadows, the more a confrontation between the two men seems inevitable. This is clinched in a remarkable passage towards the end, when Guillermin cuts between huge sweaty close-ups of the two men, each in his own respective lair (the garage, the café) but each hearing voices that suggest that, although physically separate, they are each predominant in the other's thoughts.

The theft of the car at the beginning of the film has begun a chain reaction of humiliation, charted by Richard Todd with great attention to small revealing details of behaviour (the nervous laugh, the mock military salute, the over-hearty manner that always rings a little hollow). Cummings is chided for his aggressive salesmanship by one of his regular clients, Mr. Pennington (John Le Mesurier) with, "Please don't try to sell me so hard." He is criticized by his boss for his poor sales performance (Guillermin shoots this in such a way that Cummings even looks smaller when he leaves Berger's office than when he entered). When he tries to tackle Tommy Towers (Adam Faith) about the theft, Towers' gang quickly surrounds him and Towers steals some soap from his bag and drops it in his drink. Even the unhappy Cypriot owner (Cyril Shaps) of the ironically named Freedom Café seems to sense, as he plies him sympathetically with tea, that Cummings might be a kindred spirit in this land of fear and harassment. When he steps outside, Cummings finds his way blocked by Towers' motorcycle gang who drive across his path to prevent his departure and generally behave in the menacing manner of the gangs in *The Wild One* (1954), the notorious Marlon Brando biker movie (which at the time was considered so shocking that it was banned from public exhibition in the UK). That night Cummings cannot sleep because the sound of the motorbikes and the mocking laughter continue to echo like a rebuke in his head. The aura of failure around him is accentuated by the place where he lives with his wife and two children (effective Art Direction by George Provis), a drably furnished flat at the top of a tower block, which is in sharp contrast to Meadows' luxurious living quarters. When Meadows bursts into Cummings' home at one stage, he cannot conceal his derision at the shabby surroundings.

> There's a scene in *Never Let Go,* where David Lodge, who was Peter Sellers' right-hand man in real life as well as in the film, where Peter Sellers was playing a crooked boss of a car dealership with a stolen car ring, and David Lodge goes to the garage doors, big wooden doors with a little look-out door that opens, and he opens the door and he's supposed to say, "Blimey, it's the Law!" And when they were filming this, David Lodge got a fit of the giggles and as he opened the door to say, "It's the Law," he just started laughing and Peter Sellers started giggling and their laughter was so infectious that the whole crew, with the possible exception of the director, was just rolling around laughing. As they kept trying to re-film this bit, David Lodge and Peter Sellers would break down and the rest of the crew would join in laughing. I think they wasted about fifteen minutes in attempting takes, and, interestingly, that scene does not appear in the final cut.

There is a particularly powerful scene in the middle of the film when Cummings' wife (sensitively played by Elizabeth Sellars) urges him to abandon his mission and leave everything to the police. She is not only alarmed at the beating he has received and the danger he is running; she sees it as symptomatic of a fundamental flaw in his character that he has never acknowledged. To her the car is not a symbol of Johnny's self-respect; it is a symbol of his self-delusion. It is just another example of what she calls his "pipe dreams" — all those things that were going to make a difference to his (and their) life, but which never materialized, like the photographic studio he was going to start, or the cottage in the country. Even the glasses he wears to work are an aspect of this delusion, she says; he does not need them. (Perhaps they just give an additional air of seriousness, one feels; they might even conceal the fear in his eyes behind the façade). "Let it go, Johnny," she says, reassuring him that she loves him as he is. "You're not meant to push and shove your way through life. You're not tough enough."

As she is speaking, tears of bewilderment begin to well up in Johnny's eyes; it is perhaps the most touching piece of acting in Richard Todd's entire screen career. It is as if her words are inflicting more pain than he received at the hands of Meadows' henchman, Cliff (David Lodge). The impression one has is that she has never spoken to him in this way before and that he has been unaware of her perception of him, which in turn compels him to see himself in a different light. "I only made one mistake," he insists. "I didn't hold on." If his wife can live with his weakness, and even love him for it, he suddenly realises that he cannot. Paradoxically, in tenderly trying to bring him to his senses, she only strengthens his determination to see things through, even at the cost of his marriage and possibly his life, for what is at stake now is his sense of self. Small wonder that some critics have seen echoes here of *High Noon*. A man who is steadily forced into a situation where he has nothing left to lose can become a formidable opponent.

In highlighting the character of Meadows as Peter Sellers' first dramatic role, the DVD box describes the villain as "Cummings' nemesis." One could actually see it the other way around; it is Cummings whose dogged persistence brings Meadows' criminal activity crashing down about his ears. Sellers was certainly a bold and controversial piece of casting. Some critics have suggested that the performance seems more like Sellers' impersonation of a movie gangster than a convincing representation of the real thing. With its surface swagger and false bonhomie, only thinly disguising a sense of threat just below the surface, the performance reminds me in some respects (and this is a compliment) of Lee J. Cobb's corrupt union boss in *On the Waterfront*, which also ends in a bloody hand-to-hand fight between the villain and the lone individual who has brought down his crooked empire. There are echoes of *On the Waterfront* also in the quayside brawl that concludes *Thunderstorm*. "Sellers played a heavy in *Never Let Go*," wrote Raymond Durgnat, "with immaculate technical perfection, and made us all laugh."[13] This might have been true for audiences of the time, accustomed to Sellers' comic persona and unwilling to adjust to this new example of his versatility; but to later biographers of Sellers, the characterisation seemed unnervingly close to his unstable and occasionally violent personality. "It was more than a conscious effort to extend his range," wrote Alexander Walker, "it seemed like a role chosen to match his black moods."[14] Ed Sikov noted one occasion when, coming home from the studio during the making of the film, Sellers seemed unable to shake himself free of the role and threw a vase at his wife, Anne. On another occasion, he tried to brain her with a bottle of milk and had to be calmed down by David Lodge, always one of his most loyal friends (and who was to marry Guillermin's sister, Lyn). Meadows' eruptions of violence look very authentic, and all the more disturbing because they are often preceded by a moment of calm, suggesting either that the attack is premeditated to catch the victim off guard or that the man is unable to control the rising fury within him. With a rasping voice that seems somehow caught between a smile and a snarl and explosions of rage that come from nowhere, Sellers gives Meadows a frightening and intimidating presence, the sense of someone you cross at your peril. Alexander Walker described the role as "a vivid testament to an almost pathological streak in Sellers' character."[15]

Always Too Late:
Waltz of the Toreadors

Guillermin also tapped into a different dimension of Sellers' screen persona in *Waltz of the Toreadors,* a breezy adaptation by Wolf Mankowitz of the Jean Anouilh play about a lecherous General facing retirement and old age in the period immediately preceding the First World War. Sellers' performance at first sight seems to be in a broadly comic vein (the voice he adopts is that of Major Bloodnok whom he created in the classic radio series *The Goon Show)*. Unhappily married to an invalid wife (Margaret Leighton) and partially compensating through a series of adulterous flirtations, the General senses a chance of enduring happiness through the return in his life of Ghislaine (Dany Robin), with whom he has been platonically in love since he danced with her at a ball 17 years ago. She has remained chaste out of love and loyalty but now has discovered evidence (love letters from the General's wife to her doctor) that can set him free. Yet, through a series of complications (e.g. a broken leg), libidinous encounters (e.g. with a willing dressmaker) and farcical mishaps (an attempt to climb into Ghislaine's hotel room, which ends with his falling into a water-butt), the General is never able to consummate his love, with the result that, in the meantime, Ghislaine falls for his young secretary (John Fraser) who turns out to be the General's illegitimate son. The farcical elements are handled with some gusto, particularly when the General challenges Dr. Brogan (Cyril Cusack) to a fight over his wife's honour but finds his only available weapon is an umbrella; and there is a delightful moment when the Doctor, driving through a fox-hunt in his dilapidated car, discovers that the fox has hitched a lift to avoid its pursuers.

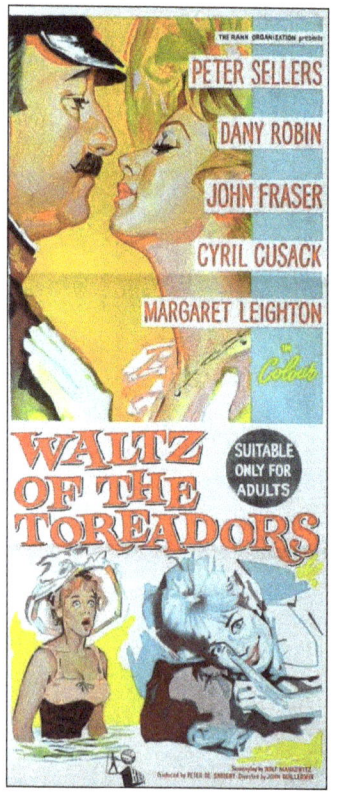

Yet, amidst the farce, there is an undertow of sadness about the fate of a man who, for a variety of reasons (many to do with weaknesses in his own character), has let the chance of happiness slip through his fingers. The General is far from blameless, of course; in addition to his flirtations with adultery, he has insisted that his wife should give up a promising operatic career, which has only contributed to her sense of ill-use through his patriarchal selfishness and has driven her to becoming what her Doctor has called "a professional invalid." Few actresses could match Margaret Leighton for conveying

> Peter Sellers was given a part in *Waltz of the Toreadors* where he had to play both his young self and an older version of himself who's supposed to be seventy. And the first thing Peter said was, "I'm not going to sit in makeup for five hours." He was such a good mimic that he mimicked the posture, gait and the voice of an old Major neighbor of his to such effect that he doesn't quite look seventy but he definitely looks way older than his younger self in the film, all without any extra makeup. Quite an achievement.
>
> The other story is that during the filming of *Waltz of the Toreadors*, in real life, Peter Sellers received word that his first wife, Ann Todd, had left him. And he was devastated. He kept breaking down during one particular scene and he couldn't say his lines. John said something to him like, "Just sit at the desk. Don't say anything." I don't know exactly what he said but basically just, be sad, and look at the revolver. Think about ending it all. And he did, and that's a very powerful scene in the film.

the anguish of sexual repression and jealousy; and her performance here was only to be surpassed later by her Mrs. Maudsley in Joseph Losey's *The Go-Between* (1971), a woman smouldering with frustration beneath the polite civilities of turn-of-the-century upper-class society. It says much for Peter Sellers' dramatic, as well as comic, prowess that his performance fully matches that of his co-star. Guillermin draws a performance of pathos and pain from him that he was never again to display on screen. How far this was accentuated by the fact that his marriage was disintegrating at this time is impossible to say. There is a moment when he is talking about his life to his friend, the Doctor, and he says quietly, "The shell is empty. There's nobody inside. I am alone, and I am afraid." The character's self-revelation feels perilously close to that of the actor playing him. Sellers was to win the Best Actor award at the San Sebastian Film Festival: and it is arguable, that in the two films he made with him, Guillermin got closer to the real Peter Sellers than any other director.

The dramatic highlight of the film should have been the marital row, in which two people, formerly in love and now bound together by mutual hatred, vie for each other in striving for the most wounding revelation that will destroy whatever remains of their romantic illusions. It is superbly acted by Sellers and Leighton, but its impact is blunted by the studio's decision to intercut the film's most powerful scene with its silliest: a riotously unfunny frolic in the fields with a shrieking Dany Robin and a palpitating John Fraser. The studio was obviously afraid that a coruscating scene of marital reproach and recrimination might not fit their conception of the film as a period sex romp, but Guillermin was justifiably livid at this interference. Fortunately, the visual highlight remains intact: the waltz that the General shares with Ghislaine will prove the summit of his happiness. Richard Addinsell's theme is one of his loveliest; the sweeping camera movement over the dance floor is

Peter Seller's General is rescued by the appearance of the new maid

the epitome of choreographic elegance; the dissolves between past and present as the General muses alone in his private room, which in itself is a sort of mausoleum of memory and past glory, are the essence of bittersweet reverie. Such remembrances will take him close to the point of suicide, but from which he will be rescued by the appearance of the new maid, standing in the spot where Ghislaine stood on her return, with a promise of fulfilment that has since been scattered to the winds (like the pages of his memoirs, blown to the floor as he opened the window to the storm outside). When he puts his arm around the new maid's waist, there is a sense of life starting up again, but perhaps in a different, more melancholy manner: an affectionate gesture that reflects less a sudden flare of lust than an imminent fear of loneliness.

Conclusion

Although he was to go on to great success in Hollywood, it could be argued that the core of Guillermin's achievement resides in the films he made between 1957 and 1965: that is, between *Town on Trial* (his breakthrough) and *Rapture* (his masterpiece). Rather like Carol Reed, he seemed more at home within an English or European environment than an American one and was at his best working in black and white rather than colour, for it seemed to offer a more expressive and exciting photographic challenge. Historically this period of British film has tended to be dominated by critical consideration of the Free Cinema Movement, the British New Wave, the Bond phenomenon and the cinema of the Swingin' Sixties. In the process, a number of British film directors who were not critically fashionable but made some of their best work during that period, have tended to be bypassed: one thinks of Ken Hughes (*The Trials of Oscar Wilde, The Small World of Sammy Lee*), Val Guest (*Hell is a City, The Day the Earth Caught Fire*), Ronald Neame (*The Horse's*

Mouth, Tunes of Glory), Bryan Forbes (*The L-Shaped Room, Séance on a Wet Afternoon*) and a number of others who deserve reclamation. John Guillermin is one of these. His idiosyncratic approach to genre, his adventurous casting, his offbeat heroes and those forceful women who struck fear and desire into the hearts of men, marked him out as a forceful and unusual talent; and his visual flair, although sometimes erring on the side of exaggeration, rarely failed to excite.

CHAPTER 5

A LOVER OF FEMININITY IN ALL ITS FULLNESS

MARY GUILLERMIN

MY HUSBAND LOVED, and respected, women in general, and he loved women's potential for soft vulnerability in particular. Soon after we married, he pulled a passport-size photo of his first wife out of his wallet dating from the early years of their nearly forty-year marriage, and said in an almost reverent and rather wistful tone, "Look at the softness in her face." He discouraged me from wearing makeup saying: "You don't need makeup, Mary. I've worked with some of the most beautiful women in the world, and I'm telling you, you don't need makeup." He took photos of me in the rolling Essex fields by our rented first home that highlighted this quality of softness. His vision created me beautiful.

His real-life relationship with women was complex. On the one hand, cherishing — how many men would still love a woman after forty years of marriage, loving her for years after she had finally left him, loving her even after falling in love with me — yet on the other hand, at times devastatingly harsh. He yelled. He intermittently bruised my soul with fierce, loud noise. I don't recall receiving attacking words of personal cruelty; just a barrage of vicious noise that left no room to breathe. His own story, in the first chapter of this book, reveals the age-old pattern that we see in the history of those who abuse; the victimized became the victimizer. He was honest about himself, and I am honest about him.

Yet what perceptiveness John had of the female of the species. Acknowledging our strengths, our desire to pull against societal limitations, as well as appreciating our gentle, conventionally feminine sides. The composite vision threading through his films of what it means to be a woman would be extraordinary in its fullness even for a man born half a century later than John, but for someone who was born seven years after the First World War ended, who was in his fifties during the Feminist movement of the 1970s — though he probably paid no attention to political movements or events — his sensibility was indeed extraordinary.

Women Inside Their Softness: A Clarion Call to Femininity

John's love of vulnerability as a core part of femininity shines through in his direction of Jessica Lange in *King Kong* (1976). The search for the lead actress had been a long one and he was pretty desperate when Lange arrived for a screen test, full of a head cold and flushed, with a runny nose. She had been suggested for a tryout by the head of the modeling agency she worked for in New York, Wilhelmina. John sent her to a hotel to recover and ran the test a few days later. When he watched the result, he yelled with excitement and kicked over the seat in front of him, blurting out, "I've found my Fay Wray!" I think what he had first seen despite her puffy eyes and runny nose, was the quality of innocence and fresh openness Jessica Lange would, and did, display in her role as Dwan.

I believe this untrained but natural actress — her long and successful acting career since *King Kong,* her debut film, is sure testimony to her talent — exemplified John's vision of a pure Femininity. Right from the moment we see her on the raft, her face and the line of her body expresses softness. As she awakens to consciousness and she describes her shipwreck ordeal, we can feel her vulnerability. As she runs along the beach in delight on first landing on the island, as she is drugged and dragged to be sacrificed to Kong, her innocence and extreme vulnerability shine in her body and her face. As she submits to the hot breath blown by Kong to dry her under the waterfall, her performance makes me at least feel her experience as a sensuous echo in my own body. Note John's careful eye directing the camera. Despite the challenge of showing a developing

Mary and John in their garden among the fields of Essex, England, 1998

A LOVER OF FEMININITY IN ALL ITS FULLNESS

tenderness between the human female and the huge ape, he doesn't stray into lasciviousness or over-sexualization, as I rather wincingly feel the portrayal of this character in Peter Jackson's 2000 version of *King Kong* does. Lange is deliciously feminine, and despite being ogled by the men on board the oil ship and, we feel, loved by Kong, the eye of the director does not objectify, does not offer her up (intentionally, at least) as prey for sexual fantasies. John celebrates her innocence and refuses to objectify her.

In *King Kong* where Dwan appears almost like a mermaid stranded on debris from the yacht's shipwreck and with the fantasy island setting, John had the freedom to wax lyrical about the side of Femininity he so loved. It's my belief that consciously or otherwise, he was reacting to the increasing rejection of the soft side of Femininity by contemporary women — the pervasive feeling that was finding its way into society that if women wanted to achieve equal rights they somehow had to emulate men, rather than find their own way into the strengths of the Feminine Principle. Although I am proud of my involvement in the British Women's Liberation Movement, especially the first ever consciousness-raising groups I helped found at the University of Lancaster, Lancashire in 1971, looking back now I am saddened by the pendulum swing towards restricting and rejecting all expression of conventional femininity, that also saw fit to laud masculine attire among women. Consciously or otherwise, 1976 was a good year to stake a claim for the value of sweet delicate femininity that was by then in danger of being lost and had already been lost in great measure.

Why this focus here on the presence and presentation of femininity in *King Kong*, one of John's later films? In John's films of the Fifties and early Sixties he didn't need to pay particular attention to the soft side of femininity — it was just there in real life in the way women saw and presented themselves. The films discussed in this chapter were made in the two decades before the political feminist turbulence of the 1970s. These actresses and their characters all bear the stamp of the conventional

Joan Rice is Peggy

Josephine Griffin is Yvonne

Sonia Holm is Moira

Vera Day is Suzy

Patricia Plunkett is Alice

A LOVER OF FEMININITY IN ALL ITS FULLNESS

femininity of the 1950s and '60s — in their facial features and expressions, their body movements and their clothes. Women were expected to be women, that is, to have a feminine presentation. Rona Anderson as Joan, the secretary-housekeeper to two brothers in *Torment* aka *Paper Gallows* (1950); Kathleen Byron as Lucienne Templar *(Four Days)* (1951); Joan Rice as Peggy, Josephine Griffin as Yvonne, Vera Day as Suzy, Sonia Holm as Moira and Patricia Plunkett as Alice, the five shop girls in *The Crowded Day* (aka *Shop Spoiled)* (1954), Carol West as Jackie, the girl who had run away from reform school and Elizabeth Sellars' contrasting middle-class wife and mother, Anne Cummings *(Never Let Go)* (1960) — all these female characters expressed in their appearance the 1950s view of women.

Yet what about their feelings and thoughts, what about these women's actions? How did the director view those? In the next section, I move on to an examination of John's ability to see women's strengths at a time when society in general chose to focus on women as helpmeets and mothers and did not acknowledge their power and strength.

You may well feel that the view of femininity as expressed by Jessica Lange under John's direction is a restrictive view of femininity, and one we should have long left behind us. Let me clarify. I am a feminist, but a feminist who loves Femininity it all its glorious aspects. I want women to have our own power, power as defined by ourselves, not men. I want women to have our own voices, voices that can be strong and strident or sweet and gentle as the need and occasion demands. Yes, John did see in me a softness and gentleness he loved. But he also saw, liked and loved the woman in me who was bold and bright, dynamic and outspoken — who could be intense and exciting as well as comforting and companionable. In fact, we loved this range in each other; from the valleys of vulnerability to the intense heights of joy and passion. We were indeed well matched. In disagreements, each of us wanted to get our own way, as couples often do, and it was John who made up a game where we playfully called each other, "Boss," in such moments. We knew we could both be centers of willful strength and this tactic enabled us to each at times give way to the other's strong desire. I admit I did more often give way to John; the desire of the retired film director for some measure of control in small things was palpable, but I wasn't resented for those times where I claimed the right to be the "Boss." A slightly amusing example is that as a member of the generation before me, he had little tolerance for the "fad" of recycling trash. I let him have his way, and within days of his death, I bought myself a kitchen-size recycling bin. Ah, what little things is freedom made of!

Women Inside Their Strength: Defying Restrictive 1950s Stereotypes

This inclusive and wide-ranging acceptance of the many faces of being feminine shines through in John's films right from the beginning of his career. He had a marvelous capacity to understand — and show through the camera's eye — the whole range of feminine experience. He did not pay lip service to the 1950s idealization of Woman as homemaker, mother and wife. He did not deal with the stereotypes that abounded at that time of the nice little woman and helpmeet there to support the central person of importance, the man. In fact, in an odd twist, he may have been freer to subvert the story as written almost because the way of presenting women's roles in the Fifties was so standardized, and perhaps a touch boring. Expanding the audience's sympathy with a deeper, more layered look at what womanhood meant was a way to be daring and take risks — and deliver something more interesting than the usual run of the mill fare.

Although by the early Sixties there was beginning to be resistance to the Fifties view of women, it was books like Betty Freidan's *The Feminine Mystique*, published a few years after all of the films discussed in this chapter had been made, that blew the lid off the growing dissatisfaction ordinary women were feeling. An article in the *French Journal of English Studies: The United Kingdom and the Crisis in the 1970s* states:

> The book was a virulent condemnation of the consumer society that fed the myth of the fulfilled housewife and mother, making women prisoners of their homes and depriving them of their lives.... The dominant view was that women's 'natural' role was to care for children at home, that men were the breadwinners, and that money earnt by women was pin money. However, these legal and social practices that were keeping women in subordinate positions were increasingly perceived as unfair and outdated especially by women.

One of John's greatest regrets as expressed to me, his second wife, was that he had insisted that his first wife did not work; she was an actress who wanted to keep acting after they started a family. Later in life, he knew that insistence had been a mistake. Mistake or not, it was an easy one for the young husband to have made in the 1950s when he had been brought up by parents in very conventional roles; his father the breadwinner who managed the London factory of a famous French perfume company; his mother, deeply involved in her role as wife and mother, lavishing love on her children, and, as John complained, not venturing outside the home with her heavily-accented English.

John's father had tried to direct him into managing the family business, which John had strongly resisted, declaring he was determined to be a film director. John's father rejected his son's creativity — becoming a film director was seen by his father as impractical because it "would never make money;" an inaccurate prediction that eventually reconciled Mr. Guillermin the elder to his son's chosen profession. Perhaps this attempt to restrict the creative artist in John later led to him showing an intuitive sympathy for those female characters who wanted to express themselves outside narrow confines.

Elizabeth Sellars, the accomplished actress who played Anne Cummings opposite Richard Todd's obsession-driven salesman whose car was stolen (*Never Let Go* 1960), once said, we are told by imdb.com, "We're expected to sink back into the background and look nice," and she was often dissatisfied with the scripts she was offered. I imagine she was delighted to be offered such a rich, deep part as that of the wife struggling with her husband Johnny's obsession to retrieve his stolen car. As Johnny becomes ever more drawn into his quest, Anne reflects back to him, lovingly but with a depth of truthfulness he has never encountered from her before, that she loves him just as he is, a dreamer who never reaches his goal. She doesn't want him to be tough, she likes his human vulnerability.

But Johnny is shocked at her words and feels misunderstood by her. He persists in believing that if only he had just hung on longer, the dream would have been fulfilled, and therefore that is what he must do this time. As an audience we watch Anne struggle with the dilemma that arises for the loved ones of alcoholics, compulsive gamblers or any other person with addictive behavior. How can she get him to stop putting himself and their family at risk from Peter Seller's gangster boss? Johnny refuses to give up trying and as a result of his "meddling" into Meadow's affairs, a menacing Sellers bursts in into their apartment with a beautifully acted display of repressed violence that is just waiting to spill out. Meadows breaks a vase and is about to attack Johnny with it, but Anne rushes to the front door and screams for help. She has her back to Meadows holding the broken vase, but she does not think of the danger; she has to end the situation so that her watching child does not see the blood that is about to be spilt. Someone shouts down from an upper floor at Anne's screams, and Meadows, still hoping to hold onto a shred of respectability as the garage owner of a "legitimate business" and not wanting to be found there by the police, drops the broken vase and leaves.

But Anne has been driven to her limit. She will not allow the children and herself to be put at further risk. She tells Johnny that if he continues to pursue the car she no longer cares about, she will take the children and leave. In true Al-Anon style, Anne doesn't make the threat to leave him until she is prepared to carry out that course of action. Al-Anon is the Twelve-Step Program for Family & Friends of Alcoholics that is the sister organization of the better known Alcoholics Anonymous, and relevant here because Johnny is addicted to his dream of getting the car back and restoring his lost masculine prowess by so doing. He refuses to stop his mission for her sake and keeps on spiraling towards disaster. Johnny returns home having recovered his car, battered and bloody, to find the apartment empty. Anne has in fact taken the children and left him (though the audience doesn't know that until we arrive back at the apartment on Johnny's coattails). The film ends on Anne returning to their home unexpectedly, without the children, and finding her husband alone and forlorn, bruised, bloody and battered, she moves towards Johnny to gently touch his broken face and enfold him in her comforting and loving embrace.

As I wrote that, tears pricked in my eyes. It reminded me of the boundaries I set when John's behavior became "unacceptable behavior"—he drank too much when he was writing scripts and became unbearably hair-trigger and loud — and I carried out the threats I made; leaving for an hour, or a day, and then returning to this man who was full of love underneath his defensive, insecure behavior. Anne's return might seem misguided or psychologically invalid; but it is not. Johnny knows now that there is a limit to her tolerance for staying around for the fallout from his obsessions. In the closing moments of the film, the camera stays with their embrace, and we are left free to imagine, if we so wish, that they resume their marriage with a new understanding.

In *Never Let Go*, there are two men who behave obsessively and spiral into destructiveness, Lionel Meadows, and Johnny Cummings. We have seen Anne as wise and forthright in her communication, accurately assessing her husband's character and the risk that Lionel Meadows presents to their family. Yet the other female character, though little more than a child, shows surprising courage towards the end of the film. It is clear that the women in this film are the ones who are brave and carry that courage as a badge.

As the film draws to a tense finish, with the two men pitched against each other, equally obsessive, where there seems to be no sane way out, it is Jackie, the teenage runaway from reform school who finally has the courage to turn against Sellers' intimidating character. Meadows has sheltered her as a runaway and used her as his "little piece of fluff." She complies reluctantly but then falls for Tommy Towers, rather attractively played by Adam Faith, a popular British pop singer at that time, as the young tough and gang-leader. It is Tommy who terrorizes Johnny with his gang riding motorbikes around him in circles. As the tension heightens as the film nears its climax, Meadows becomes increasingly menacing, and Tommy crumbles into fear of the dominant male aggressor, collapsing against Jackie's shoulder.

The ultra-young Jackie, played by Carol White at about 17 years old, later of *Poor Cow* (1967) fame, is a sulky but luminescent adolescent. After letting go of her apathetic resignation to Meadow's will, she finds the strength to face her fear of the police who will, she fears, return her to the reform home from which she has escaped. Johnny has shown interest in her safety and welfare as she declares her fear of Meadows; he has invited her to shelter at their home — and, yes, we, the audience know his interest in helping her is born from his desire for the information she may hold about where his precious car is, but we also see in Todd's facial expression that his desire to protect and help her is real. He does care for her as an individual and unprotected girl. She feels this, and the, to her, astonishing fact, that someone can hold her in his mind and think about her need and fears, enables her to break through her fear, and thus dissolve for us too, the sense we have of being stuck without any kind of resolution to such male madness. Until she finds her courage, we feel that Meadows may be falling to pieces but there is no one to bring him down. Johnny has become too similar to his enemy to achieve that end; they are both hanging on to win at all costs. Jackie convinces the reluctant and scared Tommy that their only chance to escape Meadow's influence is to go to the police with "everything we know about Meadows." Tommy is won over by her sudden confidence and resolution, and he overcomes his fear and agrees. Suddenly all the pieces are in place for the tension to break and Meadows to lose his grip and, after the film's end, his freedom.

Two other films that reveal John's empathic tolerance for women who step outside of their allotted roles in life are *Four Days* (1951) and *Thunderstorm* (1956). The female protagonist in *Four Days*, Lucienne Templar (Kathleen Byron), is a bored housewife whose husband works ceaselessly at the company he manages, and her boredom leads her into an affair with the owner's son. Her dissatisfaction and stunted daily life propel her into a kind of madness where she contemplates murdering her husband. Her husband is portrayed as a pleasant, if unaware, man and though somewhat of a workaholic, he is not a bad or violent person at all. Lucienne does not have an excuse there to think about escape by murder. The whole weight of the director's sympathy is with her narrow life; not a usual perspective in the 1950s. Instead of the audience being encouraged to condemn her in line with the stricter morals of the time, a time in Britain where the Ten Commandments still had somewhat of an influence on daily life, we are invited to sympathize with her about the narrowness of her purposeless life. And we are encouraged not to lose that sympathy even when it is clear that she is an adulteress and a murderess in the making. One particularly striking shot that helps create sympathy is where we are shown a huge poignant close-up of Lucienne's eyes filling the screen with deep shadow around her face with the framing of the shot evoking her feeling of being shut in. Her expressive eyes look right at us with a plea to see her pain and be understood. Thus, the filmmaker directs us to understand her extreme reactions in her desperation to escape boredom.

In *Thunderstorm* (1956), Linda Christian plays Maria Ramon, who arrives by chance at a small Spanish fishing village; we never know who she is or what her life was before she arrived in this out of the way place, except for Maria herself telling the men who fall for her that she brings bad luck and disaster to men. The poster tagline is, "She's lightning in the flesh . . . burning, destroying everything she touches." Two local characters, Diego (Carlos Thompson) and Pablo (Charles Korvin) come to furious blows over the strange and beautiful arrival. The would-be lovers, and all the villagers, blame the heroine for the two men being in love with her. But the director doesn't blame her. Even though she is shown at one point as a siren who draws one of the lovers to crash his boat, and despite the lurid, blaming words of the publicity, there is a feeling throughout the film of the men being the holders and creators of their own obsession.

A user's review on imdb.com from 2016 by Robert Temple says:

> Linda Christian manages throughout to maintain a strangely impassive face as all the men bang on doors to get into her room and try to rape her, fight nearly to the death over her, and basically go insane because of her. She never becomes truly personal but behaves as if she is a force of nature instead of a person . . . . [T]here is nothing sinister about Linda Christian, she does not try to drive men mad, they drive themselves mad without any encouragement from her as she looks at them without any sign of what she is feeling or thinking.

Once again John describes a woman outside the usual stereotypical roles. The male lead "without any sign of what [he] is feeling or thinking" is very familiar to us — take Humphrey Bogart in his role as Marlowe,

Raymond Chandler's detective, for example. But I am not aware of any other film of this period where the woman is the still quiet center. Of course, we are in the Fifties. Maria does not have the confidence (and social approval) of '40s and '50s male heroes who don't speak or show their feelings. She does not revel in her power to attract, as do male actors of the strong, silent type with their typically adoring audiences. She is distressed by her power and tries to warn the men. But though her impassivity means that she is seen as a witch by the villagers, she is not seen by the director as an active seductress. She is the still point at the center of the storm of male passions and the director emphasizes her stillness, siding with her in believing that the forces that arise in the patriarchal villagers and fishermen are outside her control. She is a sort of victim, not the victimizer; just as the schoolboy that was John had no control over the muddy emotional mixing of his pain with his awareness of his perpetrators' sexual arousal. The plot of Thunderstorm is just the sort of film plot where the archetype of Eve as the cause of sin is usually invoked, especially in the 1950s before women in films were more openly sexual, so there is no doubt that John's perspective is unexpected and humane.

I believe John's ability to see through the male assumption of their right to power and to being in control, which keeps company with their sense of inherent worthiness just for being male, derives from his painful experiences at the hands of men with power. Let us move to showing how John had a deep awareness of how fear at the hands of patriarchal power affects the psyche.

Women Inside Their Fear: Understanding the Female Psyche Under Threat

As a schoolboy, John was bullied for his French name — Yvon Jean — which was Ivan John in English, but which looked and sounded like the girl's names, Yvonne Jean. He was a tender, shy, very French soul and he was emotionally tortured by the blunt English schoolboy derision, as well as being physically abused by powerful men and older boys wielding instruments of correction, often for their own twisted pleasure, in the widespread system of corporal punishment that existed in British schools and was not banned until the mid-1980s in state-run schools.

I believe that this physical abuse at the hands of more powerful men, some of whom had a sexualized response, gave him a unique insight into being the one without power, something that in this patriarchal, over-sexualized society all women still experience in some almost daily way. Congresswoman Alexandria Ocasio-Cortez's response to Ted Yoho's apology for swearing at her highlights this, and — the point I want to emphasize here — we all live with it; the fear or actuality of verbal and physical violence towards us just for being women. For me, the most significant moment of her speech is: "It's just another day, right?"

> Because all of us [women] have had to deal with this, in some form, some way, some shape, at some point in our lives. And I want to be clear that representative Yoho's comments were not deeply hurtful, or piercing, to me. Because I have worked a working-class job . . . and this kind of language is not new. This is not new. And that is the problem. The issue is not about one incident. It is cultural. It is a culture of a lack of impunity, of acceptance of violence, and violent language against women, an entire structure of power that supports that. When I was reflecting on this, I honestly thought that I was just gonna pack it up and go home. It's just another day, right?

The Crowded Day aka *Shop Spoiled* (1954), a mostly light and joyful film, tells the story of five shop assistants in a large department store where the young women, as was the custom of the day, boarded in a hostel owned and run by the department store owners. They were overseen in their living quarters by the same supervisor who ruled them during their working day. The storyline follows five of these young shop-girls, and in the most somber story of the five, we see a young woman, Yvonne (Josephine Griffin), who is sweet natured and naturally genteel but is not of a high social status. She is in love with a well-to-do upper middle-class man. She discovers she is pregnant while her lover is absent from the country; a desperate predicament for a young woman in the early 1950s with its intense social disapproval, not just for out-of-wedlock pregnancies, but in the still-strong class structure of that time with its classist reactions about social mobility. But in a similar way to the director's tolerant, accepting view of Lucienne the adulteress or Maria the siren, Yvonne is not condemned for being pregnant. The director shows us the personnel officer trying to handle her inevitable dismissal with a degree of warm humanity, rather than cold blame. Such a lack of condemnation for an out of wedlock pregnancy is unusual in a film — and life — of this era. It is hard to imagine in our modern times with families of all forms and arrangements, but when I was a thirteen-year old schoolgirl living in a London suburb and I was told that some neighbors were "living in sin," I was, even though a member of an agnostic family, deeply shocked. "Living in sin" just wasn't a normal, matter-of-fact thing in 1964 or '65!

Yvonne goes to visit her lover's mother in her posh neighborhood of London to inquire if she has heard from her son, and here she does meet condemnation. She is subjugated to condemnation just for existing and daring to intrude into her lover's life, and she is assumed to be a gold-digger rather than a person with deep caring. The depth of the mother's contempt is rendered visible as we close into a tight focus on her lips spouting their fiercely rejecting words. This is reminiscent of the later camera work in *Rapture* (1965) which focuses tightly on the fast-moving lips of the prospective landlady in the scene where she tells a flustered Agnes the rules of her boarding house.

A user review on imdb.com, by hitchcockthelegend states, "When the story is of the dramatic kind, [Guillermin] and Dines [the cameraman] bring noir visuals into play, with foreboding shadows reflecting the mood of the players and canted angles enhancing psychological discord." We see this noir camerawork in the scenes where Yvonne, disoriented and desperate after her visit to her lover's mother, wanders the London streets at night. Frightened and lonely, contemplating suicide with some sleeping pills she has hoarded, she stops for a cup of tea at a café stand where she is noticed by a dowdy middle-aged man who follows her through dark, shadowy streets and chases her across a railway bridge. She escapes him by going into a church but not before the feeling of terror at being chased is invoked in many of the women watching this scene. Such images will remind most women of similar moments alone at night keeping company with fear of harm or actual harm.

At times, I host women's gatherings focusing on Femininity in all its aspects. It is striking that in any roomful of strong, successful, aware women, each of us admits to moments of fear walking alone, especially in the dark. That is not, I imagine, a ubiquitous feeling in a room full of men, not straight men anyway. The scars of patriarchal ascendency are not that obvious to the privilege holders — just as people whose skins are white gain awareness of the wide-ranging effects of their white privilege only with conscious effort and education.

Relations between men and woman are complex and division can be intensified by the deleterious effects of patriarchal conditioning with its fear of the other and desire for top-down power. John himself is a conflicted product of that conditioning. He gave me both more tenderness than I had ever experienced and directed more anger at me than I had ever experienced. And as we know, he himself had been victimized by the nasty outcroppings of the Male Principle holding power. He knew intuitively, as I do consciously, that hope for humanity, inside our hearts and as a people, lies in deepening our understanding and embrace of the strength that is used to support and the sweetness that is used to nurture — he knew that hope for humanity lies with us all loving what the Feminine Principle has to offer us in all its richness.

Conclusion: Debunking the Myth

Some readers may feel I have made too much of John's experience of being beaten at school. But here's the thing: throughout our marriage, right up until his death, if I approached John from behind without announcing my presence, say bringing food to the dining table, he would start violently, clasp his hand to his heart and shout at me, "You nearly gave me a heart attack!" It would take ten or more minutes for his heartbeat to calm down again. This is the body's response to having been attacked and going into panic mode if it is caught unawares. And he was still doing that eighty-five years after the first caning he remembered at five years old.

When I met John he was a disappointed artist, regretful that he was never powerful enough to make the films he really wanted to make, aware that not only was he not capable of "kissing up" to the producers and people with power, but worse, he often chose to fight with them. He knew he had earned his reputation as the "Wild Man," as Dino de Laurentiis nicknamed him. To me it is understandable that John had trouble with men having power over him.

When I first met Christian Ferry, a French producer and longtime close friend of John's, after John had moved from California to the Essex countryside to be near me, Christian took me aside as we walked down a London street to the restaurant where we were to eat. He told me, with an intensity that I later came to know was unusual in such a calm, even-tempered man, of how much more successful John could have been if he hadn't fought with everyone with power. This was said in

1998 and the last film of their twenty years of close association had been made fourteen years earlier. (They worked together on *Rapture* (1965), *The Blue Max* (1968), *King Kong* (1976) and *Sheena* (1984)). Christian recognized John's talent and was still frustrated that he had not been able to restrain himself, and find a way to compromise, which would perhaps have opened a path for John to make the artistic films he really wanted to make.

Before John's death, and the inclusion of well-rounded obituaries, the entry about his work in Wikipedia was almost entirely about his bad temper, as though that was all there was to him. In the little that has been written about John, there tends to be an emphasis on his temper, on claiming people did not want to work with him again, or the perception that he hated his crews. Neither he nor I would deny he had a temper, was even abusive at times. I think there are many factors to this temper though. There was the undeniable damage and stress that the trauma of being physically abused caused him. But there was also his passionate, very French personality, his enthusiastic elation (that could turn to frustration), his precise vision of what shots he wanted and the thwarting of that vision when (I'm guessing here; I was never on set) people didn't know how to translate it into perfect action. As well as at times, of course, too much alcohol but, as far as I know, not during the working day on set. John would tell a story of working on *Skyjacked* (1972) with Charlton Heston who one day noticed John's assistant bringing him a brown paper bag at five o'clock. As John told it, "Chuck said, 'What's in the brown paper bag, John?' And when I told him, 'A whisky,' Chuck said, 'I'll have one of those.' And every day after that my assistant brought two brown paper bags dead on five o'clock."

As to hating his crews, nothing could be further from the truth. He told me how hard it was when the "family" of cast and crew, perhaps 150 people, dispersed to the next job or their own homes at the end of the shoot, and the closeness suddenly vanished. And in an interview for the

BAFTA Living Director's series with Nick Redman (who with Julie Kirgo released his beloved *Rapture* as an early Twilight Time disk in 2011), Nick asked him what his favorite thing was about being a director. In reply, John said that what he loved best about being a director was that he was a bit like an on-call psychiatrist and everyone, cast and crew, came to him with their problems.

Did he deserve his reputation as a "wild man" or as someone who shouts to the point of being abusive? Well, yes, in part. But that was not all there was to him; that's for sure. And I am suggesting here that John's childhood experience of being beaten, and ordered to bend over and wait for the painful strokes, which he openly admits in his essay terrorized him, was transformed by him in his work into an understanding of the feminine psyche under threat as well as an emotional understanding of patriarchal sexism and the power held by men over women. Of course, as a director who could be volatile and loud, he himself became a symbol of the power held by men. Yet as we see in his autobiographical essay, he saw that directing self as a front, a bluff almost, that his artistic, sensitive side sheltered behind.

> When John was at Adelphi Studios, he was only 24 and he'd already co-produced a couple of films for his production company with his friend and partner as the director. And one day he saw that somebody's film had finished shooting and the stagehands were about to take down the set of a big house with an upstairs, downstairs staircase, you know, a really elaborate house. And he said, "Stop! Stop! Don't strike the set." And he went to the Adelphi leadership, to Arthur Dent himself, I believe, and he said, "Please don't take the set down. I'll write a script in three weeks and I'll film it in three weeks." John was given the go-ahead and he did write the script in three weeks, the script of *Paper Gallows*, otherwise known as *Torment*, but he took six weeks to film it. And he said, "They weren't very pleased about that."

I conclude with a brief look at John's first feature that was appropriately called *Torment* (1950). We see how even in this first effort, he pushed against stereotypical roles for women. *Torment,* aka *Paper Gallows,* was filmed in 1949 when John was only twenty-four. His passion to use the set from a just-finished film earned him his first shot at solo directing. We witness two brothers, who are both writers of crime novels who live together in their late father's home with a young woman, Joan, as their housekeeper-secretary. At one point, Jim Brandon (John Gregson), one of the two brothers who are both in love with her, says to Joan (Rona Anderson), the secretary:

> JIM: What do you want to do with your life, Joan?
> JOAN: Oh, I don't know. Drift along till I meet something that stops me.
> JIM: Why don't you get married?
> JOAN: (sharply) Why should I get married?
> JIM: Well, I don't know. I thought that's what every girl wanted.
> JOAN: Sometimes, Jim, you're rather dense.

Notice her initial response is to take the freedom to not know her path in life; such freedom can be seen as part of male privilege, as was true then, and sadly, even now. As the plot unfolds and she is threatened by the unstable other brother, Cliff (Dermot Walsh) you can see her vulnerability to his clever mind and superior physical strength. But you also have also seen her deftness in handling both men, at least until Cliff's advances become frightening.

When Joan rejects Cliff he chases her upstairs and we see a scene familiar from nightmares, where she attempts to barricade her bedroom door against Cliff and she, and we, fear she cannot prevent him pushing his way into her room. He succeeds and taunts her with how he is going to strangle her, and we resonate with her terror as Cliff gets closer to his goal. Joan is not able to escape the circumstance in which she finds herself at the mercy of the incensed and vindictive male.

Neither was that five-year old child, who had only just lost the cherubic curls of the three- or four-year-old in the photo, able to escape. He too found himself at the mercy of the vindictive male who enjoyed power too much. One of the things I deeply loved about John was his bright, bold honesty. He had no illusions about himself. That shines through in his honest self-assessment in his chapter in this book, or in his comment to me when we first talked of marriage, "Don't marry me. I'm impossible." I marvel at the power of how we can contribute to others from our deepest pain. In *Torment*, John took his trauma by the throat and transformed his childhood terror into the powerful, frightening climax of his creditable first feature, a little-known example of British Noir.

John with curls on the right, with older brother, Guy

CHAPTER 6

DOUBLE HEADER: TWO CHILDREN'S FILMS

Adventure in the Hopfields (1954)
NEIL SINYARD

Miss Robin Hood (1952)
MARY GUILLERMIN

ADVENTURE IN THE HOPFIELDS was made by Guillermin for the Children's Film Foundation in 1954. Highly praised at the time, it was long thought to be a lost film until, according to one story, a copy was discovered by an American film fan in a rubbish skip outside a television studio in Chicago. It was then acquired by an enthusiast in the UK, who organised a special showing on 8 March, 2002, almost fifty years after its original release, in the village hall of Goudhurst in Kent, where most of the filming had taken place. The fact that the film was still fondly remembered was no doubt due to its quality and to the presence in it of Mandy Miller, one of the most popular child actors of the day, particularly because of her remarkable performance in the title role as the deaf and dumb girl in Alexander Mackendrick's *Mandy* (1952). She would be remembered also for her 1956 recording of the novelty song, "Nellie the Elephant," which became (and has remained) a children's favourite.

Based on the novel *The Hop Dog* by Nora Lavrin and Molly Thorp and published in 1952, *Adventure in the Hopfields* concerns a young girl, Jenny (Mandy Miller) who, when she accidentally breaks a much-loved piece of crockery (a pot dog) that belongs to her mother, attempts to join her friends on a hop-picking excursion in the country, so that she can make enough money to pay for a replacement. When she becomes separated from her party on the train and gets off at the wrong station, a family of campers agrees to take care of her until her parents can arrive. This becomes a tall order, for the child is accident-prone, and inclined to wander off on her own. She will wind up alone and trapped inside a rickety windmill that has been struck by lightning and is beginning to go up in flames. As this is a film essentially for children, all will end happily, but not sentimentally. The naughty adolescent (Melvyn Hayes), who has locked her in the windmill as a joke but then risked his life in rescuing her, has also retrieved her pot dog at some danger to himself, but conspicuously does not stay around for thanks. He bustles away in embarrassment, as if afraid that this act of kindness and heroism might compromise his reputation as rebel and tough guy. It is a nice psychological touch, which enables the ending to be heartening without being soft.

Another reason why the film maintains its edge is that the narrative is cleverly constructed as a series of suspense scenes. Jenny only just catches the train to the hopfields, but then, disembarking at the wrong station, only realises her mistake after the train has carried on without her and left her stranded. The film will crosscut with some assurance between Jenny's often-perilous progress to safety and the anxiety of her parents who are having difficulty in tracing her. The location filming is fascinating, offering, through glimpses of bomb damage and posters, a snapshot of the times. The film also conveys, through its depiction of the simple (pre-television) leisure pursuits of the families, a sense of community and neighbourliness that one can view nowadays with some nostalgia. It is in no sense a quaint period piece, though. The camerawork is noticeably fluent, as if energised by the open air; yet the filming can also be tense and atmospheric, particularly in the scenes inside the mill, where the director makes powerful use of shadow and hiding-place to suggest that, for Jenny, this might seem a refuge but it could also become a site of danger. High spirits will contend with moments of nightmare.

> For *Adventure in the Hopfields*, John and the crew were filming somewhere in the south of England; it must have been Kent because the hopfields were in Kent. John had this props man that he loved working with because he was a Romany gypsy and if John mentioned a desire for any prop, no matter how unlikely, it would turn up within half an hour. And John wisely did not question where these props had appeared from. There's a scene where a windmill catches fire which was being filmed in a big outdoor barn. The props man somehow managed to set the barn alight, which was not appreciated by the farmer who owned the barn.

For a modestly budgeted film that lasts less than an hour, the array of talent assembled now looks remarkable. As well as its star Mandy Miller, the cast includes such fine character actors as Mona Washbourne, Dandy

Nichols and Harold Lang, and also features uncredited appearances from Jane Asher and Edward Judd who were soon to make their mark in British cinema. The score (also uncredited) is by one of Britain's greatest light music composers, Ronald Bynge; the assistant director is Douglas Hickox, who was to go on to be a successful director in his own right *(The Ruling Class, Theatre of Blood* etc.); the film is co-scripted by John Cresswell, who was soon to be nominated for a British Academy Award for his co-authorship of J. Lee Thompson's powerful anti-capital punishment drama, *Yield to the Night* (1956); and in charge of the props is none other than Eddie Fowlie, later to become legendary as (in Melanie Williams' description) David Lean's "indispensable property master, location scout and all-round-fixer" *(David Lean,* MUP, 2014, p. 5). Small wonder that the film endures as one of the most highly regarded productions of the Children's Film Foundation and a worthy addition to Guillermin's list of credits.

On one of the extras on the 2018 Blu-ray release of *Town on Trial*, focus-puller Alec Burrows shares some interesting recollections of working on *Adventure in the Hopfields*. Describing John Guillermin as "a superb director," he also found him an aloof, impatient man who "expected everything to be done in micro-seconds," despite the difficulties of wielding heavy cameras on location. Guillermin appears not to have mellowed much over the next few years. In his autobiography, *In The Arena* (1995), Charlton Heston recalled working with him on the film *Skyjacked* (1972) and finding him "imaginative and skilful, very strong on his use of the cameras" but "with an irascible streak." (Heston: 464-5) Heston was unfazed. After all, he had made two films with the great Hollywood director, William Wyler, who was renowned for his uncompromising perfectionism but who once confided to Heston: "You know, I'd like to be a nice guy on set — but you don't get to make good films that way."

In *Miss Robin Hood* the children have a lot of power. The film opens with a shot of three uniformed schoolgirls blowing open a safe — our viewpoint is from the back of the safe as their hands reach in for the goods. We soon learn that we are inside the comic of the title, watching Miss Robin Hood at work. John was one of those adults who understand that even young children are intelligent beings you should respect, and that you should not talk down to them or use a special "baby" language. It was a wonder to watch him with his young granddaughter with her little face all agog as he made up the most dramatic stories. John directed *Miss Robin Hood* from a place of identifying entirely with the children in the story with a firm belief — to be echoed in the camerawork — of them having their own separate viewpoint of value. The film is known as one of the films common in the 1950s for "adults of all ages" but it is not generally noticed that the child's viewpoint is operating from behind the camera.

Before talking about the direction, I want to talk about why modern viewers may not "get" this film. The background to the plot shows children being excited fans of a comic that tells the adventures of Miss Robin Hood, a teenage schoolgirl who steals from the rich to give to the poor, and who become so incensed when the writer of the strip quits in protest at a management decision, that they rise up and march on the publishers to demand his reinstatement. Modern viewers will not relate to this drama and excitement about a story in a mere comic — especially one of such an innocent nature. Nowadays we associate comics with superheroes with tremendous powers. But I was born in the year this film was released, and growing up in the 1950s when relatively few homes had a tiny bubble of a black and white television set (we didn't own a television set until I was twelve years old), comics were a huge part of my life. Anita O'Brien, director curator at London's Cartoon Museum,

John telling stories to his granddaughter, "her little face all agog."

states: "When comics like the Beano and Dandy were invented back in the 1930s — and through really to the 1950s and '60s — these comics were almost the only entertainment available to children." (Wikipedia).

I devoured the Beano and Dandy avidly each week as soon as they came out and the wait for the next issue was interminable. I remember a huge family argument when I was about seven when one story about a ballerina in a comic called Bunty had an episode where someone was killed in a car crash. My mother wanted to cancel my subscription because the plot line upset me and I fought for it so fiercely, explaining it was a one-off incident out of tune with the usual plot line, that I was allowed to keep reading it. I well remember the devastation I felt at its threatened extinction from my life. As a side note, it is interesting that as a young child my favourite comic strip was called "The Numskulls." It was about a team of tiny little people who lived inside the main character's head and all the adventures they got up to in there. It is interesting because I grew up to be a psychotherapist using Gestalt Therapy that could be characterized as working with internal voices and parts, the "tiny people" inside. This prominence of comics as the main source of entertainment is background to the plot that can otherwise sound contrived and even a little silly.

Margaret Rutherford is the eccentric old lady who embroils Richard Hearne (Mr. Pastry), the author of Miss Robin Hood, in an adventure to retrieve her secret family recipe for Honeycup, a whisky-based drink with an ingredient that causes a feeling of well-being from the dastardly capitalist who has stolen it. She runs a home for orphan children who all gather round excitedly to hear the latest episode of Miss Robin Hood when the comic is delivered. In trying to retrieve her family recipe, Rutherford's character runs foul of the law and it is in these sections that we see most clearly the director taking the children's point of view. At one point, the police arrive at the orphanage; they stand in the shadowed doorway, looming over the children, dark shapes with fedora hats perched on the detectives' heads. The camera shoots from below, and we look up with a child's eye viewpoint at the menacing shadows. Gone are the friendly English bobbies with their tall, rounded helmets. We are watching policemen with power.

Undaunted, a little boy plants himself in front of the inspector and blocks him, using his catapult to reduce the inspector's dignity. The other children giggle. The inspector and his minions are reduced to impotence; the children win. And Rutherford is in the background supporting their defiant, cheeky attitude. The grown ups in this film know who they should be aligning with. More power to the children.

Light-hearted though this film is, seemingly all froth and fun, we can still see John working out his personal themes of opposition to unthinking powerholders. And the child in each of us can enjoy the small child standing up to the power of the Law.

PART TWO

I only made one good film, Rapture,
and only half a dozen people have seen it.
— JOHN GUILLERMIN

John in love with bringing the script to life

CHAPTER 7

THE HEART OF THE MATTER 1965

MARY GUILLERMIN

JOHN SO LOVED THE EXPERIENCE of directing *Rapture*. Everything about it appealed to his Gallic origins and temperament — the wild coast of Brittany where it was filmed, the caves, rocks, the crashing waves and seagulls, the brooding house on the cliffs, especially built for the

The brooding house on the cliffs

Patricia Gozzi in Agnes' wool dress

A playful child; a smiling John tries to keep working

film, with the interior walls all painted black at the strong suggestion of Jean André, the art director. John was astonished at the idea and questioned his choice. "Trust me," John told me André had said, "It will really work." And he was right. The oppressive atmosphere that Agnes tries to escape with daydreaming with her doll, or running alone on the beach, is made tangible by the dark walls of the house.

On a recent podcast interview I gave about this book for "Talking Images," the official podcast of ICM Forum, one of the members (who have regularly chosen *Rapture* in their top 100 films yearly poll since one of them discovered the film after its 2011 rerelease), asked me how John came to be the director. John hadn't told me, but I hypothesized for the audience. John first worked with Christian Ferry on this film, though later Ferry was involved in producing three more of John's films, *King Kong* among them. Christian had been an uncredited production manager on Zanuck's great success a few years earlier, *The Longest Day* (1962). Ferry would have been only 30 at the time of filming and yet John told me he was "Darryl's right hand man;" perhaps unofficially. If Christian and John already knew each other then Zanuck might have listened to Ferry's suggestion of an Anglo-French director with a dramatic style of shooting for an English story reset in France.

During the filming of *Rapture*, John became violently ill from eating a bad oyster. He was lying in his tent on a camp bed, incapacitated with a high fever. Darryl Zanuck suggested replacing John and Christian Ferry, John's closest friend, said, "No, no, no, you mustn't do that. It will break his heart if you take the direction away from him. Give him twenty-four hours." Zanuck did give John twenty-four hours which probably wasn't long enough for him to fully recover, but John got the filming going again after one day's break and he did not lose control of his project.

John would always say that Darryl Zanuck was his favorite producer, even though he did not like the fact that *Rapture* was not marketed after its release. The experience of filming *Rapture* was so important to him because it was the only time that he had complete artistic control over the script and how the film turned out. He credited Darryl Zanuck for that. John said, "What I liked about Darryl as a producer was once he'd given you the job, he stayed away from the set. He didn't send you any of those [production] notes, he didn't interfere. I had complete freedom to make that film the way I saw it." And for those of you who know his whole body of work, that's interesting because there's no question that *Rapture* is the best film he ever made.

Fourteen-and-a-half-year-old Patricia listens to direction with surprising maturity

CHAPTER 8

GIRL ON THE EDGE: RAPTURE

MELANIE WILLIAMS

All winter through I bow my head
Beneath the driving rain;
The North wind powders me with snow
And blows me black again;
At midnight 'neath a maze of stars
I flame with glittering rime,
And stand, above the stubble, stiff
As mail at morning-prime.
But when that child, called Spring, and all
His host of children, come,
Scattering their buds and dew upon
Those acres of my home,
Some rapture in my rags awakes;
I lift void eyes and scan
The skies for crows, those ravening foes,
Of my strange master, Man.

A LINE FROM THIS Walter de la Mare 1912 poem "The Scarecrow" provided Phyllis Hastings with the title for her 1960 novel *Rapture in my Rags*, the tale of a young woman who believes a scarecrow has come alive at her behest. When Hastings' novel was then adapted for the screen a few years later, the full extent of the literary allusion was curtailed, and only the word *Rapture* was retained to provide the film's title. Its director John Guillermin may have had doubts about this nomenclature for his film (preferring instead *The Scarecrow* as a potential title), but the one-word title conveys very effectively the overall emotional tone of the story, a tale of euphoric wonder and of the generative power of the imagination, and as acute a portrait of female adolescence as 1960s cinema achieved.

The young French actress Patricia Gozzi played *Rapture*'s heroine Agnes, having already gathered much acclaim for her role as a preternaturally mature 12-year-old in Serge Bourguignon's *Les Dimanches de Ville D'Avray/Sundays and Cybele* (1962). Gozzi's compelling performance in that earlier Oscar-winning French film, and Daryl Zanuck's enthusiasm for it, had been the prime motivation to then cast her in a similar role in *Rapture;* indeed, the decision to relocate the story from England to France was taken partly to facilitate Gozzi's casting in the lead role. Could a British actress have played it instead? Perhaps Hayley Mills might have done the part justice, if allowed temporary respite from the grip of Disney: she had convincingly played girls shielding fugitives in *Tiger Bay* (1959) and *Whistle down the Wind* (1961) as well as disturbed teenagers in *The Chalk Garden* (1964) and *Sky West and Crooked* (1966). One wonders how the film might have worked with Pamela Franklin in the lead, the young English actress with a wide-eyed neurotic intensity akin to Gozzi's (and her exact contemporary in age) who had been a striking presence in *The Innocents* (1961), *The Third Secret* (1964), *The Nanny* (1965), and later in *Our Mother's House* (1967) and *The Prime of Miss Jean Brodie* (1969). But in the end, such alternate universes are irrelevant: Patricia Gozzi's mesmeric mercurial screen presence in *Rapture* is justification enough for 20th Century Fox's casting decision, with the 15-year-old actress completely compelling as a girl poised precariously between childhood and adulthood, plagued by fears of mental collapse but desperately craving a loving human connection even if she has to will it into being from a vintage suit stuffed with straw. The rapture described by Walter de la Mare was the scarecrow's experience of awakening in Spring; in the film indirectly inspired by his poem, it belongs entirely to Agnes as she navigates the difficult pathway from girl to woman and begins to explore new worlds of pleasure and pain.

Building on the casting of Patricia Gozzi, *Rapture* was truly international in its assembly of acting talent, with MGM studio system veterans Melvyn Douglas and former child star Dean Stockwell playing the heroine's father and lover respectively, alongside Gunnel Lindblom of Ingmar Bergman's repertory company as the brazenly sensuous housekeeper Karin, as well as British character actors Sylvia Kay and Peter Sallis as Agnes' older sister and brother-in-law. Behind the scenes, the key creative workforce on the production was similarly cosmopolitan: Fellini's frequent collaborator Ennio Flaniano had initially adapted Hastings' novel, worked on further by US screenwriter Stanley Mann, whose most recent assignments had been the ambiguous tales of female captivity *The Collector* (1965) and *A High Wind in Jamaica* (1965); other key personnel included French cinematographer Marcel Grignon, Viennese-born but British-based editor Max Benedict, and French composer Georges Delerue, whose lovely plaintive score for *Rapture* is one of the film's most powerful components. And of course the film's Anglo-French director John Guillermin exemplified the same intercontinental sensibility.

Having served with the RAF during the war, Guillermin began his career working on documentaries in France before moving back across the channel in the late 1940s and into the bread-and-butter assignments of British film production, often enlivening the crime thrillers, comedies and melodramas he directed with imaginative stylistic flourishes. Film scholar Peter Hutchings notes the "weird, expressive style" Guillermin used in certain sequences of the 1952 Margaret Rutherford comedy vehicle *Miss Robin Hood* (Hutchings 2000: 186) while Raymond Durgnat recalled the director's appellation by one French critic as "the Paganini of *mise-en-scene*" and remarked himself upon "the swing and energy of his style" (Durgnat 1971: 183, 217). Guillermin's 1959 film *Tarzan's Greatest Adventure* had been critically praised for injecting new life into a moribund franchise, and by the beginning of the 1960s, the director was being discussed favourably in the ground-breaking new film journal *Movie* — usually actively hostile to British filmmakers — on the strength of films such as *Never Let Go* (1960) and *Waltz of the Toreadors* (1962), both of which boasted strikingly different performances from Peter Sellers. But even given their positive reception, and that afforded to his subsequent claustrophobic end-of-empire drama *Guns at Batasi* (1964), it would have been difficult to predict the direction John Guillermin's career took the following year with *Rapture:* into a mode of filmmaking far more akin to the European art movie than the more mainstream material he had generally handled, and into the imaginative world of a disturbed young woman rather than the masculinity under duress that he had previously explored, eliciting anxious performances from John Mills in *Town on Trial* (1957), Richard Todd in *Never Let Go*, and Richard Attenborough in *Guns at Batasi*. Although the oppressive patriarch of *Rapture* as played by Melvyn Douglas commands attention, and Dean Stockwell's kindly young fugitive garners sympathy, it is undoubtedly Patricia Gozzi's outstanding central performance as disturbed teenager Agnes that drives the film, showcased sensitively and sympathetically by Guillermin's direction.

Rapture opens with an arresting, unsettling moment, one that immediately disrupts a cliché of feminine rapture: the blissful blushing bride on her wedding day. After presenting an aerial view of a car driving along a clifftop road, the film cuts to the same car's interior. A distinctly anxious-looking tearful bride, Agnes' older sister, is on her way to the church to get married, beside her father at the wheel (her younger sister and the housekeeper in the backseat). She suddenly erupts into helpless mocking laughter. It is not exactly the same as the sound that rings out in court in Marleen Gorris' feminist classic *A Question of Silence* (1982) but it is on a continuum with it, as another female outburst that perplexes and angers a male judge (the father-of-the-bride in *Rapture*) and exposes an element of farcicality in the roles women are expected to inhabit. We never find out the laughter's object or purpose — is it just pre-wedding nerves or some deeper realisation of her situation's absurdity? — but the weirdness and the shock of it, all the more so coming from a character who will be otherwise highly conservative in her adherence to social expectations, immediately sets the enigmatic, ambiguous tone for the film to come.

Patricia Gozzi as Agnes, looking younger than her fourteen-and-a-half years

Agnes slips away from the strangeness and discomfort of the moment by looking up at passing treetops as the car makes its way towards the church, suggesting something of her dreamy, distracted nature. The film's credits finally begin. Not a word has been spoken and yet some aspect of all four characters in the car, and their conflicting personalities and desires, have been invoked, to be played out in the rest of the film. Although the older sister will knuckle down to a "normal" married life after this brief unexpected outburst, her younger sister Agnes will find it far harder to fit in with her family's and society's expectations of what a young woman should be. *Rapture* goes on to expose and explore the paradoxical position in which Agnes finds herself, as a girl who is denied autonomy and treated as a minor but is also told, "You're not a child!" and "Stop acting like a ten-year-old!" by her father and Karin respectively. When Agnes is harassed and molested by a male guest at her sister's wedding reception, she finds herself blamed for causing a scene and making trouble, not the perpetrator: a stark reminder of the victim-blaming culture that circulates around sexual assault. No wonder Agnes is repelled by the prospect of growing into adult femininity with all the attendant dangers it poses. She listens to the noises coming through the wall detailing Karin's secret assignation with her lover, both fascinated and repulsed. She is simultaneously becoming aware of her own maturing body, smoothing out the bedcovers over its changing contours. But ultimately, she covers her ears to block out these sounds of adult sexuality coming through the wall. She seems happiest instead indulging in more childlike pursuits, playing and running along the shoreline, wearing her ragged woolen dress, splashing in the salt water, calling out and reaching up to the hovering gulls above her head who seem to possess a freedom and mobility that eludes her.

Agnes' clifftop eyrie, an abandoned concrete coastal defence post, is the place where her liminal female identity is given fullest expression. Like a child, she plays with and talks to her dolls, including her favourite

> Patricia Gozzi was fourteen-and-a-half-years old during filming. She had been in one film before this and her mother was very ambitious for her, quite understandably because she had so much talent. However, she was, even though she was from France, a typical pushy Hollywood mum, and as a result, Patricia developed an antipathy to acting. And when she was due on set, she would run away! She would go and hide in the caves. It was filmed in Brittany on the coast and there were these big caves in which she would go to hide. The whole crew would have to go and search all of the caves to find her and bring her back to the set.

porcelain confidante Thérèse, but she also surveys her own appearance in a fragment of mirror, telling herself, "Oh, you are ugly," the epitome of adolescent self-consciousness and self-scrutiny. But this precious citadel of emerging selfhood is breached by her father, who angrily grabs her doll Thérèse and throws it down onto the rocks below, smashing its china skull and thereby "killing" his daughter's only friend. Although an anonymous reviewer complained in *Monthly Film Bulletin* (January 1967) about *Rapture*'s symbolism being "thickly laid on," this seems to miss the importance of the elemental nature of the film's imagery, tonally appropriate to a fable or a fairytale; forms which incidentally often specifically address the difficulties of female maturation. The broken doll not only symbolises the impact of her father's anger and violence upon her but also offers a resonant image of Agnes' fragile and fractured psyche, as well as prefiguring another later and even more devastating demise on the same rocks. This is melodrama not in the pejorative sense of the word but in recognition of the form's ability to handle big emotions on the mythic scale required.

Melvyn Douglas' incommunicative father (whose typical utterances include "I don't know what you're talking about" and "I have work to do, leave me alone") is not only a judge, he is also judgmental to his core, particularly when it comes to his youngest daughter. Obsessed with the obscure operations of justice, the concept which provides the title of his unpublished manuscript, its principles of compassionate fairness in all judicial assessments never seem to be put into practice closer to home, and he is deeply unfair to his own child. As an impossible-to-please and punitive patriarch, he is highly reminiscent of Franz Kafka's father, as outlined in the writer's unforgettable letter written from the perspective of an oppressed son. As Kafka told his father, in words (worth quoting at length) that apply equally well to Agnes' oppressed state in *Rapture*:

> You, who were for me so monstrously the measure, did not yourself keep the parts: one where I, the slave, lived, under laws that were invented only for me, and which, for reasons unknown, I could never wholly live up to anyway; then a second world which was infinitely distant from mine, in which you lived, engaged in government, in issuing commands, and dis-pleasure when they were not obeyed; and lastly, a third world where other people lived happily, free of commanding and obeying. I was always in disgrace; either I complied with your commands — and that was a disgrace; or I was defiant — and that was a disgrace too, for how could I be defiant towards you? (Kafka 2009 [1919]: 107)

In addition to the Kafkaesque intergenerational conflict presented in *Rapture*, there exists a further level of Oedipal complexity to its central father-daughter relationship. The father's over-vehement insistence that Agnes looks nothing like her deceased mother, the beating he metes out to her after she has had her first sexual encounter with a man, even the claustrophobia of some of their moments of confrontation (rendered more unsettling by Guillermin and Grignon's close-up, low-angle, queasily mobile camerawork), allude to a specifically sexualized dynamic of desire and its denial. In their commentary on the film, Nick Redman and Julie Kirgo suggest that "sexual hysteria" of various kinds constitutes the film's thematic keynote, and this includes the fraught relationship between father and daughter. Agnes' choice of her father's wedding suit as the basis for her scarecrow, which he allows her to use in a rare flicker of parental compassion for his troubled daughter, only compounds its incestuous dimensions, imbuing her effigy with what critic Trevor Johnston describes as "maximum Oedipal impact" (Johnston 2014: 111).

Ironically, her father provided the catalyst for Agnes' creation of a new friend in whom she can confide by destroying her doll, but she has now moved on from an infant female to a life-size mature male figure instead. "I want something of my own," she states as she gathers all the materials she needs to create her ideal man. Agnes lavishes careful attention upon every detail of her creation before finally admiring her completed work as he sits propped up in a chair at the end of the bed: "You're very handsome." Silhouetted in the darkness, the blank space where his face should be no longer so glaring an absence, he is almost indistinguishable from a real man. Agnes' scarecrow becomes a screen onto which she can project her dreams and desires, and unlike when she was the frightened recipient of unwanted male sexual attention at the wedding, Agnes is able to exercise control over this man she has created for herself. This creational trope is much more familiar when enacted by a male creator and a female creation, from Pygmalion and Galatea to Svengali and Trilby, and all their cultural derivations. It is far more unusual to see it in the hands of a girl. Of course, one might sense intimations of *The Wizard of Oz* (1939) in a teenage girl's mental confusion between a scarecrow and a real man, but the idea of bringing to life an inert body in a gothic storm, enacted by a bolt of lightning, also recalls the work of another highly imaginative 15-year-old girl, Mary Shelley, and the creation myth she inaugurated with *Frankenstein*.

Just as Mary Shelley's Frankenstein insisted on his propriety rights over the man he made, Agnes is similarly possessive of her creation, crying out, "He's mine! I made him!" When Karin goes to touch the not-yet-alive scarecrow, Agnes warns her to, "Leave him alone!" (Karin's dismissive response is that, "It's not a he, it's just a bunch of old rags."). Once her scarecrow has come to life, Agnes' possessiveness only deepens, shading into murderous rage aimed at her creation when she feels threatened by his autonomy: "I could take you to pieces again. I could destroy you!" Of course, we can see more clearly that Agnes' scarecrow is less mythic in his provenance than he initially appears to be. Joseph, a sailor up on a minor charge with the military authorities, is being transported into custody when the van he is in crashes, springing open the door, offering him a means of escape. But when he accidentally injures an officer trying to apprehend him by shoving him away — an injury that later turns out to have been fatal (the man strikes his head on a rock) — his fugitive status suddenly has much higher stakes. The fact that the character's first onscreen words are an expression of solicitous concern for the man he has hurt ("Please could you help him?") help to make him a deeply sympathetic figure, further compounded by the casting of sweet, soulful-eyed Dean Stockwell in the role. He represents

Sweet, soulful-eyed Dean Stockwell

a softer, more sensitive model of masculinity than any of the other men encountered in the film up to that point. This may be why Agnes colludes in her myth that she has made him, despite knowing deep down that it is untrue, and that he has just put on the scarecrow's suit to provide himself with a dry set of clothes and a disguise: he is the answer to a maiden's prayer, and she wants to believe in her unique connection to him, that he has been hand-made just for her. However, as Redman and Kirgo point out, Joseph is not only welcomed and idealized by Agnes: both Karin and the father also project their desires onto the stranger; Karin's baldly sexual in nature while the father's are a more abstracted longing for a case study and sounding board for his theories of compassionate justice.

As Agnes takes care of Joseph, brought in from the storm cold, hungry and injured, he is both bemused and fascinated by the girl who claims

Patricia Gozzi as Agnes feeling adolescent anguish

to have created him. Despite her eccentricities, Joseph also begins to intuit that Agnes has been the victim of a kind of "gaslighting" campaign, encouraging her to see herself as mad and believe that her ultimate destiny must be the local lunatic asylum. As Joseph later comments to Agnes' father, "She's not as odd as she's been told she is." Rather, her adolescent mood swings have been pathologised, all the madness and unhappiness of the family romance has been projected onto her, and she has been deprived of any independent authority that might call that diagnosis into question. Removed from school at age twelve for daydreaming rather than concentrating on her lessons, she has been left to lead a feral, formless and very solitary kind of existence thereafter. But acknowledging these contextual factors in her malady's formation does not deny the harrowing extent of the emotional and psychological agonies Agnes experiences, which are vividly depicted through Gozzi's heartfelt and intensely physical performance. As she writhes and twists in pain on the floor, gnawing her knuckles, having narrowly avoided killing Karin in an uncontrollable jealous rage, or rattles the asylum gate begging to be admitted, she is truly a soul in torment; indeed, as Trevor Johnston suggests, "Gozzi puts so much of herself on screen you almost worry for her." (Johnston 2014: 111). She provides a definitive performance of adolescent anguish *in extremis,* painful to watch at times.

But Agnes' trusting, gentle, slowly-coalescing relationship with Joseph offers a way out, and a sense of possibility beyond the mental and social confines of the family home. She follows him onto the ship he is hoping to escape on, but he feels obliged to disembark in order to bring her back home safely — already lessening his chances of evading capture, with the ship's gangplank thudding onto the quayside decisively to underline this loss. However, the seeds of their future elopement as a couple have been sown, and the next time Joseph breaks away, to Paris, he will take Agnes with him. The aspiration is that they will be able to continue the idyll of their loving relationship, finally consummated, with great mutual joy, in

Agnes' clifftop hideaway. The age gap between the lovers (Gozzi fourteen and Stockwell in his late twenties at the time of filming, with both playing roles that approximate to their real ages) is one of the reasons, Julie Kirgo suggests, that *Rapture* is not as well known or celebrated a film as it might be, due to being centered on a relationship that could be viewed with discomfort in different cultural contexts (indeed, this may have been another reason for relocating the action to France, where the age of sexual consent is lower than in Britain). If this presented a problem in the 1960s, it seems even more pressingly pertinent to a contemporary viewer of the film. And *Rapture* built upon the even more pronounced entanglement with pedophilia in Patricia Gozzi's previous film *Sundays and Cybele,* with its depiction of a close relationship between an older man and a pre-teen girl which verges on romantic at times. This is very challenging territory for any filmmaker to navigate, but Guillermin on *Rapture*, like Serge Bourguignon before him on *Sundays and Cybele,* traverses it with remarkable sensitivity and nuance and a refreshing avoidance of its sleazier potentialities. In *Rapture*,

Agnes and Joseph's relationship is carnal but still youthfully innocent and is clearly presented as one of reciprocal physical desire and enjoyment. Gozzi's performance is extraordinary in its evocation of pain but she is equally skilled at suggesting her character's delight at receiving Joseph's caresses and discovering a whole new realm of pleasure in life. Many other iterations of the older man/younger woman relationship in 1960s cinema tend to focus much more on the perspective of the man being reawakened by a destabilizing but revitalizing younger girl, in a forerunner of the "manic pixie dream girl" trope. By comparison, *Rapture* places its emphasis firmly on the young girl's awakening and growth, and though her lover is older there is never any intimation of sexual exploitation as he is played as touchingly boyish and chivalrous, a rather malleable figure just like the scarecrow that Agnes claims him to be.

In spite of their affection and their closeness, once they try to set up a makeshift home in Paris, it becomes clear that the sheltered Agnes is ill-equipped to cope with looking after herself independently while Joseph is at work and in one particularly harrowing sequence, superlatively framed and filmed by Guillermin, she loses their hard-earned money down a storm drain when it gets blown from her grasp and races down the gutter in a fast-moving gush of water. The rest of the money had been thrown at a potential landlady in supplication after she smashed her vase in a panic (these sequences are particularly powerful in their suggestion of rising anxiety, and how the escalation of noise — pneumatic drills, noisy trains, incessant talk — can give rise to terrible claustrophobia and terror). Realizing that she is unable to cope and that she is jeopardizing Joseph's freedom, Agnes hitchhikes back to the family home in Brittany. Its state of disrepair and disorder suggests how her father has been bereft since her absence. But Joseph comes back too, and this proves his downfall as the police discover him, give chase and pursue him along the cliff edge, through the trees — all soundtracked by Delerue's poignant main theme — before one of their bullets hits its target. This causes Joseph to fall to his death on the rocks below, this time the real skull of a real man irrevocably smashed rather than the head of a china doll. Having experienced love, Agnes is now alone again, although there is at least the suggestion that her father will be able to show far greater humility and sympathy towards his grieving daughter than he has been capable of in the past. That minor consolation aside, it is undeniably a tragic, pitiful ending.

John Guillermin's next film, the aviation epic *The Blue Max* (1966), would also conclude with its male lead suffering a fatal fall to earth but that film's cynical ironic approach was a world away from the tone of tender, compassionate sincerity that defined *Rapture*. In an article staking a claim for the director as a "master manqué," film critic Olaf Möller defined John Guillermin as "something of a melancholic" and continued:

> There's nothing conventionally uplifting about his films; his tales of violence, grimy glory, and defeat concede with stoicism, don't make for easy viewing experiences. At their finest, Guillermin's films are howls from the soul's darker recesses — there is a savage heart. (Möller 2014: 20-21)

Möller doesn't mention *Rapture* in his account of Guillermin's work — a sign of the film's disappearance from view and lack of availability prior to its 2011 rediscovery and revival (it was released in the UK in 2014) — and his emphasis is much more on Guillermin's male-centered war films and thrillers. But in many respects *Rapture* perfectly exemplifies the darkness, savagery and melancholia Möller identifies as the keynotes of the director's work, albeit leavened by an empathy and hopefulness in its evocation of first love, coming of age, and sexual discovery.

Rapture is indebted to the French New Wave as well as the chamber drama of Ingmar Bergman (not only in the casting of Lindblom) but it is also its own unique transnational triumph, bringing together its diverse components into a satisfying whole. Its emotional power and stylistic virtuosity prompted critic Trevor Johnston to ask: "Why and how did something of this quality essentially disappear from view for almost 50 years?" (Johnston 2014: 111). The question is a very pertinent one for historians of film concerned with questions of canonicity. John Guillermin, like other directors of his generation and nationality, simply did not fit the template of an *auteur*, and, as Johnston justifiably suggests of *Rapture*, "Had it been shot in French and billed as 'Un film de Jean Guillermin,' it's easy to imagine it being regarded now as another treasure of the French New Wave." (Johnston 2014: 111). Perhaps also Patricia Gozzi's truncated subsequent acting career, resulting in only one further film, *Le*

Grabuge/Hung Up (1973), contributed to the film's obscurity. She is one of that select number of former child stars who leave film completely to lead a "normal" life instead, possibly to the benefit of their wellbeing but to the detriment of cinema. Neither Gozzi nor Guillermin, each with careers of vastly varying longevity, ever did anything like *Rapture* ever again. It was "a distinctive outlier in the oeuvre, a road never to be travelled again" (Johnston 2014: 111), and as an uncategorizable one-off, its evasion of the usual marketing hooks was probably yet another factor in its disappearance from view for many years. But even via the restricted channels through which it was available upon release, it still made an impact on those cinemagoers who did manage to catch it, as this 1967 letter to the British film magazine *Films and Filming* attests:

> John Guillermin's *Rapture* is surely the "sleeper" of the year. Understandably, it has had no West End showing because of its lack of commercial appeal and it was pure chance that enabled me to see it as the supporting feature to *A Guide for the Married Man*. Not being sure of what to expect, I was riveted by it. The outdoor shots of seashore and landscapes are wonderfully atmospheric and the acting of Melvyn Douglas, Gunnel Lindblom, and the newcomer who plays the daughter, is superb. (Butler 1967: 50)

In 2011, with its reclamation as a lost classic and the release of a pristine print onto Blu-ray, the sleeper finally awoke and received some of the rapturous critical attention it was long overdue. *Rapture* attested to the extraordinary richness of that mid-1960s moment of transnational production, when Hollywood studio product became more permeable to experimental tendencies that had previously been the exclusive preserve of the art film. It also triumphantly demonstrated the skills hidden in plain sight possessed by a director like John Guillermin, whose loving presentation of Patricia Gozzi's astonishingly honest performance offered a definitive depiction of teenage girlhood, poised on the edge of a precipice.

CHAPTER 9

FILMING RAPTURE

Style and Technique in John Guillermin's Masterpiece[16]

BRIAN HOYLE

WHEN JOHN GUILLERMIN DIED in September 2015 the numerous obituaries in both the British and American press almost universally characterised him as what *The Daily Express* called "a master of big-budget action fare" with a "reputation for craftsmanship and perfectionism."[17] Film Studies, however, largely remains in thrall to the *auteur* theory, and calling a director a craftsman is, at best, a backhanded compliment. Kevin Lyons, in one of the very few sensitive obituaries, summed up the filmmaker's current critical reputation by arguing that, "detractors have too often accused Guillermin of merely being a journeyman, lacking in any real style."[18] To put it another way, Guillermin is not considered an *auteur,* and by extension not a great filmmaker, because he made films about a wide variety of themes, rather than a single one, and he did not have an instantly recognisable signature style that he brought with him to every film. But just because he never developed a single visual style does not mean that his individual films are lacking style. On the contrary, Guillermin is one of those filmmakers, like John Huston, who altered his style and technique to best serve the project he was working on.

Lyons justifiably argues that the "defence [for Guillermin as a stylist] would do worse than to offer *Town on Trial* (1957) as its Exhibit A, drawing particular attention to its breath-taking PoV shot of the killer stalking a second victim that anticipates the camera gymnastics of Dario Argento."[19] While I cannot disagree, I must also argue that, at least at first glance, *Town on Trial*, with its *film noir* aesthetic, has little in common stylistically with the film this chapter will be concerned with, *Rapture* (1965). Perhaps this is the way it should be. *Town on Trial* is, after all, a murder mystery set in the Home Counties of all unlikely places, while *Rapture*, to use Lyons' own description, is "a hard-to-categorise coming-of-age drama set on the Brittany coast,"[20] which combines elements of a love story, a fairy-tale, a horror movie and the European art cinema of Ingmar Bergman. The protagonist of the former is a hard-boiled Scotland Yard detective, played by John Mills, while that of the latter is an innocent fifteen-year-old girl with an overactive imagination, played by Patricia Gozzi.

According to Mary Guillermin, the director's widow and the editor of this volume, *Rapture* is both Guillermin's "best and least-known work."[21] The fact that almost none of the many obituaries that followed Guillermin's death even mentioned the film easily bears out the second half of that statement. The first half, however, is perhaps in need of substantiation. *Rapture* is a strange film to be sure, and it is certainly not without its problematic elements, especially in regard to its depiction of underage sexuality (an examination of which will be left in more capable hands elsewhere in this volume). But it is also, I would contend, both Guillermin's masterpiece and a masterpiece in the sense that it is a work made with consummate skill and artistry. *Rapture* is a film in which content and form perfectly cohere. It is above all else a work made up of contrasts. Thematically, it is about the contrast between young Agnes' rapturous, childlike view of the world and the disaffected adult world she is painfully introduced to. Visually, Guillermin echoes this binary opposition by emphasising *chiaroscuro* lighting and juxtaposing stasis and movement through virtuoso camerawork. It is this final aspect, or what one might call Guillermin's film style in *Rapture,* that this chapter will focus on through a close examination of the camerawork in a handful of shots and sequences in the film and the relevant annotations in Guillermin's personal shooting script.

This approach is necessarily limiting. But as this is a book about the work of John Guillermin, this chapter will unashamedly focus on his contribution to the film at the expense of collaborators such as cast members Gozzi, Melvyn Douglas, Dean Stockwell and Gunnel Lindblom; the composer George Delerue; and cinematographer Marcel Grignon, amongst others. This narrow focus is also necessary because Guillermin's contribution to the film has genuinely been underappreciated. The film was given its belated first release on a home video format in the United Kingdom in 2014 by Eureka!, a company specialising in high-end DVDs and Blu-rays often featuring new restorations and bespoke extra features. It is worth noting, however, that the film, which Eureka! touted as "one of the most striking and neglected studio projects of the 1960s" was not released as part of the company's flagship "Masters of Cinema" series. Although no doubt unintentional, this oversight can clearly be read as a snub to Guillermin, one that is further compounded by the failure to mention his name at all on the back cover copy. Even the accompanying essay by Mike Sutton spends little more than one paragraph discussing Guillermin, and despite insightfully linking the film's depiction of "fatalistically doomed romance"[22] to numerous other Guillermin films, including the remake of *King Kong* (1976), nothing is said about his direction outside of brief mentions of the "beautiful black and white scope photography" and his "sensitivity to place."[23]

To help redress this imbalance, I would like to begin my appreciation of Guillermin's stylistic contribution to *Rapture* by starting at the very beginning. The opening minutes, which include the titles, wordlessly but eloquently establish the setting and several central characters. The former is introduced with twenty seconds of an extended helicopter shot which traces the coastal road, with its sheer cliff-face as Larbaud (Melvyn Douglas) drives towards the small coastal town where his elder daughter, Genevieve (Sylvia Kay), is to be married that day. The film's first interior scene is inside the car. As the process shot projected behind the actors shows, the shots inside the car were filmed in a studio. Guillermin uses this to his advantage and introduces all four characters in the car in a single shot. Larbaud sits in the driver seat and a pan left reveals Genevieve sitting in the passenger seat next to him. She is wearing a wedding veil, and her facial expressions show a host of emotions ranging from nervousness to excitement. Behind her, in the back seat is Karen (Gunnel Lindblom), the family's housekeeper. But rather than do the obvious, and cut to a close up of her, Guillermin slow zooms the camera past Genevieve and then has Sylvia Kay's car seat pulled to the left so that only the edge of her veil remains in the shot. The camera then pans once more, from left to right, to reveal Agnes (Patricia Gozzi), the film's protagonist, next to Karin, who gently adjusts the young girl's hair. By filming all four characters in a single shot, he links them together as a family unit. At the same time, the unusual decision to move Genevieve out of the shot gives the shot a slightly strange, dream-like quality. This is a tone that will be maintained for the entire film. This dream-like quality continues over the opening titles as Guillermin again goes slightly against the grain in his depiction of Agnes' point of view. At first, he shoots conventionally, alternating a close up of Agnes looking out the window with a travelling shot of the scenery she sees. After this, however, Guillermin opts to superimpose the shot of the moving scenery over the close up of Agnes, meaning the viewer sees her and what she is looking at in the same shot rather than in two separate ones. The camera therefore becomes both objective and subjective at the same time, and here one first gets the sense that the film will generally show one thing through Agnes' innocent and singular gaze. This is immediately reinforced in the single, economical tracking shot in the interior of the church, (which follows aerial shots of the village and the building's exterior). Here, Guillermin once again does something unexpected. The shot begins conventionally, with a track in towards the groom. But just as one would expect it to stop and hold position on the ceremony, it makes a dramatic ninety-degree turn away from the seeming focal point of the scene and instead tracks to the front row of pews, where it ends on a tight close up of Agnes. By this point, a mere three minutes and fourteen shots in, there can be no doubt who this film is about.

As impressive an opening as this is, the first true sign that *Rapture* may be something of a technical *tour-de-force* comes in the wedding reception scene that immediately follows the shot in the church. Guillermin films this scene in a single, unbroken take lasting exactly two minutes. Over the course of this shot Guillermin shows the party in full swing, Larbaud reluctantly agree to dance with his newlywed daughter, then a young man wanders through the house and finds Agnes hiding in the kitchen where he tries to force himself on her. This is the kind of virtuosic long take that would be justly celebrated and studied had it appeared in a film by a more canonical filmmaker like Kenji Mizoguchi, Orson Welles or Martin Scorsese. Indeed, Guillermin's camera may travel a little less distance and contains fewer extras, but this shot nevertheless contains at least as much visual information as the often-cited Copacabana sequence in *Goodfellas* (1990), which Scorsese filmed in a single three-minute Steadicam shot. Like its more famous counterpart, which shows the bustle of the Copacabana's kitchen, the long take in *Rapture* is densely packed with figures including a small orchestra and numerous wedding guests, many of whom are either dancing or helping themselves at the buffet table. The shot also contains a great deal of essential character information, establishing Larbaud's emotionally distant relationship with his two daughters and his continued obsession with his dead wife, and Agnes' naiveté, extreme social awkwardness, and her sexual vulnerability.

This shot is all the more impressive when it is compared to the camera directions given in the original shooting script by screenwriter, Stanley Mann. Mann breaks the wedding banquet sequence down into at least three scenes, and therefore at least as many shots, marked as scenes number three through five. The sequences begin as follows:

3. INT. SITTING ROOM — NIGHT

—Where the reception is taking place. The room is crowded with WEDDING GUESTS. A SMALL ORCHESTRA is playing its heart out, and people swirling and stamping. THE COMMANDER [Larbaud in the finished film] is standing apart from the group watching the activity wearily. There is perspiration on his face from the heat of the room. GINA [Karin in the finished film] is the centre of attention as she dances with a YOUNG MAN who is making a large display of dancing technique. AGNES is not seen. [. . .]

4. MED. CLOSE SHOT — A YOUNG MAN

CAMERA MOVES with him as he pushes through the crowd, heading for THE KITCHEN. He is a skinny, pimply young man with his thin wrists sticking far out of his sleeves.

5. INT. KITCHEN — NIGHT

A large room with a huge centre table heaped with plates and food. On a chair, pressed back into a corner of the room, sits AGNES.[24]

Guillermin filmed everything that Mann describes, and adds a great deal of telling detail beyond that. According to his handwritten annotations, Guillermin originally planned to film this sequence in five shots that he details on the back of the first two pages of his shooting script. He wanted to begin with a tracking shot that gave off the "strong *provincial* [his emphasis] atmosphere of a small wedding." His notes read: "start [with] dancing couples, then 3-piece band, then people talking, eating, hand on buttocks, child peers at food, gills stuffed [. . .] people drinking too much, talking too much. Gina talks with young man [. . .] ending on Commander, apart, weary, joined by Genevieve and Armand, moving away from them as he speaks, other people passing, talking across them." This was to have been followed by a "Full shot [of the] room. Pimply faced man in the foreground as Commander and Genevieve start to dance, track . . . pimply faced young man, unsuccessfully eying girls." The third shot would show the young man in a "corridor or hall" leading to the kitchen. The fourth shot was to begin with a "cut [to] kitchen" when the camera "tracks to the back" with the boy before he "hears a noise from a dark corner and sees Agnes sitting in half-darkness, rigid." After Agnes has fled his advances in the kitchen the fifth shot would take place in the corridor as the young man follows her and "pulls her into the living room" saying, "Oh no, you're going to dance with me."

Since Guillermin's notes, which are incredibly detailed, make no mention of his changing his mind and deciding to shoot this sequence in a single take, one can only assume that the decision was made on location. The choice may have been a pragmatic one. While long, mobile shots like this take longer to block and light than shorter, static ones, they can, ironically, prove to be faster in the long run as they bypass the stop-start nature of filming coverage and multiple set-ups. Indeed, once the camera was rolling Guillermin would have been able to film two full pages of script in as many minutes. This consideration aside, I would argue that Guillermin had several other reasons for filming the scene this way. Firstly, it is telling that he always intended the opening shot of this sequence as a tracking shot. He knew that a coolly observant

John giving instructions for the long single take

FILMING RAPTURE

establishing shot taking in all of the guests from a distance would not convey the "strong *provincial* atmosphere" as forcefully as his notes show that he wanted. Rather, he understood that by placing the camera in the middle of the wedding reception and having it effectively mingle with the guests, he could show the audience small but telling details that establish character and the tone of the film, as well as the required atmosphere of the party.

The shot begins with an older couple in the foreground, greedily eating fruit tarts with their mouths open. Everything about the couple, from the food on the sides of their mouths, to the man's comb-over haircut, to the woman's garish dress sense, is deliberately grotesque. In the background, to the extreme left of the frame Larbaud enters through the living room doors, aloofly watching the guests and looking less than amused by what he sees. While to the right of the couple, in the middle ground, Genevieve and Armand dance. The camera at first seems to follow Genevieve and Armand as they dance, and in the process it shows us other guests in the foreground standing at the buffet table, including a woman who sneaks some food into her purse. But as the newlyweds disappear amongst the other dancers, Guillermin has the camera tilt down to show a bored young girl try to pick a cherry of the top of a clafoutis before being admonished by her mother; then up to show Karin's midriff being pawed by several male admirers; then back down to show the musicians; then a man places his hand on a woman's thigh, only to have the advance quickly rebuffed. Once it has reached the end of the buffet table and beyond, the camera turns 180 degrees, first circling Armand's weeping mother and her friends, and then panning and pulling back to show Armand being told off by Genevieve for dancing too excitedly.

At this point the shot is only one quarter of its way through, but in this time Guillermin has already established Larbaud, whose aloof but always dignified manner stands in stark contrast to the couple gorging themselves, as an outsider in this community. He has shown Armand to be a buffoon, and Genevieve to be impatient with him, hinting that her marriage was more about escape than love. But even more pointedly, by showing us the bored child, Karin's flirtatious behaviour, and man placing his hand on the woman's thigh, he has already subtly established two of the film's key themes: the contrast between the world of adults and children, and the key role that sex plays in distinguishing the two. Even the two lines of seemingly inconsequential dialogue that accompany these moments, the mother saying, "Leave that alone," to her daughter, and the woman saying, "Not here," to the man who touches her reinforce the control that adults have over children and the presence of sexuality in everyday encounters.

The next thirty-five seconds of the shot comprise Genevieve asking her father to dance, and his reluctant acceptance. Guillermin's blocking is discreet, but highly skilled. As Genevieve and Armand approach Larbaud, the camera tracks with them until Larbaud is situated in the foreground at the right of the frame with his back largely turned to the camera. As Genevieve says, "It's your turn now, Father," Guillermin has Larbaud turn and try to walk away from them, with the camera (and the couple) tracking his movement. This not only shows his discomfort and displeasure at being asked to dance, it also blocks the actors so that all three are facing the camera. As Larbaud rebuffs his daughter by saying, "Genevieve, you know I don't dance," Guillermin has Larbaud come to a halt and slowly pivot to face her. As he does the camera, for the first time in the shot, also stops just as Genevieve catches up to her father. The two now make eye contact and are filmed in profile dominating the right two-thirds of the frame, with the gawky Armand standing between them in the background and their guests visible in the left third. This configuration, which feels entirely natural, not only helps to establish character, it also allows Guillermin to avoid having to break up his sequence shot with the conventional over-the-shoulder shot-reverse shot pattern that one has come to expect in dialogue exchanges.

Guillermin's notes do not specify what kind of camera he wished to use for this particular shot, but only a few pages later he specifies the use of an Arriflex for a particularly unusual shot (discussed below). It is, however, very likely that he used the same camera here. Ronald Denning, writing for the professional photography website *Red Shark*, has noted that Arriflex cameras, which were much lighter and more compact than competing 35mm cameras made by companies such as Mitchell, were often used "as a second camera, often on location in places where a Mitchell just would not go, attached to cars or boats, used in confined spaces or hand-held, but from the late 1960s onwards, it was increasingly used as the primary camera as a new wave of directors wanted to shoot fast on location."[25] Denning argues that "the Arri 35II half-answered the dream of a small, portable cinema camera that you could handhold,"[26] and qualifies "half-answered" by noting that:

> Although the 35II was a lightweight camera that took great pictures, it was strictly what Americans call a MOS camera ('without sound'): it made far too much noise for useable sync sound to be recorded. Arri released a blimp for the 35II in 1953, enabling it to be used for sync sound, but it made the camera much more cumbersome, adding 42lbs(19kg) to the original weight of 13lb (5.8kg).[27]

With this in mind, it is worth noting that the dialogue between Genevieve and her father appears to have been dubbed in during post-production. This makes it even more likely that Guillermin shot his long take using an Arriflex with the Arri 35II. The decision to do so would have been practical as well as artistic. As Denning notes, an unblimped Arri 35II was a very noisy camera, but also a very light and mobile one. By removing synchronised sound from the equation, Guillermin was able to use the Arriflex without a blimp, and the 5.8kg camera could unobtrusively glide through the crowded wedding reception. The lack of synchronised sound would have had other advantages. Most obviously, it would have prevented the sound of the band and the numerous extras cluttering up the soundtrack and making the important dialogue hard to hear. More importantly, however, the lack of direct sound would have allowed Guillermin, his First Assistant Director (who usually deals with extras), and cinematographer, Marcel Grignon, to speak to the actors, other crew members and each other while the shot was being filmed. Critics like Sutton have noted echoes of Ingmar Bergman in the film's

A tense moment at the wedding party

focus on a dysfunctional unit living in an isolated location, its stark close ups and the casting of Gunnel Lindblom. I would argue, however, that the wedding reception, with its bustle, its rogues' gallery of local grotesques, and its sweeping camerawork, comes far closer to the work of Frederico Fellini. Indeed, the Italian director once told Guillermin's contemporary, John Boorman, that the secret to his unencumbered visual style came from shooting without direct sound, quipping that "if the Americans find out about dubbing, we are finished."[28]

Once Larbaud has agreed to waltz with his daughter, Guillermin starts to move his camera again, following the pair as the guests make room on the dance floor. He does not linger on their waltz, however, and Armand's brother, known as the "pimply young man" in the script and Guillermin's notes, almost immediately walks past Larbaud and Genevieve and the camera follows him all the way to the other side of the room. He asks a young lady who is standing by the entrance to dance but is rebuffed. By this point Guillermin's camera has travelled up and down the length of the living room twice, but when the woman declines the boy's request, Guillermin takes the camera out of the living room and through a small hallway into the kitchen, where he encounters Agnes. Before discussing their encounter further, it is worth noting two other technical details about the shot so far. Firstly, one must mention the considerable depth of field that Guillermin and Grignon achieve, which, for example, allows the gorging couple, Genevieve and Armand, and Larbaud to all be in focus across three planes of action. In addition to using a wide-angle lens with a small aperture to achieve this deep focus aesthetic, they must have employed a great deal of light, from both available and artificial sources. But just how much light they are using only becomes apparent when the pimply young man leaves the living room and crosses into the far more dimly lit hall and kitchen. Secondly, the smoothness of the camera is remarkable. Indeed, the lack of camera shake might lead one to think that the camera is on tracks, but when it turns on a right angle from the hallway to the kitchen no tracks are visible on the kitchen floor, so this is clearly not the case. The camera could be mounted on a trackless dolly, but even the smallest crab dolly would get in the way in such a crowded room. The camera therefore almost certainly has to be handheld; but just how Guillermin and Grignon achieved what feels like a Steadicam over a decade before Garrett Brown's invention was used in Hal Ashby's *Bound for Glory* (1976) remains a mystery.

While in the kitchen preening himself in a mirror, the pimply young man catches Agnes' reflection as she hides in a dark corner behind a table stacked high with boxes. As he approaches her and introduces himself as Armand's brother, Guillermin simply pans with him and for a moment keeps the camera at a discreet distance. But as his behaviour becomes more predatory, and Agnes stands up and pins herself against the wall the camera pushes into a tight two shot. Everything about this moment stands in contrast to what has preceded it. Bright lights give way to shadows, wide shots full of extras have been replaced by an uncomfortable claustrophobia and unwanted sense of intimacy, and, most importantly, the constant sense of movement, be it of the camera or the bustling party-goers, has come to a notable halt. Pinned against the wall by this would-be teenage Lothario, Agnes' body language is just as Guillermin described it in his note, quoted above, "rigid" and for a few moments the camera, relatively speaking, follows suit. It is, however, only a momentary lull. As soon as the young man moves in to kiss Agnes, she breaks away, initiating a cut and the end of this extraordinary long take. The next shot, which is a good deal shorter at only twenty-three seconds, nevertheless contains almost as much movement as the one that preceded it. The movement this time is far more aggressive. It begins with the camera looking through the kitchen doorway as Agnes runs out into the hallway and the boy follows her, grabbing her arm and dragging her into the party in the living room. After panning close to 180 degrees from the kitchen door into the living room, the camera, which is now notably hand-held to accentuate Agnes' feeling of woozy confusion, darts after them and begins to run rings around the two young actors as the boy spins Agnes violently around. The effect is dizzying, with the camera making at least two 360-degree turns and the two actors a good many more. When Agnes is finally able to break free, she charges out of the living room with the camera, moving in a notably unsteady manner, chasing Agnes until she bursts through a second set of doors.

After this display of kinetic energy Guillermin cuts to a wide shot of the living room with the camera clearly mounted on a tripod. Bar Agnes, all the major characters are visible, as well as Armand's parents, who apologise to Larbaud for their younger son's lack of decorum. This would be the kind of establishing shot a less imaginative filmmaker may have begun the party sequence with. By placing the shot where he did, Guillermin establishes one of the film's key visual strategies. From this point forward, Agnes will be associated with Dutch angles and liberal, often highly imaginative camera movement. By contrast, the adults who surround her will be associated with comparatively sober camerawork and more classically conventional techniques. Indeed, the long shot of the living room appears to be locked off on the tripod until it makes two discreet pans to show Larbaud move towards Karin and Karin runs out to follow Agnes. By this point, the young girl is in a crowded street running in a confused and agitated state, and Guillermin again finds the camerawork to match. In his notes for this sequence, on the back of page four of his shooting script, he writes, "Long 'mad' tracking shot with Agnes through crowds, people and noise, she's terrified. Cam panning sometimes following her on one side, sometimes another." This is intercut with a second tracking shot taken from Agnes' point of view, which similarly pans violently from side to side and moves in and out of focus as it pushes relentlessly forward. Again, the difference between this shot and the almost entirely static one that preceded it is pronounced. Guillermin seemed to have had a strong understanding of dynamics, rhythm and the almost musical relationship between shots in a film. Take, for example, the opening of his war movie, *The Bridge at Remagen* (1969). He begins by showing a German ambulance train arrive at a rail bridge crossing the Rhine. Overflowing with wounded soldiers the train moves at a slow pace and is filmed with a largely static camera from a handful of angles. The pace of the editing is stately (ten cuts in seventy seconds), and there is relative quiet on the soundtrack. There is then a cut to a helicopter shot of a column of Sherman tanks moving at full speed down a dusty road, followed by six more shots (in forty seconds) showing a seemingly endless line of American vehicles from a number of angles. The camera is always moving at speed and the sound the column makes is cacophonous. A return to a single ten-second static shot of the German train inching its way across the bridge immediately slows the pace again, before more shots of the American column, now approaching the bridge, reaccelerate things. The German retreat and the Allied advance are contrasted not so much through editing (the pace of the cutting is only marginally faster in the sequence showing the Allies) but rather through the speed of the movement within the frame and the pace and amount of camera movement. Guillermin is doing something very similar at the start of *Rapture,* albeit on a far more intimate scale, with Agnes being represented by movement, and the adult world by relative stasis.

One notable exception to this comes around forty-one minutes into the film when Larbaud and Joseph talk in the former's study. Throughout the scene Guillermin cuts to close ups of Agnes who is watching Joseph with wonder through a window from outside. Neither of the men notices her. Guillermin's framing, particularly involving a prominent mirror, is exquisite, but the camera movement is sober with a few pans and tracks to follow the characters as they talk. Only a reasonably quick track in on the money in Larbaud's desk drawer in any way calls attention to itself. But when Larbaud moves to the back of the room to refill his drink the camera, which seems to be handheld, moves in towards Joseph. At first it moves slowly, at a pace which matches the previous movements in the scene, but as he reacts to something he sees out of the corner of his eye the pace of the camera very suddenly increases with a fast zoom in. It darts towards him for a close up but before the zoom has stopped there is a cut to an equally fast dolly shot moving towards Agnes, who smiles at him from the other side of the window in the rain. By cutting from the middle of the zoom into the middle of a dolly in, Guillermin gives the impression of one continuous movement. This is effectively the first time that Joseph has noticed Agnes and the splicing of the two camera movements forms a visual bond between them. The significance of the moment is compounded by a subtle manipulation of the soundtrack. Larbaud, who is no longer in shot, is telling Joseph about how the locals ignore his pamphlets and ideas about the law. "It is impossible to talk to anyone here," he says, but when he continues, his dialogue is suddenly cut off mid-sentence, with him saying, "I haven't talked like this..." Joseph, having seen Agnes, stops listening to his host, and the sound of the rain beating against the window intensifies.

It would be impossible to discuss Guillermin's technique and film style in *Rapture* without giving due attention to the second sequence in the city, which takes place nearly ninety minutes into the film after Agnes has run away with Joseph. This sequence shows that the film is full of strong visual echoes and subtle repetitions as well as meaningful visual contrasts. Indeed, the second scene in the city is both a contrast to the rural idyll Agnes created for herself, and, at first, a direct echo of the scene discussed above when Agnes runs from the wedding reception into the city streets. On her second visit to the city she is, however, not alone. Rather, Guillermin places her and Joseph in a two shot with his arm around her. She is nevertheless clearly agitated, and soon she breaks away from Joseph in a panic and starts to run. Guillermin once again includes shots taken from her point of view. The pace of the camera movement may be slightly slower this time, but the combination of quick cuts from shots panning from one direction to another, soft focus, and intense lighting make the scene every bit as disorientating as the earlier example. The point is clear. Agnes may now have Joseph, but she is in many ways still the anxious child she was at the start. When Joseph catches up to her, she begs him to find a room. A dissolve takes the action to the couple together in bed. The sounds of the street outside give way to George Delerue's marvelous score. This, however, is one final moment of peace before the film gives way to its darkest, but arguably most striking section. The six minutes that follow, which depict Agnes' and Joseph's ill-fated attempt to start a life in the city, is a technical *tour de force,* which features some bravura direction on Guillermin's part.

Everything in this sequence is amplified and taken to its extreme. The sound design is at its loudest and most cacophonous. Delerue's score is at its most atonal. On Guillermin's part, his camera angles are at their most canted here. Indeed, of the sixty-one shots in the city that follow that of the couple in bed only two are in any way close to being level. The remainder tilt noticeably. Certainly, there are Dutch angles in the rural scenes in *Rapture*. There are, in fact, a great many of them. In the city sequence however, Guillermin crams so many canted angles into such a short sequence that the effect is overwhelming. Moreover, the film's rectangular CinemaScope ratio makes Guillermin's angles all the more conspicuous. This sequence also features Guillermin's most sustained use of the Franscope zoom lenses that the film's end credits make reference to. Zoom lenses that were compatible with an anamorphic process such as CinemaScope were relatively new at the time. The French lens designer, Pierre Angénieux produced the 35mm Angénieux Zoom. 35-140 f/3.5 in 1960, and by 1961 Franscope modifications of these lenses were being used by cinematographers like Raoul Coutard on *Nouvelle Vague* benchmarks such as Jean-Luc Godard's *Une Femme est une Femme* (1961) and *Le Mépris* (1963) and Francois Truffaut's *Jules et Jim*

(1962). Guillermin and Grignon were therefore availing themselves of the latest technology and keeping up with the most innovative techniques in European filmmaking. But if the zoom lens is generally used discreetly in most of *Rapture*, Guillermin lets it call attention to itself in this sequence.

A brief look at his notes on the back of page 105 of his shooting script, which detail the shots of the pair arriving in the city, make it clear that this was entirely intentional. He writes:

3. Tracking from behind Agnes & Joseph in full mid-shot as they walk down the dingy streets of the town outskirts.
4. FULL MID-SHOT from front tracking back, camera slowly tracks in (zoom lens) to MS Agnes and Joseph.
5. MID-SHOT tracking fwd [forward]. Busier part of town.
6. MS tracking back, track in (zoom) to MCS.
7. MCS tracking fwd on their backs. Busy street.
8. MCS tracking back, zoom in to CS Agnes [. . .].
9. CS tracking fwd on their backs. Very busy.
10. CS tracking back. Zoom in to Agnes, fast.
11. CS tracking fwd, Agnes' head big.
12. Tracking back. Zoom into MCU Agnes.
13. Tracking fwd, Agnes' POV. Distortion.

Although he would alter this shot pattern quite significantly in the finished film, this nevertheless shows how prominently Guillermin wanted to exploit the qualities of the zoom lens to its full advantage in this section of the film. At times he uses it conventionally, to hone in on something that Agnes is looking at, like the zoom in towards the café where Joseph finds a job. He uses it more psychologically to increase tension, like the zoom in toward the gendarmes and the construction jackhammer, even when Agnes is not looking at them. He exploits the varifocal lens' ability to distort perspective, perhaps most obviously when he zooms in towards the sweeper truck as it drives towards the camera. He uses it to exaggerate the grotesquery of the snooty landlady with unflattering extreme close ups. At other times he uses the zoom in deliberately counterintuitive but effective ways. Perhaps the most notable example of this comes at the end of the series of shots with Agnes standing outside the café trying to communicate with Joseph, who is less than pleased to see her. The first shot shows her arriving outside the café. Guillermin frames her in the window from inside the building, but just before it cuts to a reverse angle he includes a mere six frames of a zoom in towards Agnes. This may initially seem like a strange decision, but when the cut to the reverse angle begins in the middle of a zoom in on Joseph from over Agnes' shoulder, it becomes clear that Guillermin is merely being a consummate professional. Indeed, select any practical guide to filmmaking or editing and it will somewhere tell the reader to "avoid cutting between still (static) shots and moving images (panning, titling, zooming, etc.), except for a specific purpose."[29] For four shots Guillermin obeys this rule, cutting from zoom to zoom. The six frames of a zoom in on Agnes transition to the zoom in on Joseph, then a closer zoom in on Agnes' face, then a return to the previous zoom in on Joseph as his boss chastises him and he motions for Agnes to leave. The fifth and final shot in this short sequence is a final shot of Agnes, but this time Guillermin has broken the rule and he cuts from a zoom to a static medium close up of the girl, who turns from the camera to walk away. About sixty frames into this shot, however, Guillermin once again zooms. But he does not, as one might expect, zoom in towards Agnes as she walks away, but rather zooms out, as if she is being pulled further away from Joseph. This scene is also a subtle but very telling variation of the one discussed above when Joseph first meets Agnes' gaze when she is again looking at him from outside a window, and the two are linked by a zoom. Here, once again, zoom ins are spliced together, but they are noticeably slower and less dramatic than before. Moreover, this time Joseph does not want to meet Agnes' gaze, nor does he want her to be there. The cold water of reality has begun to dampen their passion, and if the audience did not already know, it can see this relationship is doomed.

Perhaps the most resonant visual echo in the film, however, is the recurring overhead shots that look directly down on Agnes. Indeed, I would go so far as to say that this is nothing short of a motif through which Guillermin attempts to film the feeling of rapture itself. This overhead shot is first glimpsed around seven-and-a-half minutes into the film when Agnes is first seen on the cliff near her pillbox hideout. She is shown looking up at the sky and whistling at the seagulls that circle above her. After a shot of the birds Guillermin cuts to an image he describes in a note on the back of page five of the shooting script in the following way: "GUNNING RIGHT DOWN on to Agnes (CAM Arriflex on rope?), as CAM twists round on its own axis, as she makes gull noises." Guillermin is once again taking advantage of the small, light Arriflex to create an image that would be next to impossible with a more conventional 35mm camera. Although he only mentions this shot once in his notes, Guillermin intercuts it with upward shots of the seagulls and returns to it no less than four times in this scene. Clearly he realised that the shot worked even better in reality. Patricia Gozzi does not merely emulate the sound of the gulls, she reaches upwards. While she may simply be trying to connect with the birds, she is also reaching up towards the sky, or the heavens (if you prefer). At the same time she is also reaching out

> John really wanted to capture the lyrical scenes where Agnes turns in circles with the seagulls circling and calling above her. He had a special apparatus built to hold the camera and capture just the shot he wanted. But the birds were silent, and refused to circle in the air. They tried everything, including special food bait. In the end, the sound man had the idea of playing a recording of sea gulls, and that did the trick. I suppose another director would have used a recording all along, but John always wanted things to be real. He told me that when he started filming in 1949, it was customary to physically lower the height of furniture for the convenience of the camera shots. John refused to bow to that convention. He always wanted everything to be as real as possible.

towards the viewer, who is placed in the dizzying position of the spinning camera. For a moment it seems like the laws of gravity no longer apply. As an image of childhood wonder, or indeed rapture, this is every bit as transcendent as the crane shot in the opening minutes of Andrei Tarkovsky's *Ivan's Childhood* (1962) in which the young protagonist is chasing a butterfly and then spontaneously levitates above the forest.[30]

At several pivotal moments throughout the film Guillermin offers up variations on this overhead shot. The first and most subtle occurs when Agnes and Joseph first kiss in the pillbox. As he places his arms around her waist, she leans her head and body back and the camera moves in towards the couple but then also moves upwards so that it is almost looking straight down on Agnes' face as she feels a rapture of an entirely different kind. The second instance comes when the couple are living in a grimy one-room flat in the city. The room's sole light is a naked bulb which dangles from the ceiling and keeps going out. At one such moment, Guillermin places the camera overhead, where the ceiling should be. In keeping with the aesthetic of this section of the film, however, it is looking down on Agnes who is sitting in the dark, and the failing lightbulb, from a distinctly canted angle. As she approaches the light and climbs on to a chair, the camera both twists on its axis and zooms in towards Agnes and the floor. In a direct echo of the earlier scene with the seagulls she reaches her hands upwards to touch the light, which buzzes on before fizzling out again. The expression on Agnes' face is a far cry from the look of wonder and elation it showed earlier when she reached towards the sky. Like the scene at the café it is another fine example of Guillermin echoing an earlier scene to show Agnes' painful induction into the adult world. The final and most moving repetition of this overhead shot is also the most direct. It comes in the final moments of the film after Joseph has been killed by the police. The gendarmes take the body away, and Agnes tells her father to head back to the house. As he moves out of the frame she looks up. A shot of the gulls circling above, almost identical to the ones earlier in the film is followed by

The finished shot of the two lovers

The camera setup for the shot

another overhead shot taken with a suspended camera turning on its axis. The angle is the same as before, but there are several important differences. Agnes is no longer smiling, her sweater is covered in blood and her hands remain fixed by her sides. The camera also turns far more slowly, and spins less than 270 degrees before the image cuts back to the seagulls. In the next shot, the camera is no longer bearing straight down on her, but instead directly level with the bottom of her chin as she slowly looks down from the gulls and just past the lens out to sea. Tears run down her cheeks. At the same time however, she almost smiles. The child who gazed upwards in wonder has been replaced by an adult who looks straight ahead. Or as Guillermin puts it on the back of the final page of the script, "she is sad, but confused. A woman."

When *Rapture* was released in 1965, it was sadly not a commercial success. Had it been, John Guillermin's career may have looked very different, as might his critical reputation. Indeed, the anonymous reviewer for *Time* argued that *Rapture* will "boost the artistic stock of English Director John Guillermin, whose feature films have covered such varied terrain as *The Day They Robbed the Bank of England*, *Waltz of the Toreadors* and *Guns at Batasi*."[31] One certainly sees their point. In *Rapture* Guillermin became one of the first filmmakers to bring the influence of the European art cinema of Bergman, Fellini, Truffaut, Godard and Tarkovsky to bear on a studio project. Had the film made more of a splash it may have led to more scripts like *Rapture* for Guillermin to direct, and by extension, more opportunities to stretch his artistic muscles and we may then have spoken about him in the same breath as say, Arthur Penn or Joseph Losey. *Rapture* instead went on to become a genuine cult film and Guillermin returned to the "varied terrain" of his earlier career with *The Blue Max* (1966), *P.J.* (1968) and *The Bridge at Remagen* (1969) before moving on to his blockbusters of the 1970s he is now best remembered for.

Rapture is one of those rare films that bears shot-by-shot examination and which reveal new details each time you watch them. But even if it is

Guillermin's "art film," the artistic flare he demonstrated in it cannot be a one-off. So as tempting as it is, we must not view *Rapture* as an anomaly. Rather, I would suggest that the quality of filmmaking on display here should encourage us to revisit his other films in the hope of finding more of the same. Indeed, I noted towards the start of this chapter that there was, at least at first glance, not much to link *Rapture* with a film like *Town on Trial*. On closer inspection, and having examined the film style Guillermin brings to *Rapture*, I would argue that what the films have in common is what Lyons called "camera gymnastics."[32] Such virtuosity might be sporadic, as it is in *Town on Trial* or *The Bridge at Remagen*, or sustained as it is in *Rapture*, but there should be no doubting Guillermin's ability to use his camera expressively. If, in the end, his work is too disparate for him to ever be classed as an *auteur*, such expressive camerawork is also not the hallmark of a mere journeyman. Indeed, if we are to continue discussing Guillermin's work, and it is well worth discussing, we should qualify the term "craftsman" with the prefix "master."

One of the caves where Patricia Gozzi hid

Up Close and Directing

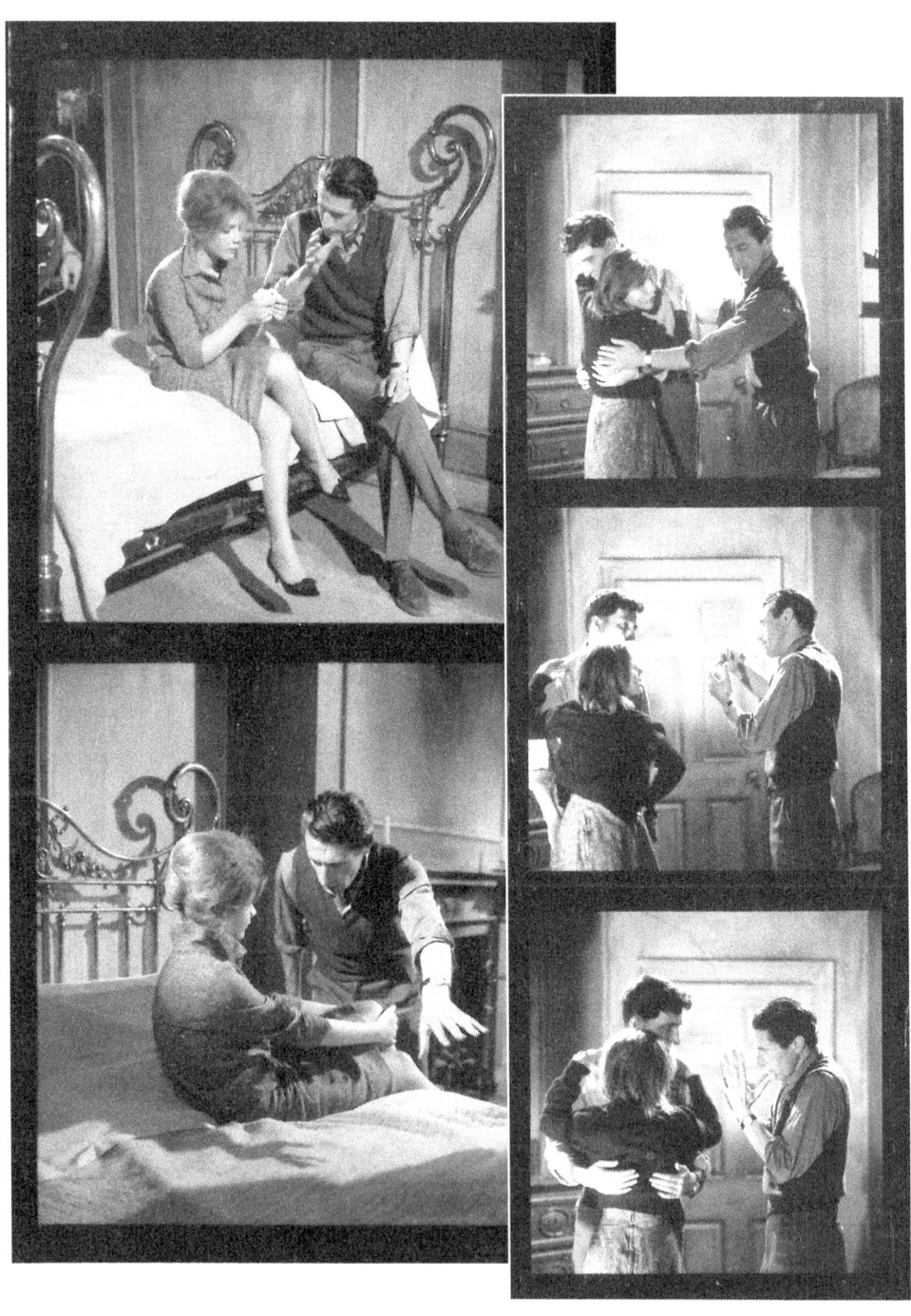

CHAPTER 10

RAPTURE IN THE #METOO ERA

MARY GUILLERMIN

My feelings watching *Rapture* in this #MeToo era are complicated. After all, I was Patricia Gozzi's age at the time she was filming *Rapture* when I was groomed by a schoolteacher for sexual activity that I experienced at the time as consensual, and the shame about which gave me lifelong difficulties with my sexuality. Surely Agnes' pairing with a twenty-nine-year-old man, played by Dean Stockwell, should have disturbed me — my particular perpetrator was thirty-six when he first noticed me. Yet each time I watched this film — originally on a special VHS professionally copied for the director with Fox's blessing — as I did repeatedly from 1999 onwards, it being John's favorite among his own work, I was so moved by Gozzi's performance and the tender relations between Agnes and Joseph that I was moved to tears. And after each viewing, I felt cleansed and healed.

Julie Kirgo raises the issue of the unequal age difference between the two actors in her program notes to the 2011 release of *Rapture* by Twilight Time:

> And it is here, with its own insistence on Agnes' childlike belief, that *Rapture* becomes most problematic. Gozzi is a 15-year-old

girl playing a damaged, infantilized young woman; Stockwell, for all his restrained, dewy-eyed gentleness, is a man twice her age; when their relationship turns sexual, the discomfort — despite the high level of tastefulness in operation — is palpable. Isn't he — and aren't the filmmakers — somehow taking advantage of her vulnerability? However "true" the situation (and it's hard to deny that teenagers are a maelstrom of hormonal yearnings), doesn't Agnes' blighted emotional state, her inability to distinguish fantasy from reality, render her even more vulnerable than the average young girl? And does the argument that the relationship is consensual — true on the film's terms and sometimes equally true, if often disturbing, in life — justify its relatively casual portrayal? *Rapture,* while not an exploitative film, does raise questions of exploitation that it never really answers.

Earlier in her program notes, Kirgo says:

[T]his intoxicating cocktail was overseen by Twentieth Century Fox's Darryl F. Zanuck, a longtime Europhile who, after catching the then-12-year-old Gozzi's extraordinary performance in *Sundays and Cybele* (1962), became so determined to cast her that he ordered the locale of *Rapture* changed from the English countryside to the French.

John told a different story about Zanuck's determination to cast the by then fourteen-year-old which I will characterize as "over-interest" in the young actress. According to John, one of the reasons the film received little attention or distribution — the other was John's insistence on filming in black and white just as color was gaining ascendency — was that Darryl Zanuck lost interest in the whole project after John, by his own telling at least, and using rather more colorful language, interfered with Zanuck's excessive interest in the fourteen-year-old.

The earlier *Sundays and Cybele* (1962) with a luminescent Patricia Gozzi at twelve years old, presages some aspects of the innocence and tenderness of the relationship between Agnes, who is still a child, and the sensitive Joseph. In a review for Criterion Cast, written by David Blakeslee for the DVD rerelease of *Sundays and Cybele* (1962; 2014), he states:

> Their meetings are idyllic, magical moments out of time: an extension of a dimly remembered childhood for one partner, and for the other, a miraculous surrogacy of an absent father coupled with a tender courtship for her affection that can only be characterized as "reverent."

And Blakeslee sees "the essential beauty and purity of this friendship between two souls who find respite from the tragedy and injustice of their lives, despite the suspicion and disdain of outside observers."

In an interview in 2014 filmed for the rerelease of *Sundays and Cybele,* Patricia Gozzi recounts how she asked her father the day before the interview took place whether he had been concerned about her acting with a much older man.

> I asked him, "What do you think about the film where I was acting this relationship between a man and a little girl? What did you think as my father?" And he said, "No, no problem. They were just friends." And he told me, "You know in '62, we didn't speak about all this, this kind of, let's say the word, pedophilia..." I said, "You let your daughter be in this kind of film. What did you think?" He said, "No, it was just a relationship between the two people, very nice without anything bad or anything wrong. So, for me it was just two kids playing together."

Fifty-five years later it would not be possible for a contemporary father to respond in this manner — the awareness of sexually predatory behavior is societally so much greater. I suspect many perpetrators had a free rein in that more innocent age, but on the other hand, cross-generational friendships that were deep and not exploitative could be and were accepted as possible and innocent. I think there are reverberations of this in *Rapture*, and it is a testament to how extraordinary a film this is, that we can feel there is a sense of innocence, even when the love becomes sexual. If this story were being filmed in the current century, it would inevitably, in this less innocent age, be seen as being about sexual abuse. Yet in all the showings of *Rapture* I have organized among my friends, several of whom are themselves survivors of sexual abuse, none have ever seen the film as being anything other than about love and loss.

I think the core reason that the love scenes in *Rapture* were healing to me is that as the viewer, I was convinced of the tenderness, rather than lust, that you felt between the two characters. John described to me how off the set Dean Stockwell was protective and affectionate in a brotherly way to Patricia. I admit though, I did feel some discomfort for the sexualization of the young actress; you can't undo the sensual touching once it has been instigated for the sake of the film. But I did not feel any trepidation for Agnes within the story. She has a strength of her own; her toughness as she challenges and almost blackmails her companion over the noises she hears as Karin and her boyfriend make love, her determination to follow Joseph when he leaves for the city. She is a wonderful mystery of a being, showing, in line with the thesis of my chapter on John's view of Femininity, a multi-layered picture of an adolescent girl on the verge of womanhood. Agnes needs the love, and in the story, she blossoms under Joseph's loving caresses.

That my tears were healing is not necessarily what you might expect. As a fifteen-year-old schoolgirl I had been groomed by my 37-year-old history teacher who initiated a sexual relationship of sorts that lasted for three years till I left school. (He told me later that he used to watch my fourteen-year-old schoolgirl hips swaying as I walked down the school corridors). I was desperately lonely, not fitting in with my peers, a middle-class outsider, and once physical contact was initiated by him, I was hooked by a desperately intense, and bewildering, physical attraction. I shared this part of my life story in my one-woman play that premiered in early March 2020 as part of Solofest, the largest solo show festival on the West Coast of America. Here is an excerpt from my show, *From Crazy to Sane: Or Am I? A Tale of Feminine Mysticism, Magic & Madness*. I include it as a way of presenting, perhaps more lightly than serious prose could in looking at such dark subject matter, the psychological complexity of this kind of mutual attraction amid predatory and abusive behavior. By way of explanation, in a solo show one plays all the characters oneself.

MARY: My best friend in high school was Sally... and I did anything and everything to stay in favor with her. Sally had lost her virginity when she was only eleven to her older brother's best friend and she'd been having sex ever since. We were too young to realize that that was sexual abuse. And it was the Sixties; no one talked about sexual abuse in those days.

Keeping in with Sally meant lying to my mum about sleeping at Sally's house on a Saturday so we could stay out all night to pick up boys, well, men actually. It meant losing my virginity at fifteen and having sex with different men in cars, Sally in the back seat, me in the front, with the steering wheel and everything, just to stay in her good books.

By the time I was sixteen, I was crying into my pillow at night, "I might as well become a prostitute. I couldn't feel any worse. I've lost my self-respect."

By now I had a bad problem with mood swings. I was so determined not to be like my depressed and anxious mother that any time I felt happy or excited, I deliberately exaggerated my feelings. I just couldn't understand it when I got very depressed. I'd been feeling so marvelous. Actually, I had a big secret. And that didn't help my ups and downs. It was Ron Gould.

I was fifteen and Ron was my History teacher and 37 years old. One day he gave me a ride home from school. He parked the car and turned to look at me.

Oh my god! What's this? I'm on fire. It's spreading all over me. It feels marvelous.

I'd had my very first orgasm, without being touched physically, and I was so young and naive, I didn't even know what had happened.

So, Ron and I began our little game. I would hang around the street at the side of the school. He would pull over in his car and ask me,

RON: Would you like a ride home, Mary?

MARY: Then we would drive to Valentine's Park where it was a bit private, and kiss and he would touch me between my legs, until I said, No! Stop! It's too intense. I was very confused.

I was still lying to my mother. And Ron was married. I felt disgusted with myself, and ashamed. When the guilt got too much for me, I ignored Ron. I would try to resist the seductive stares he gave me, but in the end, I couldn't.

This on-again, off-again behavior went on for three years, between fifteen and turning eighteen. The whole time I felt so grown up I thought it was consensual. I didn't understand how Ron was betraying his position of authority. It took me another thirty years to realize he had abused me.

As I said, there was little if any awareness of sexual abuse as an issue in the early Sixties. As third formers, we schoolgirls giggled together as we passed the chemistry lab. We knew about the chemistry teacher who went into the stock cupboard with the pretty sixth form girl (12th grade) for kissing sessions. Everyone knew. The math teacher, Mr. Spitz, came to me one day and told me in a slightly admonishing tone, "I know what's going on between you and Mr. Gould." A friendly warning to look after myself, I expect, I don't remember. But I also suspect he did not deliver the same warning to the true offending party. Awareness at that time was such that the responsibility almost lay more at my door.

Despite my many viewings of *Rapture*, despite knowing John intimately as a person, I still don't quite understand how he transformed the bald facts of a fourteen-year-old sleeping with a twenty-nine-year-old into a story about purity, love and tenderness that doesn't — even in our more aware age — make (most of) us squirm on our justifiably politically correct seats. (In all my showings of *Rapture* to friends, Kirgo's understandable comment about discomfort is the first I have heard). I have written about my own reminiscences of my at-the-time unacknowledged abuse, because it is such a difficult area of life, then and still, and my experience illustrates how — I say this somewhat reluctantly but such is the complexity of real life — the most exquisite sexual moments in my life, sadly, came within this cruel and harmful relationship.

But back to John. In fact, John makes his position clear from the opening shots. After the car ride in tense silence, punctuated only by the giggle of the bride-to-be, we are in the church as the wedding commences. The camera pans past a young man who turns to look at Agnes sitting in her family pew with a strange expression on his face. It is this same young man at the wedding party scene that is the film's proper opening, who finds Agnes huddled in a corner hiding from the noise and the strangers. As he moves towards her with the intention of kissing her and thus taking advantage of the vulnerable girl, he looks over his shoulder to make sure he is not observed. Thus are we told he is up to no good. When Agnes resists and he drags her out onto the dance floor, and spins her rather viciously around, his father interrupts his bullying of Agnes, prompting the young man to say, by way of excuse, and somewhat plaintively at being called out for his behavior in front of the whole wedding party, "I was just teaching her how to dance." The excuse of male privilege. Always a lie that is often accepted. The neurotic girl or woman is blamed for making a fuss, as indeed Agnes is here. "I told you not to bring her, father," her older sister hisses at Melvyn Douglas.

In thinking about my husband over the five years since his death, I have come to believe that he put many of his vulnerable feelings

Agnes, held captive against her will, is whirled around the room

into the hands of his female characters; cf. my description in this book of John's understanding of the Feminine psyche under threat, such as Yvonne being chased in *Crowded Day* or Joan's attempted strangulation in *Torment*. In *Rapture,* consciously or otherwise, John also put his heart into expressing all his dreamy, sensitive yearnings, which would be seen as feminine by a gender-rigid society, into the role of Agnes.

It is Agnes who runs on the beach, plays with dolls, and through her gestures at the sky, plays with soaring seagulls. It is Agnes who makes the scarecrow, in her intense yearning for something of her very own, an intensity of desire that matches John's intensity about this film. Witness the transcription of John's hand-scrawled notes on the title page of the script on the next spread.

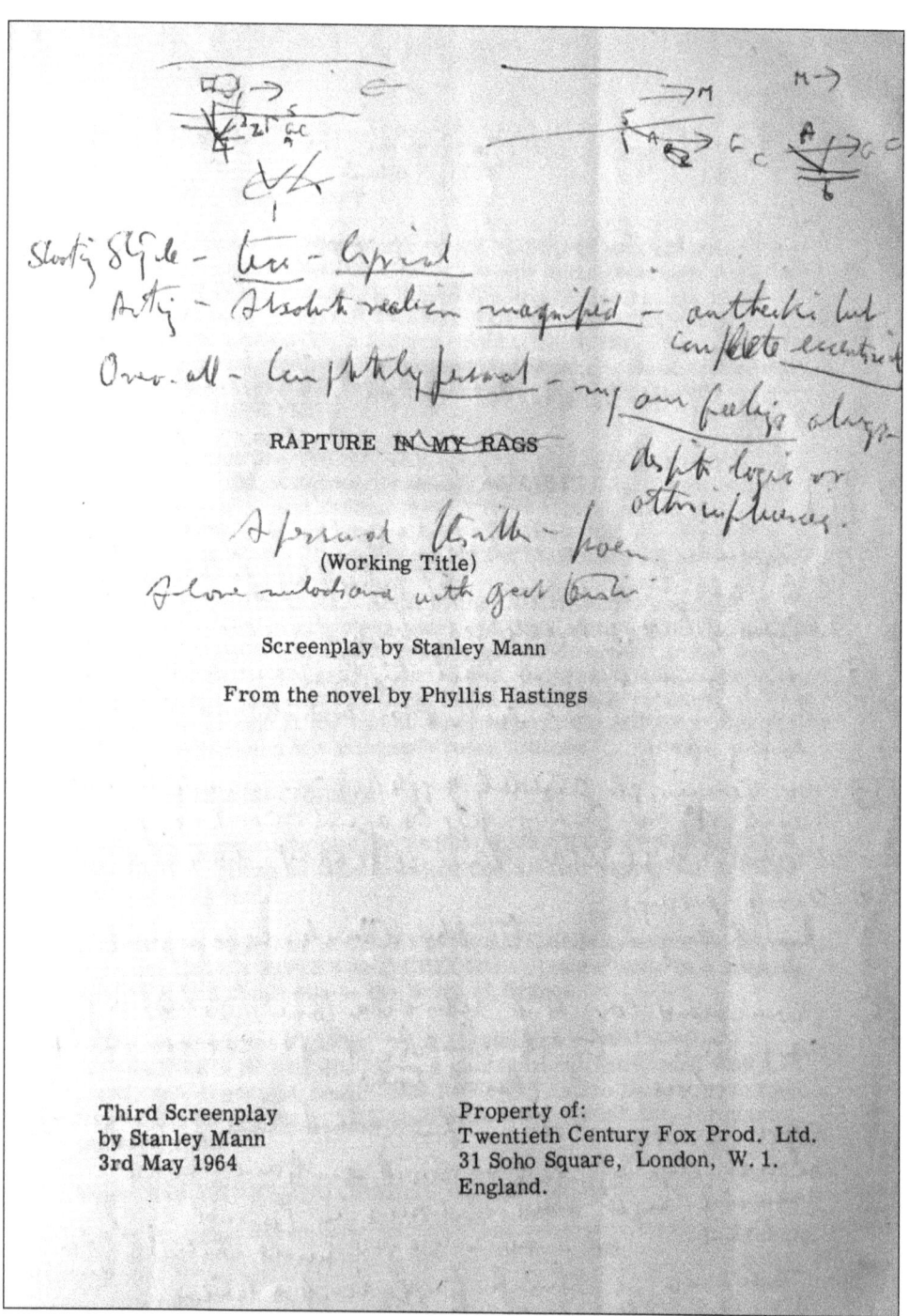

John's scrawled thoughts on shooting style and emotional tone

Shooting style - <u>tense</u> - <u>lyrical</u>
Acting - Absolute realism <u>magnified</u> - authentic but complete <u>eccentricity</u>
Over all - Completely <u>personal</u> - my <u>own feelings</u> always despite logic or other influences

RAPTURE IN MY RAGS

A personal thriller-poem

(Working Title)

I love melodrama with great tension

Screenplay by Stanley Mann

From the novel by Phyllis Hastings

Third Screenplay
by Stanley Mann
3rd May 1964

Property of:
Twentieth Century Fox Prod. Ltd.
31 Soho Square, London, W.1.
England.

Transcription of John's scrawled feelings about Rapture

> There's a very poignant scene in *Rapture* where the character, Agnes, is talking to Joseph, Dean Stockwell's character, and telling him, perhaps telling someone for the first time, what her internal experience was that made her agree that she was in difficulty with her mental health. She was quite new to acting and John made a few suggestions, one of which was that she should lie on the floor for part of the scene and he demonstrated how she could raise her hand to the wallpaper pattern and run her fingers down the wallpaper. This Patricia Gozzi did, and that scene is so powerful. It's just interesting to know that John's capacity as a director extended to really understanding the interior of a disturbed fourteen-year-old's mind.

I believe, and I only came to see this in the process of writing this paper, that John put all his dissociated tenderness and sensitivity into his ardent desire to film this story; everything that he had pushed under the surface in himself in his struggle to fit the gender-role expectations of a world at war in the 1940s as he learnt to be a man among men. He would say, "Being in the Air Force was the making of me." It is John's soul who yearned for something of his very own and found it in this extraordinary film. It is John's soul who panicked in the streets as Agnes and Yvonne do, who felt himself a victim to chastising words of whom? Schoolmasters? We do not know. But I feel he had somewhere seen lips moving with the incessant criticisms of the landlady in *Rapture* or the mother of Yvonne's lover (*The Crowded Day*) that the camera closes in on so effectively. It is John who wanted to unpack the chest in the attic filled with treasures and remembrances; John who poetically expressed all his subterranean yearnings, the running on the beach, watching the world turning with the seagulls, even running up to the iron gates of the mental asylum and battering on it, "I'm mad, I'm mad. Let me in, let me in."

I watched *Rapture* repeatedly to heal the exploitation, guilt and shame that had dogged my own life. Interestingly, for the first five or six viewings, I really had trouble knowing whether Agnes knew that Joseph was separate from her creation and was *not* the scarecrow come to life. Each time I saw the film, I would fall into a state of reverie, fall into being in her world where her creation myth was believed by me. The spell of the scarecrow coming to life was woven in me, and even though she tells us the secret at the end, whispering to the dead Joseph, "I always knew you were real," I would look at John and say I still didn't know what to believe. Did she know? Did she know?

I now think John watched *Rapture* repeatedly so that he too could sit with his own inner sensitivity come alive — his own version of the trauma

John directing the oppressive nature of the father-daughter relationship

healing this film performed for me. He may have seen his sensitivity personified by Gozzi's wonderful performance, and as Joseph crashes down onto the rocks and his death — mimicking the earlier destruction and death of Agnes' doll-self when the dominating patriarch snatches the doll away from her with a scornful, "You're not a child!" — I believe John saw his own "dewy-eyed, sensitive" body crashing to destruction on the rocks of what patriarchal society expects from its men. No room for the evocative, for blurred edges of reality, for deep inner feelings that are hard to share. In *Rapture,* John shares with us "[his] own feelings despite logic or other influences."

CHAPTER 11

INTERLUDE: SAVAGE SPECTACLES

*Hidden in plain sight, John Guillermin's
36-film career deserves a closer look*

OLAF MÖLLER

COME AGAIN? Yes, John Guillermin, the guy who made *The Towering Inferno*. Today Guillermin is mainly remembered (if that's the word) for that remarkable 1974 disaster film, the Dino De Laurentiis-produced 1976 *King Kong* remake, and *Death on the Nile* ('78). He also made *Never Let Go, The Blue Max, Tarzan's Greatest Adventure, Guns at Batasi*... I know what you're thinking: you would never have guessed that they're all directed by the same guy.

Why has Guillermin's career gone unrecognized? Easy: bad timing. Guillermin hit his stride at the end of the Fifties, just as a post-studio system style of filmmaking was arising with the French New Wave, Britain's Free Cinema, and so on. For the admirers of these idioms, Guillermin's meticulously executed and unapologetically classical works, such as *The Blue Max* ('66) or *The Bridge at Remagen* ('69), were anathema. The only Guillermin film that was somewhat in synch with the fashion of the day is *Never Let Go* ('60), an excursion into England's

underworld that functions as a perfectly constructed parable about the new middle class' fear of falling—a kitchen-sink noir. The problem wasn't so much the disdain of new wave hipsters, as it was one of the director's attitude. Guillermin is something of a melancholic: in his coolly unflinching cinema, tired, traumatized men in desperate situations fight with dour determination for a few shreds of dignity. There's nothing conventionally uplifting about his films; his tales of violence, grimy glory, and defeat conceded with stoicism, don't make for easy viewing experiences. At their finest, Guillermin's films are howls from the soul's darker recesses—theirs is a savage heart.

The opening of *The Blue Max* is quintessential Guillermin: a barren landscape littered with the debris of trench warfare; a low skyline of leaden blue, soiled with puffs of black smoke; everything is still, but the faraway noise of artillery, machine guns, and exploding grenades tells a grim story of mechanized butchery. Title card: "1916. Western Front." In the distance, three soldiers emerge from the ravaged earth and run toward the camera. Two are mown down, and the third makes it into a muddy crater. When the roar of airplanes begins to fill the air, he looks up yearningly; meanwhile, the sweetly forlorn score suggests that this man's hopes are beautiful and doomed. For the opening title sequence, the camera rises above the clouds, where the planes seem to frolic on white pastures. When the credit "Directed by John Guillermin" appears, the gunfire is heard once more and we realize that we are in fact watching aerial combat.

Men often look heavenward in Guillermin's films. At the end of *The Bridge at Remagen,* a Wehrmacht officer listens mournfully to the drone of Allied planes while a firing squad takes aim at him; at the end of *Skyjacked* ('72), Charlton Heston's wounded airline pilot looks up from a stretcher at a plane taking off, smiling ruefully. This calmly composed professional might be the closest thing to a Guillermin self-portrait, down to the pipe perpetually dangling from his mouth, and the director's then-wife (Maureen Connell) as the cautious hero's spouse.

Born in 1925 in London to French parents, Guillermin (pronounced "GILLer-min") belongs to the underappreciated generation of British filmmakers, most of whom fought in World War II, started making features in the immediate postwar years, and had a knack for the tough and the nasty. Think the Bond practitioners Terence Young, Guy Hamilton, Lewis Gilbert, and Peter Hunt, in addition to J. Lee Thompson and Michael Anderson.

Guillermin served with the RAF and went to France after the war to make documentaries, and "documentary" seems to be one of his guiding ideas. One of his stylistic constants, an expert use of handheld camera to add grit and muscle to key scenes, may be rooted in those early efforts, and they function as counterweights to Guillermin's penchant for forceful lines, a very plastic sense of interior spaces, and use of overhead shots. In one of his few extant interviews (*American Cinematographer*, January 1977), he repeatedly employs the word "documentary" to define his notion of realism: *The Towering Inferno* for him is "documentary." Guillermin's interest in conveying how people and spaces relate to one another and how decisions are reached and carried out suggests a spark to his filmmaking that one might call Griersonian— even if the grandfather of British documentary focused on social development and progress as opposed to collapse.

Guillermin was reportedly a demanding director, and it appears that he antagonized many of his collaborators with his will for perfection (few people worked with him more than once). Just study the opening Allied tank column attack on a Wehrmacht train full of wounded soldiers as it slowly crosses a bridge in *The Bridge at Remagen*. The impeccable

John with some of the tanks used in The Bridge at Remagen

clarity of the breakdown of the action coupled with the means at Guillermin's command—armored vehicles and artillery galore, tons of steel in full-tilt motion, and a vast landscape in which to deploy and arrange it all—make for a truly fearsome spectacle, born of a filmmaking ethos forged in battle and planning, where the tiniest oversight may lead to disaster. Here, self-preservation and self-realization can become one and the same.

> John was filming *The Bridge at Remagen* with quite a big international cast in Czechoslovakia in 1968. One day John was in the hotel with his wife and two children and he heard the sound of gunshots and tanks in the street so he hurried his children underneath the table and he and his wife watched from the window as Russian tanks rolled by. It was really difficult to get out of Czechoslovakia. The British Consulate was taken aback by the sudden crisis. Some of the leading stars of the film requisitioned taxis and saved their own skins without thinking about people like John with children there. Anyway, he did get his family out safely.
>
> And then the hunt was on. Where and how could they finish the film? John and the producers had location guys scouting all over Europe. And eventually word came back that a match had been found for one end of the bridge. It was on a lake near to Rome, called Lake Albano. They all decamped production to the shores of this lake where the mountains behind the lake were well matched with those left behind in Czechoslovakia. They wrapped the film with one end of the bridge at Remagen being built on the shores of the lake.

Returning to England, Guillermin made his feature debut with *High Jinks in Society* ('49). Only half of his dozen or so subsequent films (he also directed some episodic television) are readily available. They show a director looking for his voice: Guillermin had a stab at comedy with the pleasantly quirky *Miss Robin Hood* ('52) and the carefree *Song of Paris*

('52); revealed his taste for more somber hues with *The Crowded Day* ('54), a cross-section look at postwar society set among the employees of a department store during the grueling days leading up to Christmas; and even tried his luck at the meta-moviemaking game with the endearingly puzzling *The Whole Truth* ('58). These films are of interest in relation to

the strange emotional tone of *Waltz of the Toreadors* ('62) and *House of Cards* ('68), two dazzling oddities from Guillermin's Sixties heyday, and to the flourishes and offbeat touches that add a casually disturbing edge of hysteria to sober-bordering-on-grim films like *The Day They Robbed the Bank of England* ('60) and *Guns at Batasi* ('64). Perhaps the first example of prime Guillermin is *Operation Diplomat* ('53), a 70-minute programmer so tautly directed that every image counts, every detail matters, every actor's movement feels perfectly timed—a true gem. The same goes for *Town on Trial* ('57), a police procedural in which the lead investigator, in true Guillermin fashion, tears a community to pieces to expose every last lie. Imagine an English Mike Hammer, finding corruption wherever he goes, but too serious and proper to mix it up with the dames and too civic-minded to go ahead and torch the whole town.

Guillermin's winning streak begins with *Tarzan's Greatest Adventure* ('59), the most relentless and brutal Tarzan film ever made—it's Guillermin's *Heart of Darkness,* with Tarzan as a Marlow character who behaves like Kurtz. The only subpar film during the subsequent decade is *P.J.* ('68), a New York-set, mellowly goofy private-eye mystery starring George Peppard, a swing of the pendulum away from the fairy-tale-like Euro mystery *House of Cards* (also starring Peppard), whose landscape of palaces and ruins, rooftops and cellars, and eerie undertones of all-pervading perversion and menaced innocence echo his Gothic fable *Rapture* ('65). Perhaps *Tarzan Goes to India* ('62) is also mildly underwhelming—but be that as it may, Guillermin could do almost no wrong throughout the Sixties, regardless of the period's cine-cultural tastes.

Guillermin's career continued for another 20 years, with shakier results. His Seventies output is still remarkable—for the most part. *Skyjacked* and *Death on the Nile* are the high points, followed closely by *The Towering Inferno* and *King Kong,* but *El Condor* ('70) is a mess—Guillermin had no feel for screenwriter Larry Cohen's ironies. The Eighties are another story, even if his final film, a stark TV Western about revenge and self-discovery called *The Tracker* ('88), marks a surprising return to something resembling form.

It's difficult to imagine how a master manqué like Guillermin—a professional maudit with a maverick's heart—could have continued working in the current era. What he stood for means nothing today.

"Olaf's World," *Film Comment* Jan-Feb 2014
Used with permission from Film Comment
and the Film Society of Lincoln Center.
© Film Comment 2014

PART THREE

There's really nothing like an exciting film on a big screen.
Hopefully, I've made a few in my career.
—JOHN GUILLERMIN

John sizing up the shot

CHAPTER 12

THE AMERICAN YEARS 1968 TO 1988

MARY GUILLERMIN

J OHN'S TALK ABOUT his working life centered around stories that happened around the people in the films. He didn't talk much about actual directing itself, which was sad for me, as I would have loved to hear about his work as a director. Some of those stories are scattered throughout this book. His later life was deeply affected by the death of his only son in a car accident in 1984 while he was directing *Sheena*. Mike had been with John for six weeks in Kenya, prior to returning home and having the fatal accident, and John would reminisce about the pranks he got up to.

When I met John in 1998, he still, he told me, cried every day for his son, and his face was etched with deep pain lines from this loss and the divorce that had been thrust upon him. I was pleased when the heavy pain in his eyes lightened and then disappeared as we fell in love and started to live together. And when he showed me photographs of the sailing he and Mike had done together in the South Seas around Tahiti, I reminded him how many fathers didn't get to spend all that time with their 18-year-old sons and how special that time had been for them both.

John was grateful to George Peppard for being his passport to Hollywood. Although John had made a few films for US companies, it was through Peppard's determination to work with John again that he was able to get a firm foothold in Hollywood. Peppard wanted John to direct *P.J.* (1968) and when he got him the job, John agreed, though he expressed reservations about directing a film that was set partly in a New York he did not know at all. *House of Cards*, also 1968, followed which is a tight, nifty film, superior to the rather muddled *P.J.*

John behind the camera on King Kong Lives

In *House of Cards*, Orson Welles played the head of a Fascist conspiracy. He was very overweight and not in good health. One of the scenes involved a shot from the top of the Coliseum and as filming was about to begin, cast and crew were rushing around looking for Orson Welles who was nowhere to be found. Eventually he was discovered. He had climbed, ever so slowly and all alone, the many flights of stairs that led to the chosen location for the shot. Orson was pleased he had made it to the top, pretty much on determination and grit alone. Everyone else was horrified that he had risked his health.

The Bridge at Remagen (1969) was also filmed in Europe, as was *El Condor* (1970) but by now John was safely working for US companies and his family lived in Los Angeles. John, literally, followed the money as the American dollars and US-UK partnerships that had subsidized the British Film Industry dried up. He took his role as the provider for his family very seriously, and he put that before his artistic yearnings. I remember him running *Sheena* (1984) for me, a movie panned by the critics, saying, "I really tried to make it artistic; look at the wildlife shots." Some critics write about the film losing its way in the second half. I always think about the courage and discipline it took for John to return to Kenya to finish the film after organizing his son's funeral and cremation.

After *El Condor* (1970), which was not much liked by the critics either, John's career hit a low patch. Barbara Holsopple, film critic of the

John directing The Bridge at Remagen

Pittsburgh Press, said, under the headline, *"El Condor* is a Movie that Could be Forgotten;" "Another Grade B Western has hit town . . . . Only Lee van Cleef adds talent to the mélange created by director John Guillermin." John had just bought a large house with grounds in Brentwood with an at-the-time huge bank loan of $300,000. John admitted to me he had always had a penchant for large houses that were a stretch financially and he had made that mistake several times in his life. The months went by and the interest and payments piled up. The house was put up for sale, and John became very depressed and anxious that his career might be over. He resorted to building a brick wall around the swimming pool, imitating Winston Churchill who laid bricks during his "dog days" as he called his depressions. One time a house-viewing party came when John was doing this work, and, humiliated, he pretended to be the gardener. The house eventually sold for what he had paid for it.

Then Chuck Heston, a friend and neighbor, suggested him as the director for *Skyjacked* (1972). John described walking into the Polo Lounge at the Beverly Hills Hotel to meet with Chuck and the producers, his palms sweaty, feeling like he was walking to his execution. To his relief he was offered the job, and though it wasn't very much money, he took it gratefully.

John's career did take off again. He made nine movies between 1972 and 1988 — including his three blockbusters, *Towering Inferno* (1974), *King Kong* (1976) and *Death on the Nile* (1978) — after which film there was a downward slide until the final made-for-TV cowboy film *The Tracker* in 1988. This downward slide was a mixture of giving in to Dino di Laurentiis' ardent desire to get another blockbuster hit with the dismal *King Kong Lives* (1986) — John tried to dissuade Dino from the mistake — and the fact that he was dealing with acute grief and a failing marriage strained by his son's death, his temper and his refusal to give up drink. Although John regretted that he fulfilled his artistic vision only in *Rapture* (1965), he was proud of the many audiences he entertained and the huge scope of the productions he managed.

Filmography 1968 to 1988

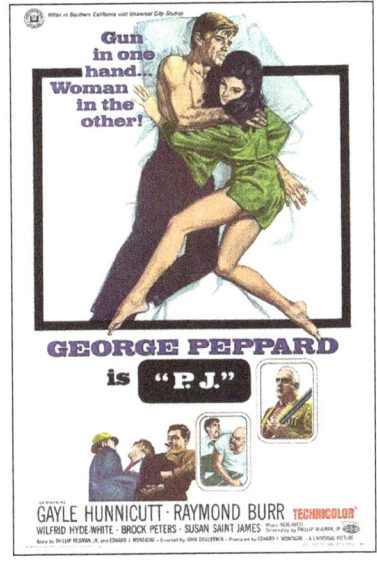

1968
P.J.

1968
HOUSE OF CARDS

1969
THE BRIDGE AT REMAGEN

1970
EL CONDOR

1972
SKYJACKED

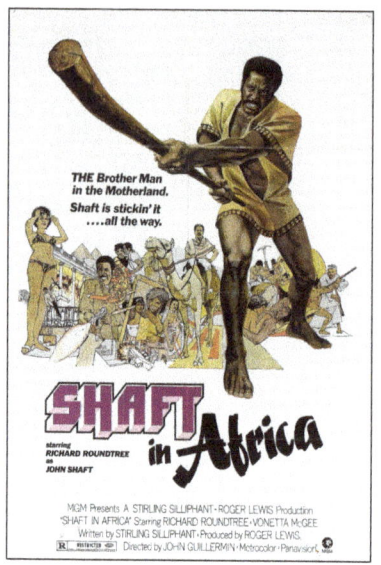

1973
SHAFT IN AFRICA

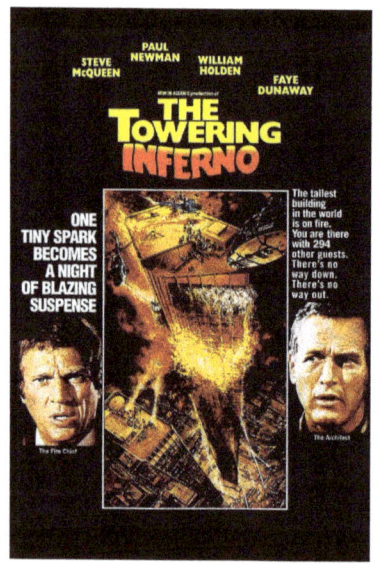

1974
THE TOWERING INFERNO

1976
KING KONG

1978
DEATH ON THE NILE

1980
CROSSOVER (MR. PATMAN)

1984
SHEENA

1986
KING KONG LIVES

1988
THE TRACKER (Made for TV)

THE AMERICAN YEARS 1968 TO 1988

CHAPTER 13

THE TOWERING INFERNO: SAVED BY A FIERY VISIONARY

BRETT A. HART

WITH A ROSTER OF thirty-four titles spanning a period of nearly 40 years, director John Guillermin brought more than a few exciting box office hits to the big screen during his career. One of which was *The Towering Inferno*.

Next to his remake of *King Kong*, Guillermin is perhaps most known for this 1974 all-star epic disaster film, and one that he repeatedly dismissed during his lifetime as one of his least favorites. During the last years of his life, he even went so far as to turn it off within 10 minutes during any attempted private screenings where he was present.

The Towering Inferno was a difficult project from the start. Producer Irwin Allen, fresh off the box office success of his ocean-liner disaster feature *The Poseidon Adventure*, first sought to option the rights to Richard Martin Stern's book *The Tower*. But much to his chagrin, Warner Brothers had already purchased the rights for reportedly $400,000. This would have forced most Hollywood producers to concede defeat, but not Allen. Known as passionate if not equal parts convoluted in his actions, Allen instead secured the rights to Thomas N. Scortia's and

Frank M. Robinson's *The Glass Inferno,* published in 1974 (one year after *The Tower)* with an almost identical storyline. Purchased with 20th Century Fox and for the reduced rate of $300,000, Allen set out to greenlight his project before Warner Brothers had even scratched the surface with theirs.

After a persuasive pitch to both Warner Brothers and 20th Century Fox, Allen made the then-unheard-of suggestion of doing a coproduction and merging both projects. He suggested that rather than compete for box office seats with two very similar films, that they split the cost of making the film and he would oversee all production. Impressed by Allen's vision, dynamic storyboards and his usual chutzpah, they agreed.

The box office success of Allen's previous disaster epic *The Poseidon Adventure* may have helped him strong-arm the two studios into giving him what he wanted: to be the creative force bringing his next vision of a disaster epic into being and to finally wear another cap on set that he had desired all along, that of director.

Allen, arguably more of a showman than a storyteller, was held back from this inspired dream by the studios. And fortuitously, John Guillermin stepped in as director.

Smoke & Mirrors

Though no stranger to filmmaking, Guillermin was still relatively new to the Hollywood system, having moved to the United States in 1968. He'd enjoyed a highly successful run in Europe that spanned almost twenty years, but like many talented artists, decided to move to the "Land of Dreams" where he found himself constantly hunting and foraging for new directorial assignments. And these ran the gamut of genres, from modern noir to espionage thrillers to blaxploitation. But Guillermin was a man with one constant: he lived to be behind the camera. He poured his energy into steering a set and telling a story, regardless of narrative or budget. John Guillermin had a reputation for creating works of lush cinematography with first-rate performances.

His pictures were made with passion and focus, and covered immense variations on narrative: jungle men fighting the laws of nature and man, or obsessed middle-class WWI German fighter pilots who would do anything to capture the respect of peers and nation, and artistic explorations of young girls and the death of their innocence as they transform into women. His were arguably some of the most beautiful films of the time, driven and married with musical scores that remain unparalleled.

Never imagining having to reinvent himself after box office successes like *The Blue Max,* John began to have his doubts after a while in Los Angeles. Down to his last savings and working on his own home in Brentwood that was put up for sale (John was even on occasion mistaken for a workman), he was understandably anxious when Hollywood legend Charlton Heston called on him to meet him at the Polo Lounge at the Beverly Hills Hotel about directing his next picture, *Skyjacked*.

Little is known about why Heston had chosen Guillermin for this directorial assignment. One can only surmise that perhaps he had seen Guillermin's aerial opus, *The Blue Max,* and was so impressed that he wanted the director to take the helm with the thriller *Skyjacked*.

Guillermin went into that meeting, feeling the financial stress that he absolutely had to walk away with the studio's confidence and secure the directorial position. And that he did. The results were well received. Critic Vincent Canby surmised that,

> "... a basically standard melodramatic movie situation can be made diverting and occasionally gripping. Aerial hijacking is a shocking fact of life these days and *Skyjacked,* a straightforward, simple thriller, which, if memory serves, is the first in this genre, treats it without glamour and as the madness it is .... John Guillermin, the director, handles an essentially familiar plot with speed and efficiency."

Heston wrote, "*Skyjacked* looks surprisingly good, I was relieved to see... it seems very tight. A pleasure for a change to be in a film that runs under two hours... it's been some time." Even if the storyline of a hijacked airline would eventually become formulaic, John led the charge with one of the very first in the genre, and he did so with his traditional flourish.

Next under Guillermin's Hollywood belt would be the blaxploitation picture *Shaft in Africa*, which had mixed reviews and box office success. So it would seem that Guillermin's success with *Skyjacked* is how he ended up at the top of 20th Century Fox's list as director of *The Towering Inferno*. This decision must have been difficult for producer and director to embrace. The producer, Allen, had visions of being the single auteur of the first-ever epic fire disaster picture, and it was his very own passion project. The studios wisely denied him the tremendous responsibility of sole direction; he would have to share direction with a British director. Guillermin walked in with eyes wide open, realizing that he was going to have his work cut out for him if he was going to steer this ship.

John directing the actors in Skyjacked, pipe in mouth

In March 1974 John Guillermin was announced as the director of *The Towering Inferno,* and production would begin three months later and last for only four months. With his usual forceful demeanor, Allen had been able to convince the studios to let him direct the action sequences. This not only must have felt like a slap in the face to Guillermin as an accomplished filmmaker by this point in his career, but also robbed him of what he had built his reputation on: outstanding action set pieces.

> John had a really difficult time on *Towering Inferno,* because of the push-and-pull with Irwin Allen. And there's a sad and a happy story about that. The sad story is that John had what could be called a nervous breakdown under the pressure of working with a less-talented, wannabe director, as second director, and he told me he often refused to have a driver take him to the studio, because he cried the whole way into work. That's how painful making that film was partly because he didn't have clear authority.
>
> The amusing story concerning Irwin Allen is that Irwin Allen bought a brand new Rolls Royce and he took John for a spin and as John got out of the car, the passenger door fell off its hinges! I don't know whether John controlled his laughter or not, but he said that the horrified look on Irwin Allen's face was priceless. And it turned out that the mechanics had given it a service and forgot to put the bolts back in the door.

The production design would occupy over 11 locations. There were a total of four film units shooting, which perhaps added to Guillermin's frustration. He was quoted as telling Allen that more cameras were needed for certain scenes, and this fell on deaf ears. He was concerned that the fire scenes needed four cameras, rather than two. Less coverage meant fewer angles to cut to; then less pacing in the editing room; and fewer of those gorgeous close-ups on his stars that his films had previously been known for. However, with four crews working simultaneously, the budget would have risen even further with the addition to each and every camera, cameraman and assistant cameraman. With an already over-inflated multimillion-dollar budget, it's easy to understand how Allen couldn't justify any further production costs. And this is just the beginning of the many ways the two men differed in their aesthetics on how sequences and films should be made. This was a bone of contention to Guillermin throughout the entire production and his lifetime regarding this film.

Playing with Fire

During the four-month production, sixty stunt people performed more than 200 stunts. These were led with precision by stunt coordinator Paul Stader, who worked with Allen on most of his films. Paul had a reputation for not only being a consummate professional, but taking good care of his people. This would be obvious by the end of filming, as little to no mishaps would occur with a production that was centered on one of the stunt community's most dangerous effects, filming with stuntmen on fire.

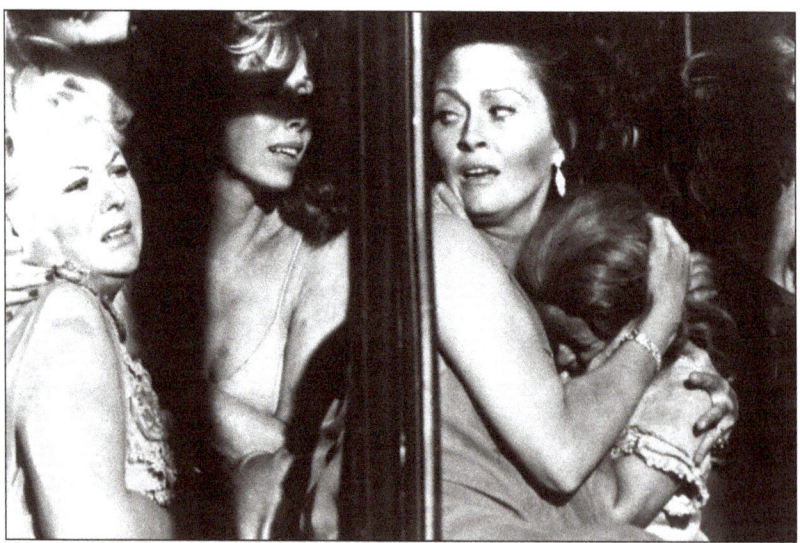

Terror inside the elevator

On the Fox lot, a crew constructed a three-story replica of the glass elevator explosion. L.B. Abbott and A.W. Flowers were the architects for the practical effects. Some of the cast inside the elevator included Faye Dunaway, Jennifer Jones, and Shelia Matthews, Allen's fiancé at the time. Allen directed the blast sequence, and the explosion was so intense the women could feel the heat waves. The explosion also caught other parts of the set on fire, including the trees behind it. The future Mrs. Allen shared her safety concerns with Irwin, and he decided to do no further takes. What you see in the finished film was the only take needed.

Although the production had to juggle multiple units, the results are some of the best slow-motion cinematography of fire sequences up to that time. The decision to shoot on film stock that captured the orange brilliance of the flames can't be overlooked or applauded enough. Oftentimes filmmakers with less attention to detail preferred to go with faster film stock that made it easier to shoot interiors with studio lights. This resulted in fire that resembled milky white candles, losing all of the natural beauty and grandeur of the flames. However, if you go back to a period a few decades prior in cinematic history during the Golden Age and watch the burning of Atlanta in *Gone with the Wind,* you'll witness just how sublime cinematography of infernos could be in the hands of passionate craftsmen. And *The Towering Inferno* exalts here if anywhere. The epic shots of the miniatures, shot under L.B. Abbot's supervision, hold up to this very day. And Robert

Wagner's death scene of being overcome and engulfed in a room ablaze is nothing short of breathtaking. The demise of his character Dan Bigelow, and Lorrie, his secretary and mistress, really is the glowing highlight of the film. The pure visceral beauty of the cinematography, stunts, and John Williams' music all come together with tragic beauty as Wagner is overcome in sumptuous orange flames, and Flannery's scantily-clad character jumps to her demise out of the high-rise windows in flames.

The Art of Good Directing

Inferno was filled with an onslaught of directorial decisions. If one reads about John Guillermin's personality, they're bound to eventually stumble upon a less-than-complimentary evaluation of his temperament. Like the quote often gleaned from his October 1, 2015 obituary in the *New York Times* by Daniel E. Slotnik,

> "Regardless of whether he was directing a light comedy, war epic or crime drama, Mr. Guillermin had a reputation as an intense, temperamental perfectionist, notorious for screaming at cast and crew alike. His domineering manner often alienated producers and actors... but Mr. Guillermin's impeccable eye and ability to capture both intimate moments and large-scale action scenes usually overcame that reputation."

Were these rumors, half-truths, or truths? If one reviews on-set footage of Guillermin directing (as can be found in the "Extras" section of the DVD), you'll find quite the opposite personality guiding the performances of cast and crew. What you will see is a man of patience, vision, and yet with a strong enough personality to handle the egos of a cast of thousands.

The Towering Inferno had one of the largest casts of megastars at the time. The ensemble included four Oscar winners: Paul Newman, William Holden, Faye Dunaway, and Jennifer Jones. There were also

Oscar nominees Fred Astaire, Robert Vaughn, Steve McQueen, and Orenthal James "OJ" Simpson, known only at that time as a beloved pro football player venturing into acting.

Katharine Ross, Raquel Welch and Natalie Wood were all offered the role of Susan Franklin, Doug Roberts' (Newman's) fiancée, which was eventually played by Faye Dunaway. Records state that Wood declined because she was pregnant with her second child, and that she found the script "mediocre," a sentiment Guillermin would later concur with.

> John's story about Fred Astaire is that John had, and I still have, a hand-carved full-size pool table. John told me a few stories about stars that played on that table, including the quartet of John, Steve McQueen, Paul Newman and Faye Dunaway. But a combination that happened quite often was Fred Astaire and John because Fred adored pool. And he had to be on the set at 11 a.m. and John had to be on the set at 6 a.m. According to John, Fred Astaire would keep him playing pool until 4 o'clock in the morning.

Lead Cinematographer Fred J. Koenekamp stated that both directors had a completely different working style, and that a DP was only as good as his director. Koenekamp recalls that, "...Guillermin was a soft-spoken man. If he showed any temper at all it was done in a quiet way...and usually on how he wanted something done in a certain way and when...whereas when Irwin walked on set everyone knew he was there. Generally, with an entourage."

Actress Susan Flannery warmly recalls that John Guillermin was a wonderful director, and that she felt very fortunate to work with him, as did the entire cast.

Guillermin's trademark on set was the pipe constantly hanging out of his mouth while giving directions in a thick British accent. After Allen visited him on set and complained that he wasn't moving the camera enough, actress Susan Flannery witnessed an irritated Guillermin biting clear through the tip of the pipe wedged between his clenched teeth. It's understandable how he would be incensed by Allen's observation, as Guillermin was known for sweeping dolly and crane shots, but when reduced to shooting dialogue scenes, what was he supposed to do? Guillermin was far more than a director who moved his camera just to show off. He wasn't a young up-and-comer attempting to prove himself with cinematic tricks. There needed to be motivation for his characters and camera to move. And in this movie often the expository dialogue forced everyone to be tethered to phones while the characters worked hand-in-hand both inside and outside to save lives.

McQueen was on record as saying he wouldn't be wearing a fire helmet at all. His main concern was that when filming, his helmet dwarfed his head and made him look less than heroic. Guillermin was on great work-

ing terms with McQueen, and figured out a way of tricking him into wearing a helmet. One day off set while having drinks with one of the consulting firemen, Guillermin spied a unique helmet behind him. This helmet had actually seen combat with the fireman's father and didn't match any of the previous ones created by the production design team. Guillermin asked if he could borrow it for McQueen, who by that time had already been going out with the fire fighters and assisting them while researching his character. One look, and McQueen knew that was the one. The dilemma was that production design would have to make all new helmets for the rest of the actors, and this would cost around another $50,000. McQueen could not care less about that, for he had found his "heroic" look. And the studios, producers and directors were all interested in making their star happy.

> *Towering Inferno* is interesting because of John's stories about Steve McQueen. Apparently, when Steve McQueen met a new person in his life, he liked to put them on the back of his motorbike and drive at full speed, I'm sure cutting all the corners, down Coldwater Canyon (Coldwater Canyon is a curving hilly road that runs between the San Fernando Valley and Hollywood). And John told me he was absolutely terrified. Steve McQueen's little test was when his guest got off the motorbike at the end of the ride, Steve would say, "Want to come out with me another time?" — most people didn't — and John replied, "Yeah, sure." And because he didn't show his fear, he and Steve were really tight after that.
>
> Another Steve McQueen story is that when Steve first got the script, he said "I'm not doing this shit" about the part of the architect. He said, "I'll play the fire chief. Rewrite it." So, the script was rewritten to give Steve McQueen as the fire chief a much bigger part. John told me how he listened to the actors when they made suggestions. There's a scene in *Towering Inferno* where Steve sits silently, leaning against a wall, exhausted after fighting the fire. Steve read the lines in the script he was supposed to say and told John he wanted to say nothing at all. John was a bit startled, but he liked Steve's idea that the fire chief would be exhausted, and said, "Okay, let's try it." He liked the result and told me Steve had a better feel for the scene than he had.

Contrary to tabloid predictions of the time, McQueen and Newman had a tremendous camaraderie with one another, often pulling pranks and busting takes. Much of this bonding can be attributed to Guillermin's ability to work with personalities of all types on their level so that the set continued to move forward.

Both Steve McQueen and Paul Newman did most of their own stunts, including one with Newman climbing up and down a bent stairwell railing surrounded by flames. This scene is filled with suspenseful opportunities, yet they are suspiciously absent. It's hard to pinpoint exactly why. Was this an "action" scene directed by Allen? Or was it Guillermin working with the actors? If Guillermin, then many of his signature camera techniques are missing: sweeping crane shots, tight close-ups and pacing. No matter who directed the scene, it's easy to understand why it might have less coverage if one of its top stars was doing the stunts. One slipup and the production would be shut down. So, here's a case of where some of the egos may have been a detriment to the film. One can't help but notice similarities in the stairwell sequence with many sequences from *The Poseidon Adventure*. A few characters in search of an exit, with one slip-up costing them a terrible fall to their demise. Arguably, *The Poseidon Adventure*'s action sequences remain some of the better ones of Allen's disaster pictures. However, with the lack of additional cameras that Guillermin had requested and the clock constantly ticking with production dollars burning with every minute, it's understandable how some of the action sequences might feel as though they lack some of the flourishes usually associated with a Guillermin feature.

Also stacked against John Guillermin was working with a convoluted script, complicated by the fact that Stirling Silliphant had to merge two story lines, and also the tremendous power that Steve McQueen wielded at that point in time in Hollywood that had transformed a secondary character originally written with around 10 pages of scenes to the lion's share. McQueen's demands for accepting the role included that his lines had to match Paul Newman's in number.

Though John Guillermin didn't like the end results, you can feel his hand guiding and striving for greatness. And yes, it's obvious that Allen was in love with the material as well, but often he managed to turn the spotlight onto himself on all his productions. Even going so far as firing a handgun into the ceiling without warning the actors, to either get the frightened look he wanted on camera or possibly make sure everyone knew he was running the show during the action sequences.

The Fire Still Burns

It's too bad that Guillermin never wanted to watch his film during his later years. For its many failings, the film doesn't lack for panache or suffer from execution. But it does seem to have an almost split personality. The film feels like it's directed by two directors, and that's where Allen's self-absorption arguably could have been said to have failed the film. After all, he had hired one of the strongest visual craftsmen in Hollywood of that time, but didn't allow him to do what he did best. Guillermin's films up to that point in his career had a synergy and dynamic that remains breathtaking to this very day. Just watch *The Blue Max* to imagine what *The Towering Inferno* could have been if left alone without meddling from a frustrated armchair director. Among the onslaught of industry rumors about George Lucas' early cuts to *Star Wars* is that he was inspired by the aerial sequences in *The Blue Max* when designing the dogfights for the attack run on the Death Star. This would make logical sense as Guillermin's cinematography, when married to scores from some of the finest composers the world has ever known, continue to instill an adrenal rush to this very day. Yes, some of Allen's dramatic directing was powerful. But in today's Hollywood machine, he might just well have been given the title of Second Unit Director. And it's because of this difference in visual technique that one could only surmise why the film often feels stilted.

Allen must have done something right, though, for *The Towering Inferno* was and remains one of the most financially successful of the 1970s disaster pictures. Allen had a vision, and cast and crew have gone on record with accolades to both directors for the final product.

The Towering Inferno opened on December 14, 1974 and was a hit. The film enjoyed commercial success unlike few others. Roger Ebert of the *Chicago Sun-Times* praised the film as "the best of the mid-1970s wave of disaster films." It enjoyed a one-year theatrical run and AFI (American Film Institute) went on to list it on the "Top 100 Thrills" list.

And it's easy to understand why. From the first frame, the film is epic and slick. An opening music track drives the imagery with pulse-pounding excitement as a helicopter races against the San Francisco skyline, revealing both the titular tower and delivering architect Doug Roberts atop his very own creation. Roberts (Paul Newman) makes his way out of the chopper and into the 138-story high rise, while the titles continue to splash across the screen, and the first of the cast of thousands is revealed. This is one of John Williams' finest scores, and arguably the finest of all the disaster-movie soundtracks. And yet, Irwin Allen originally did not want to use music during the first five minutes of the helicopter sequence. Williams, one of the finest composers of our century, told Allen that he could come up with five minutes of music for the beginning. When Allen heard it, he agreed with Williams. But it's hard to say who was responsible for this strong and dramatic opening. Almost all of Guillermin's films have unmatched soundtracks by the finest of composers. Sure, Allen had the connection to Williams with *The Poseidon Adventure*. But to not see the opportunity to open with a lush score and the aerial footage during the title sequence reveals that Allen may have needed both of Guillermin's hands involved to really capture the viewer from the opening frame and not let them go until the lights came up.

Of all of Irwin Allen's disaster films, many critics felt that *The Poseidon Adventure* was a better film. But the box office didn't match that of *The Towering Inferno* (around $140 million). This too, shows the imprint Guillermin had on his films. Even on his bad days, Guillermin was a driven artist who was able to reach and pull out strong performances from almost all personalities. Stories of him being a tyrant on set are counter to what many cast members have said about him, and the stories about

Newman and Guillermin in bitter arguments appear to be just what Newman needed from a director. Newman's method approach required a different type of director. Hitchcock and he had already butted heads on *Torn Curtain*, and though Newman and Guillermin argued, other actors (such as Richard Chamberlin) surmised it was almost like a coach firing up his fighter before a round. And that's what Guillermin also brought to set: an ability to intuitively know what each actor needed in order to get the best performance. Having to share a film with what appeared to be an egomaniac producer, work with a constrained budget, and keep the egos in check show that Guillermin was a strong but gentle force. The perfect choice of director for a disaster film was the one who didn't let it become a disaster.

In 1975 *The Towering Inferno* was nominated for eight Academy Awards, and won three: Best Cinematography, Best Film Editing, and Best Original Song. The other films nominated for Best Picture that year were *Chinatown, The Conversation, Lenny,* and the winner, *The Godfather Part II.*

One of the final cues to John Williams score for *The Towering Inferno* is called "An Architect's Dream." This is a beautiful and ardent piece that seems to not only capture the spirit of the film, but of the filmmakers as well. And though John had to share the director's chair, he always remained the architect of his films. Despite any outside interference, his

> John hated *Towering Inferno*. He hated the result; he thought the fire scenes needed four cameras and that Irwin Allen's work with a two-camera set up "just crawled!" He did respect his audiences, and he knew he'd given a lot of entertainment to millions of people but personally that particular film was so difficult for him. I don't know if this is true but the story went, according to John, that after the making of *Towering Inferno*, those elevator warnings saying don't use the elevator in case of fire, but go down the stairs, were a direct result of *Towering Inferno* and that was what he took pride in. He said, "I'm proud that my film achieved that."

pictures still managed to capture his passion. Perhaps Guillermin should have been most proud that he directed Fred Astaire's Oscar-nominated performance and Golden-Globe winner as well as having had his first and only nomination for best picture. With each viewing, you can tell *The Towering Inferno* was helmed by an artist who loved his craft.

The Towering Inferno was the forefather of the Epic Blockbuster. Even though "fire films" had been around since the early silent films, and executed with equally-chilling expertise, Guillermin's disaster picture is still a hallmark for films like *Deep Water Horizon, Backdraft, Volcano,* and even *Armageddon*.

John Guillermin's imprint on cinema was much stronger than he realized. Even with all the meddling and hassles he had a success. His signature is on a film that has now grossed a reported $200 million and is beloved by many.

The Next Spark

In closing, it is Mary Guillermin, John's lovely and immensely brilliant widow, who perhaps captured his prowess the best in one of her collages paying tribute to her late husband with the words:

John Guillermin, 1925–2015
"A Man's Man."

John was that, and a fiery visionary leader. His vision was so strong that it seemed to foreshadow his next picture. In 1975–1976 life seemed to imitate art, the art of *The Towering Inferno* and Guillermin's next film. Not two months after *The Towering Inferno*'s release, a fire broke out in the World Trade Center in New York City. And if one studies the poster for *The Towering Inferno,* it seems to foreshadow the next directorial assignment that Guillermin would be asked to do, another epic film that climaxes atop skyscrapers: the 1976 remake of *King Kong*.

CHAPTER 14

HOW JOHN GUILLERMIN INSPIRED AND INFLUENCED ME

BRETT A. HART

ON MARCH 10, 1975, my parents took me to the local movie theater in St. Ann, Missouri to celebrate my seventh birthday. I was ecstatic to see the film that had been highlighting the marquee for several months: *The Towering Inferno*. Now over 40 years later, I still have vivid memories of the opening frame and the impassioned score that seized my childhood attention until the house lights came back on. I can still feel the enthusiasm and hear the buzz of the audience as they left the theater. This was the first of many birthdays celebrated at the cinema as well as my first exposure to the magnificence of John Guillermin's work. And it would certainly not be my last.

One year later our family migrated to Michigan with the addition of my newborn brother. In December 1976, during a brutal winter, my parents would once again change my life forever by surprising our entire family with a trip to see the film that I had been consumed with, a new remake of *King Kong*. The giant cardboard Kong artwork loomed in the lobby. The vast theater was so overcrowded, my parents allowed me to sit off to the side by myself in order to get a better view. The theater lights dimmed, and the projectors illuminated the silver screen with John Guillermin's imagery. John Barry's music triumphantly echoed throughout the theater and I was hooked. When the house lights came back some two hours later, I was forever altered and would never be the same again. I had just been delivered from Skull Island to the top of the World Trade Center and experienced my very first bittersweet tragedy on screen. John Guillermin had grabbed hold of my passions, my primal fears, and my hopes. And to this day, he still has hold of that eight-year-old boy's imagination.

> I was struck when I read Brett's childhood story as to how closely his story mirrored John's own story of being inspired to be a director. As John told it, when he saw *Treasure Island* at the local cinema as a seven-year-old, he knew, just as Brett did two generations later, that he just had to be a film director. When John was twelve, he was given a movie camera and he spent hours filming simple stories with a friend. He said it was a simple script with the movie set in a cemetery and they used Bach's music as background music.

Understandably, for many, the original *King Kong* (1933) is untouchable. After all, it was the first of its kind, redefining the genre and visual effects. But for myself, John had done something with the 1976 remake that the original had not. It opened my eyes to how a filmmaker can truly move an audience by putting them directly in the center of their vision. John's *King Kong* is less about effects than it is about the glory and tragedy of Kong and those whose lives the creature touched. Every frame of the film is filled with the passion of a filmmaker who wants his audience to deeply feel the movie. In that theater in 1976, Guillermin had inadvertently shaped how I saw filmmaking: a series of heart-wrenching performances captured with cinematography that subjects the audience to the experience. And the technical beauty of it all was enthralling: the sweeping dolly shots, crane shots, gorgeous close-ups, and dynamic low and high angles. Unlike the original *Kong*, which had to lock off the camera to allow the magic of special effects to come to life, John put his camera and the audience in the heart of the emotion. The action. The tragedy. And to this very day, if I hear even a few bars of Barry's score, I'm immediately inspired.

By my second Guillermin film, I was already a tremendous admirer of his work. And although I was only eight years old, I knew then that a career had chosen me. Directing would become my life. I set out to write and storyboard ideas that I would eventually begin experimenting with once I got my hands on a camera and editing gear a few short years later. Moved more by intuition than conscious decision, I began to take on many of John's stylistic filmmaking techniques. For example, much like the technique Steven Spielberg used for *Jaws*, Guillermin created an atmosphere of dread by simply withholding showing the monster and letting the audience fill in the gaps with their imagination. And the revelation of Kong during the ceremony is nothing short of masterful craftsmanship. It is a visual and musical opus as suspense builds while trees collapse, natives dance, torches blaze, and a damsel arduously awaits her impending fate. The titular creature is seen initially through an extreme close-up on his eyes, and just as the audience can wait no longer, the sequence crescendos in silence and a low angle reveals Kong in all his glory, beating on his chest and staring down upon his new bride.

The sequence is executed with sweeping crane and dolly shots, extreme close-ups and syncopated with a driving score that creates an adrenal and almost subconscious visceral response. This is what I took away from John's work: his ability to move audiences through the careful orchestration of building atmosphere by pulling strong performances out of actors, set in dynamic locations, shot with panache and always edited and married with exceptional music. This standard of poignant and visceral storytelling is what I have committed to throughout my entire life.

After my family eventually settled in Houston, Texas, I spent a large portion of my teen years honing the skills that I had learned while falling in love with John's work. Of course, there were several other filmmakers whose craft influenced me as well and eventually, through kismet, I was fortunate enough to cross paths with Richard Franklin while he was directing *Cloak & Dagger* in San Antonio. New to the States and fresh off the success of *Psycho II*, he was surprised that a 15-year-old aspiring filmmaker knew who he was. He graciously took me under his wing and gave me guidance and tools to equip myself for one of the wildest careers imaginable.

At age 17 I discovered another film directed by John Guillermin, *The Blue Max,* specifically, the score. While listening to a weekly radio program that showcased soundtracks, I heard Jerry Goldsmith's exquisite music to the film for the very first time and was speechless. Just how had I missed this score and feature?! I made it my mission to correct this transgression. By the final frame of *The Blue Max,* I not only recognized and cheered all of John's signature flourishes, but also for the very first time related to a character unlike any other. Bruno Stachel's obsession with winning the Blue Max was on par with my obsession with filmmaking at all costs.

John's beautifully tragic WWI love note illustrated how our unwillingness to compromise in our obsessions can lead to alienation and eventually tragedy. The very first CD I purchased before heading off to film school was *The Blue Max*. This score would end up being a driving force not only during the long road trips to college, but throughout all of my tenure in Denton, Texas. And in tribute, John's film had such a profound hold on me that I eventually named my first dog Denton Von Stachel in honor of George Peppard's character and the city in which I was attending school.

John characteristically directing with his hands

Years later, I began professionally directing and chasing visions that would lead me from Dallas to Los Angeles. Shortly after the release of my debut feature film *Bone Dry,* I was delighted when one of my dramatic tornado promos caught international attention while being showcased on Jon Stewart's *The Daily Show,* and eventually led to winning my first Emmy. I went on to produce and direct 37 episodes of *Ain't It Cool with Harry Knowles,* a PBS TV Series sponsored by IMAX that celebrated and educated audiences about all facets of cinematic history. It was during this time that I felt an obligation to finally reach out to John Guillermin. While wrapping *Ain't It Cool,* I made a definitive effort to contact John and left a voicemail on an answering machine for a number that was his in Topanga, California. Afterwards, I was destroyed when I discovered that John had in fact passed away one year prior. But John's hold on me took an interesting twist of fate after I found the love of my life.

I fell in love with my wife, Bonnie Hart, at first sight and six months later we were married and living in Los Angeles. Perhaps through kismet, destiny, or some other hand of fate, Bonnie would end up at a home in Topanga for a meeting. All around her were pictures of a director who she thought she had heard me mention before. And one picture in particular caught her attention, a photograph from the set of *Kong*. This was the house of Mary Guillermin, John's lovely and brilliant widow.

A few short weeks later we would all have the pleasure of getting to know one another and becoming fast friends while screening John's films at his and Mary's home. When I had attempted to call John just a couple of years earlier, I had intended to thank him for inspiring an eight-year-old boy. A boy who, in 1976, fell in love with filmmaking largely due to the impassioned works of a filmmaker in whose house he now stood. And while I never had the opportunity to meet John in person, I do feel that by having crossed paths with Mary, I've finally had an opportunity to champion an outstanding visionary: an artist with heart, vision and soul that has forever changed my life and countless others through his cinematic legacy.

CHAPTER 15

THE BIG ONE: KING KONG

RAY MORTON

"Yeah, I know what to do with the monkey." With those words, John Guillermin undertook what became the highest profile—as well as one of the most challenging—films of his career: the 1976 remake of *King Kong*. That Guillermin would helm the redo may have been inevitable, since *King Kong*'s producer Dino De Laurentiis was initially inspired to update the 1933 RKO-Radio Pictures classic by the success of Guillermin's *The Towering Inferno*.

De Laurentiis got his start in his native Italy in the years following World War II. Beginning his career as an actor, De Laurentiis eventually moved into production and both in partnership with Carlo Ponti and on his own generated a steady stream of popular movies and art house fare from 1946 until the early 1970s. He won Academy Awards for Best Foreign Language Film for his productions of *La Strada* (1954) and *Nights of Cabiria* (1956); created epic international blockbusters such as *Ulysses* (1955), *War and Peace* (1956), *Barabbas* (1961), and *The Bible: In the Beginning* (1965); and sponsored offbeat cult films like *Barbarella* and *Danger: Diabolik* (both 1968). In the early 1970s, financial setbacks and turmoil in Italian politics motivated De Laurentiis to move to the United States, where the expatriate mogul immediately generated three big hits: *Serpico* (1973), *Death Wish* (1974), and *Three Days of the Condor* (1975), all of which were released through Paramount Pictures.

In January 1975, De Laurentiis met with Paramount chairman Barry Diller to discuss what movies they might make next. Impressed by the tremendous box office being generated by *The Towering Inferno* (which had been released at the end of 1974), they talked about making a disaster movie. However, after *The Poseidon Adventure* (1972), *Earthquake* (1974), *Airport 1975* (1974), and *Inferno*, all of the best natural and man-made catastrophes had already been filmed, so De Laurentiis and Diller decided to make a giant monster movie instead. They figured a massive creature rampaging through a crowded city would allow them to generate the same level of crowd-pleasing, special effects-fueled, big screen mayhem that capsized ocean liners, seismic upheaval, crashed airplanes, and burning skyscrapers had been turning into box office gold. At the time of this initial discussion, De Laurentiis and Diller did not have a specific giant monster in mind, but—after allegedly spying a poster for the original 1933 *King Kong* on his daughter's bedroom wall—De Laurentiis soon settled on the giant ape god of Skull Island, the legendary monster created by adventurer and filmmaker Merian C. Cooper (who co-directed the film with his longtime partner Ernest B. Schoedsack) and brought to life with stop-motion animation created by visual effects pioneer Willis H. O'Brien.

After obtaining the necessary remake rights from RKO-General (the successor company to RKO), De Laurentiis hired his *Three Days of the Condor* screenwriter Lorenzo Semple, Jr. to pen a script that updated Kong's story to the 1970s. In the original movie, the giant ape was discovered by a filmmaker who leads an expedition to Kong's uncharted island home to shoot a natural drama. In the new version, Kong would be found by an expedition sponsored by the Petrox Oil Corporation that journeys to an uncharted island in search of fossil fuels. Kong was the villain in the 1933 film, but in the forty-three years since he has become a beloved cultural icon, so there was no way the new movie could present him as anything other than a hero. Thus, Semple's script made Kong the story's tragic protagonist. As he did in 1933, the giant ape would fall for a female member of the expedition, get captured, brought to New York City, and put on display. Kong would then escape and cause much havoc and destruction before finally climbing to the top of Manhattan's tallest building—originally the Empire State Building but now the newly-completed World Trade Center—where he would finally meet his doom.

With the script underway, De Laurentiis went in search of a director. Although a John Guillermin movie was the impetus for De Laurentiis' *Kong* and although Guillermin was already working for the producer preparing an adventure film about an oil supertanker caught in a hurricane, the director was not De Laurentiis' original choice to helm. Instead, De Laurentiis approached Roman Polanski, then a hot property following the critical and box office success of *Chinatown* (1974). Although initially interested, Polanski eventually passed, claiming he "didn't know what to do with the monkey." At that point, De Laurentiis then turned to Guillermin. Their supertanker movie was having script problems, so De Laurentiis asked the director if he was interested in taking on *Kong* instead.

Guillermin was definitely interested. He had seen the 1933 *Kong* when he was a child and loved it (in an interview with *American Cinematographer* magazine, Guillermin called it "just a sheer piece of brilliant technical hocus pocus"). And, while Guillermin was known in Hollywood primarily for making action movies, he also had a poetic side (as evidenced by *Rapture*, which Guillermin always considered his best picture) and had always wanted to direct a fantasy film. When Guillermin signaled his enthusiasm for the project, De Laurentiis asked him if he knew what to do with the monkey. After the director answered in the affirmative, De Laurentiis signed John Guillermin to helm *King Kong*.

Although Guillermin was excited by the project, he was wary of the situation. When he took the *Kong* assignment, Guillermin knew he was joining a unit heavy with De Laurentiis loyalists: the producer's company was run by his longtime aide Frederic M. Sidewater; De Laurentiis' son Federico was the movie's executive producer; and the day-to-day making of the picture was being supervised by veteran production manager Jack Grossberg, whom De Laurentiis had handpicked to line-produce the picture. Not wishing to be steamrolled by De Laurentiis—a very strong personality used to getting his own way—or his team, Guillermin wanted someone on the film to look out for his interests, so he insisted De Laurentiis hire Christian Ferry, with whom Guillermin had worked on *The Blue Max,* to be the film's co-executive producer. De Laurentiis agreed. Guillermin also insisted on selecting the film's cinematographer (Richard H. Kline), editor (Ralph E. Winters), and second unit director (William Kronick, who had worked for Guillermin in the same capacity on *The Bridge at Remagen).*

There was also the issue of credit. Dino De Laurentiis was a powerful, flamboyant, high profile producer. Guillermin had just worked for another powerful, flamboyant, high profile producer on *The Towering Inferno* and it had been a difficult experience. Irwin Allen had desperately wanted to direct *Inferno* himself, but neither Warner Bros. nor 20th Century Fox, the two studios that co-financed the film, were impressed by Allen's directorial abilities and insisted he hire Guillermin instead. Allen did so begrudgingly but persuaded the Fox and Warner executives to allow him to direct some of the film's second unit action sequences. The producer then manipulated the publicity to give the public the impression that he had helmed the most important parts of the movie and that Guillermin had been little more than a dialogue director on the project. Feeling he had been denied proper acknowledgement for his work on the very successful blockbuster and determined not to be overshadowed again, Guillermin negotiated a possessory credit with De Laurentiis that would identify *King Kong* as "A John Guillermin Film."

John running on the beach in Kauai

Despite Guillermin's efforts, the huge wave of publicity that accompanied the film through its production and release was focused primarily on De Laurentiis, for whom *Kong* had become a passion project. Once again, the impression was given that the producer was the major creative force on the picture and Guillermin was just a director-for-hire. This was not the case. While De Laurentiis was unquestionably the initiator of *King Kong* and its prime mover, Guillermin's artistic contribution to the film was significant. In fact, he began to flex his creative muscles as soon as he signed on.

- Guillermin had a strong hand in the development of the film's screenplay. In Lorenzo Semple, Jr.'s initial outline, the female lead was a documentary cameraperson hired by Petrox to photograph its expedition to Kong's island. De Laurentiis liked this concept, but Semple himself was dissatisfied, feeling it was "too television." The screenwriter came up with a new approach that made the object of Kong's affection a shipwrecked actress discovered adrift in a raft on the high seas. Semple's thinking was that the movie needed to bridge the reality of an oil company expedition and the outrageous fantasy of a giant ape and the best way to do that was to link the two with the smaller fantasy of finding a beautiful girl all alone in the middle of the ocean. De Laurentiis didn't care for Semple's new idea and was set to overrule the screenwriter when Guillermin intervened. The director loved Semple's concept and insisted they incorporate it. Seeing how strongly Guillermin felt about the matter, De Laurentiis deferred to his director and eventually came to embrace the idea.

Guillermin and De Laurentiis both liked Semple's first draft of the *Kong* screenplay very much. However, as is always the case with the initial version of any creative work, they also felt there were a few things that needed work. These criticisms sparked a crisis of confidence in the screenwriter, who made radical changes to the script in his second pass. Neither the director nor the producer cared for the rewrite, so Guillermin insisted they go back to the first draft and then worked closely with Semple to fix that script's problems and preserve its considerable qualities in the screenplay's third and final draft.

• Once the screenplay was finished, Guillermin spent five months working with illustrator Mentor Huebner to storyboard all of the movie's big action and special effects sequences. The majority of Guillermin's initial shot conceptions ended up in the finished film.

• Prior to hiring Guillermin, De Laurentiis had brought an old friend and colleague, production designer Mario Chiari *(Doctor Dolittle)*, over from Italy to design the film's sets. However,

Guillermin did not care for the look Mario Chiari was developing for the film and insisted he be replaced by Dale Hennesy, who had won an Academy Award for his work on *Fantastic Voyage* (1966).

Guillermin then made a major contribution to the look of the film when—inspired by photos of the primitive native village of a tribe of Stone Age warriors living in modern New Guinea called the Dugum Dani the director came across in anthropologists Robert Gardner and Karl G. Heider's book *The Gardens of War*—Guillermin insisted the great wall separating the native village on Kong's island from its jungle interior be a vast wooden structure as opposed to the stone construct Chiari had favored.

- Guillermin worked closely with De Laurentiis to cast the film. After initially approaching Chris Sarandon, they gave the lead role of primate paleontologist/photographer/former med student Jack Prescott to recent Academy Award-nominee (for *The Last Picture Show* and *Thunderbolt and Lightfoot*) Jeff Bridges. Director and producer cast Charles Grodin, who had made a big splash with his role in 1972's *The Heartbreak Kid* and had just been nominated for a Tony for his performance in the 1975 Broadway hit *Same Time, Next Year*, as the film's villain: exploitative oil company executive Fred Wilson. Guillermin was also instrumental in "discovering" newcomer Jessica Lange, who would ultimately be given the film's most important human role—Kong's inamorata Dwan.

After considering a number of both well-known and up-and-coming actresses for the part, Guillermin and De Laurentiis were close to awarding the role to '70s starlet Deborah Raffin when they received a call from Wilhelmina Cooper, the head of New York's famed Wilhelmina modeling agency. Aware that Guillermin and De Laurentiis were looking for someone to play Dwan, Wilhelmina recommended Lange, a new addition to her stable of models who had expressed an interest in becoming an actor.

When Lange first arrived in Los Angeles, she had a bad cold, so Guillermin booked her into a hotel for a few days and asked her to come back when she was better. Several days later, Guillermin—knee-deep in pre-production—asked second unit director William Kronick to supervise the now-recovered Lange's initial test. Kronick spent a day shooting with Lange and was very impressed by both her look and abilities. Kronick alerted Guillermin and when he screened the test, the director was knocked out by it—when he saw the footage, Guillermin reportedly kicked over the seat in front of him and happily exclaimed "I've found my Fay Wray!"

Guillermin's most important creative contributions to the project involved shaping the character of Kong—who he saw as a "beautiful, marvelous monster who was also intensely human"—and determining the ways in which the giant creature was depicted on screen.

- In the original 1933 movie, Kong was brought to life primarily through the process of stop-motion animation. Willis O'Brien's techniques were revolutionary for their time, but to replicate them would have been time-consuming and cost-prohibitive. In addition, De Laurentiis did not care for the herky-jerky movements animated figures tended to make on screen—the producer wanted his monster's movements to be smooth and life-like. For these reasons and because he wanted to differentiate his movie from the original as much as possible to avoid negative comparisons, he decided to use a performer in a Kong costume to play the creature. The performer would be made to appear gigantic by having him tear around miniature sets and by using a variety of optical effects processes to insert him into the same shots with normal-sized humans. Rick Baker, a young make-up artist who had just won an Emmy Award for transforming fifty-year-old Cicily Tyson into a 110-year-old former slave in the 1974 television movie *The Autobiography of Miss Jane Pittman,* was hired to create a test costume. A protégé of Academy Award-winning make-up artist Dick Smith *(The Exorcist),* the twenty-five-year-old Baker was a pioneer in the nascent fields of special effects make-up and animatronics who had already created a number of creature suits and masks for several low-budget movies. He was also a gorilla aficionado who made ape suits at home for fun.

In the 1933 movie, Kong is depicted as being a giant species of ape closely resembling a gorilla. Since the 1976 film was going to focus heavily on Kong's sexual attraction to Dwan (the notion that a giant ape could be romantically interested in a normal-sized human female may seem odd today, but in the mid-1970s it was the reigning critical interpretation of the Kong story), the creative team's initial idea was to present Kong as a primitive humanoid—more of an oversized Australopithecus than a giant ape—so as to avoid overtones of bestiality. When Baker was originally hired to create a test suit for the film, this was the creature he was instructed to realize. However, Baker felt this was the wrong way to go. A great fan of the original movie, he thought Kong should be simian rather than human and so built a prototype gorilla suit. When the production team first saw his sample costume, they were upset he had not created the asked-for humanoid. By then, Italian special effects artist Carlo Rambaldi—another old colleague of De Laurentiis'—had joined the production and was asked to come up with a suit more in line with the original conception. Rambaldi did, but as soon as Guillermin saw Rambaldi's suit, he decided Baker was right. Aligning himself with the young make-up artist, the director insisted Kong be a gorilla and so a gorilla he became.

- Once Baker's concept was chosen, he and Rambaldi worked together to create a final Kong suit to be used in the movie. Although the two had a tempestuous relationship, they eventually crafted four body suits made from bearskins and five articulated foam rubber masks that were used to create the many facial expressions Kong displays in the film. Baker sculpted, cast, and produced the masks and Rambaldi outfitted them with cable-controlled mechanisms that could contort the masks into the desired expressions. The mechanisms were operated by a team of Rambaldi's assistants (who spoke only Italian).

The original plan was to have a tag team of three actors play the part — performing in the suit was going to be a physically taxing affair, so the thought was to have one actor play Kong until he got too tired, then bring in the next actor, and then the next. To that end, two actors were actually hired: Albert Popwell (whose most famous role was the "punk" to whom Clint Eastwood delivers his initial "Do you feel lucky?" speech in 1971's *Dirty Harry*) and Hampton Fancher, who later became famous as the screenwriter of *Blade Runner*. However, while the filmmakers were waiting for Rambaldi to create his humanoid suit, Guillermin began shooting lighting and special effects tests with Baker's costume since it was at hand. As Baker had built the suit to fit himself, he was hired to play Kong in the tests. During this test period, Guillermin became enamored of the way Baker pantomimed the role. When the decision was made to make Kong a gorilla, Guillermin insisted Baker play the part. Popwell and Fancher were let go and Baker somewhat reluctantly accepted the role. Later, a second actor named Will Shephard was hired as a back-up for Baker, but Guillermin could tell the difference between the two actor's movements. Preferring Baker's interpretation, Guillermin relegated Shephard to stunt ape status and used Baker in the majority of the Kong shots.

As much as Guillermin loved Baker's interpretation of Kong, the two clashed over the monster's walk. Baker wanted Kong to move about on all fours like a real gorilla, but Guillermin wanted the beast to walk on two legs as he did in the original picture. Baker complained that the director was asking for a "movie gorilla" rather than the real thing, but he eventually acquiesced and came up with a unique, slightly bow-legged, move-from-the-hip gait for the great ape that Guillermin loved.

- One of Guillermin's most significant decisions regarding Kong was to deal with the creature as a performer rather than as a special effect. Action and special effects sequences are highly technical and involved, and usually take a long time to shoot. It's therefore standard procedure on many big movies to deploy a second unit led by a separate director to shoot these sequences, leaving the director and his main unit free to concentrate on the film's primary dramatic sequences involving the principal cast. The role of a second unit director is usually considered more of a technical position than a creative one.

King Kong's original shooting plan called for all of the scenes involving the "miniature" Kong (as the man-in-the-ape-suit was known) to be directed by William Kronick, thus relegating the great ape to secondary status as an effect and/or a stunt. However, as production ramped up, Guillermin realized that the success or failure of the film was going to depend largely on how real Kong seemed to audiences and on how strongly they responded to him emotionally. For the movie to work, Kong was going to have to intrigue, frighten, amuse, and ultimately move his viewers. In other words, he was going to need to be a fully-realized, three-dimensional character, not just a visual effect. Therefore, soon after production got under way, Guillermin decided to treat Kong as a principal cast member and to shoot the majority of the great ape's scenes himself. Kronick and his crew were retained to shoot a few stunt-heavy sequences (primarily Kong fighting the giant snake, breaking through the great wall, and being attacked by a flame thrower atop the World Trade Center) using Will Shephard in the suit, but the bulk of the Kong scenes in the movie were directed by Guillermin utilizing Rick Baker.

And direct Kong Guillermin did. Numerous behind-the-scenes photos exist showing Guillermin working with the costumed Rick Baker on the set—acting out the precise movements he wanted Kong to make and the exact expressions he wanted to appear on the great ape's face (one photo, showing Guillermin demonstrating the pained expression he wanted Kong to display as the helicopter gunships riddle him with the bullets that will eventually kill him, is particularly poignant). Some of this performing was meant to show Baker, Carlo Rambaldi, and Rambaldi's non-English-speaking crew the behaviors and expressions Guillermin wanted Kong to exhibit, but mostly it was to convey the heart and soul he wanted his simian protagonist to communicate to the audience. Comparing these production shots to scenes in the finished film, it's clear that Guillermin is as much responsible for Kong's on-screen characterization as Baker, Rambaldi, and the technical operators were.

- To pull more emotion out of his star, Guillermin made a deliberate decision to focus as many shots as possible on Kong's eyes, which were actually Rick Baker's own, masked by scleral contact lenses that were painful to wear but made the pupils look more animal-like. The notion that Kong's eyes would be the windows to his soul and therefore the key to his characterization was so important to Guillermin that he made the first shot of the giant ape in the movie an extreme close-up of those eyes.

To keep Kong's eyes looking as natural as possible, Guillermin chose to film most of the miniature Kong scenes at a normal frame rate of twenty-four frames-per-second. Miniature work is often filmed at a faster speed, which has the effect of slowing down the action when projected and so in turn generates the impression that the miniature objects being filmed are actually of great weight and size. There are some shots in the movie in which this is done with Kong and they are very effective, but most of the monster's scenes were filmed at twenty-four f.p.s. so that his eye movement and thus the emotion they projected would not be distorted. As a result of this decision, it can be argued that some of the long shots of Baker and Shephard in the Kong costume look too "normal;" too much of a regular human size and weight; too much "man in a suit." What cannot be argued is the intensity of emotion Kong's eyes display in the picture and so in that respect Guillermin's decision was right on.

• As instrumental as Guillermin was in presenting a believable characterization of Kong on screen, he was also inadvertently responsible for the film's least believable representation of the creature. When Dino De Laurentiis originally opted to use a man in an ape suit to portray Kong, Guillermin was amenable. However, intent on successfully creating the illusion that a giant ape was interacting with normal-sized humans, the director insisted they also create a full-scale representation of Kong to use in a few key shots in the film. This insistence kicked off a process that eventually led to the creation of the movie's most notorious prop and its most effective source of publicity.

Rick Baker wearing contact lenses gives Kong his expressive eyes

Initially, the production team decided to create a full-sized Kong puppet. This is what led De Laurentiis to call in Carlo Rambaldi. An artist and special effects technician whose specialty was using cable-controlled mechanical devices (devised along with his assistant Isadore Raponi) to bring puppets to life on screen, Rambaldi's most famous creations were a Pinocchio he created for Italian television and the razor-toothed dolls for *Barbarella*. Rambaldi began preliminary work on the giant Kong puppet in the summer of 1975, just as Steven Spielberg's *Jaws* debuted in theaters and became an immediate smash hit. That film's pneumatically-operated mechanical shark fascinated the public and was generating a massive amount of publicity for the picture. His showman's instincts activated, De Laurentiis conferred with Rambaldi and before long the two had decided to create a mechanical monster of their own — a full-size, fully--functional King Kong robot who would be able to walk about, pick up the girl, and generally raise lots of havoc.

Despite the insistence of special effects experts both inside and outside the production (including Rick Baker) that such a device could not be created with then-current technology, De Laurentiis was determined to have his robot and to use it to film the majority of Kong's scenes in the movie and Rambaldi was determined to give it to him. Guillermin wasn't certain such a construct could be realized, but optimistically went ahead and storyboarded a number of sequences featuring the anticipated mechanical marvel. Rambaldi developed a design for an electronically-operated robot, but his plans proved to be impractical. At that point, veteran Hollywood special effects man Glen Robinson—who also had experience creating hydraulically-controlled amusement park rides—was called in to develop a simpler, hydraulically-operated creature. It took Robinson eight months to build his Kong. Although Robinson did the best he could, the technology of the day was simply insufficient to create the fully-functional machine De Laurentiis wanted. The construct wasn't completed until the very end of the production schedule and therefore could only be used in one scene—the "presentation" scene in which Kong is presented to the public at a New York stadium and then breaks loose and escapes. During filming the mechanical ape broke down constantly and was eventually used in only six shots in the finished film. Despite this, De Laurentiis shrewdly used his robot as the centerpiece of a massive publicity campaign to promote the movie. By the time the film opened, there was hardly anyone in its potential audience who wasn't aware of and curious about Dino's mechanical marvel and this made him worth every ounce of his six-and-a-half tons in gold.

However, Robinson and his assistant Eddie Surkin did craft two hydraulically-operated Kong hands designed to carry and caress Jessica Lange that worked as well as the Kong robot didn't. So, while Guillermin didn't get the full-sized Kong he'd hoped for, he did get a pair of wonderfully dexterous Kong paws he was able to use to great effect in the picture.

> John's hero was Ingmar Bergman, and to John's delight, when he was filming some of the scenes of *King Kong*, I think the New York scenes on the set at the huge Culver City studios, Ingmar Berman was on the lot filming something else, and he was fascinated with how the mechanical parts of King Kong worked. John said Bergman would come and sit next to him, dressed in a camel hair coat, and watch the proceedings. I think this was one of the high spots of John's career that he got to hang out with his hero. He told me he once asked Ingmar Bergman how he got the ideas for his films, and Ingmar replied that he just filmed his own dreams.

The *Kong* shoot was a difficult and often grueling one. To begin with, there was a terrible time crunch on both ends of the production schedule. As the movie entered pre-production, Universal Pictures was also preparing to film its own version of the story. Inspired by the success of *Jaws,* the MCA-owned studio was interested in making another giant monster movie and had approached RKO-General at the same time that De Laurentiis had, also seeking to obtain the remake rights to the original picture. Both De Laurentiis and Universal entered into negotiations with Daniel O'Shea, RKO-General's representative. Both sides then made offers and RKO-General accepted De Laurentiis'.

This infuriated Universal president Sidney Sheinberg because—as the studio's lawyers later alleged—when Universal submitted its offer, O'Shea had verbally assured the company it would get the rights. However, while O'Shea was in charge of negotiating on RKO-General's behalf, he was not actually empowered to make a deal. That authority lay solely with RKO-General's president, Thomas O'Neil, who opted to accept De Laurentiis' proposal because, while both entities offered RKO-General $200,000 plus a percentage of the film's profits, De Laurentiis offered a percentage of the gross, whereas Universal had only offered a percentage of the net. Feeling misled, Universal filed a breach of contract lawsuit against RKO-General and De Laurentiis. The lawsuit was dismissed, so Universal took a different tact. Claiming that a 1933 novelization of the original film's script was now in the public domain because its copyright had not been renewed (which it had not been), the studio announced it was going ahead with its own production, which it claimed was an adaptation of the novel rather than a remake of the original film. De Laurentiis and RKO-General filed countersuits, but while the battles were being waged in court, De Laurentiis and Universal both began preparing to make their films. Not knowing how the courts would rule and knowing the marketplace would only support one version of Kong, both sides knew that whoever got into production first would win the war.

De Laurentiis' original plan was to begin shooting in April 1976, but when Universal announced it was going ahead with its own version of *Kong,* the producer moved the start of filming up to January. This forced Guillermin to start shooting before the production had been fully prepared and well before any incarnation of Kong was anywhere near ready. Working with production supervisor Jack Grossberg and production manager Terry Carr, Guillermin hastily prepped the only fully non-Kong portion of the movie—the oil company expedition's departure from Surabaya, Indonesia and its initial sea voyage to Kong's island. The movie began filming on the evening of January 15, 1976 at a dock in San Pedro, California (just south of Los Angeles) with the very first shot of the film: a complex establishing shot of the *Petrox Explorer*—the ship that would carry the expedition to the island— preparing to set sail. The company then spent two weeks at sea filming the ocean journey in the waters between San Pedro and Catalina Island. It had taken a Herculean effort to get the movie started prematurely, but Guillermin's efforts paid off. As soon as the De Laurentiis *Kong* was underway, Universal abandoned their version and legally settled their differences with the Italian producer. Once the ocean shoot was finished, the production shut down for three weeks so Guillermin could properly prepare the rest of the picture.

Filming resumed in mid-February on the Hawaiian island of Kauai, where scenes set on Kong's island were shot. Although Universal was no longer a threat, there was no time to relax. Just prior to the start of production, De Laurentiis and Paramount had decided that the movie would premiere in December 1976. This gave Guillermin only ten months to shoot, edit, and complete the film. It would have been difficult to complete a small-scale film on such a schedule so to complete a special effects-filled epic in such a tight time frame seemed impossible. Guillermin was quoted in the press as wondering why the movie had to come out so quickly—he felt it was more important that it be good rather than be fast. But De Laurentiis and Paramount were determined (and in fact had already begun accepting unrefundable advances from theaters wishing to book the film), so Guillermin pushed on, vowing to do the best he could in the time allotted.

The logistical aspects of the production were a challenge:

- Creating the perpetual fog bank that surrounds Kong's island required three boats mounted with fog-generating machines to move back and forth in the channel between San Pedro and Catalina in a specific pattern. When the crew members manning the boats had a hard time creating the right pattern, Guillermin—an experienced sailor—took charge and guided them to a satisfactory result. He was required to do the same thing when the unit moved to Hawaii.

- While in Kauai, the cast and crew stayed in a half-finished hotel with few amenities. Most of the island locations were quite remote and only accessible by helicopter, which meant that the cast and crew had to fly out in shifts starting at dawn each morning and then wrap filming early each afternoon so everyone could make it back before dark. This severely limited the amount of work that could be done each day. Filming was often delayed by Hawaii's unpredictable weather and on one occasion Guillermin and some members of his team were nearly trapped in a remote valley when a rapidly-approaching storm made it questionable as to whether or not they would be able to fly out before the rain hit. Luckily, they were able to escape, but not before the film's cinematographer was almost decapitated when a sudden wind gust caused the chopper to kick just as the team was climbing aboard. As it turned out, that same valley was also inhabited by a motley collection of hippies, draft dodgers, pot growers, and other societal dropouts who would emerge from the jungle each day at lunchtime and help themselves to the unit's food.

- After wrapping in Hawaii, the unit moved to the MGM Studios in Culver City, California, where the production occupied most of the studio's soundstages. Guillermin found himself working long hours filming scenes involving the principal cast during the day and shooting the miniature Kong sequences at night (whenever possible, Guillermin preferred to shoot the full-scale and miniature portions of a given scene concurrently). The sacrifice sequence — in which Dwan is offered to Kong by the island's inhabitants — was filmed on MGM's historic Lot 2 on an outdoor set of the native village that included a 47-foot-tall wall made of telephone poles, eucalyptus trees, and vacu-formed plastic. The scene required the director to choreograph 300 extras in an elaborate production number than took several nights to film.

- In July 1976, the production travelled to New York City, then at its 1970s nadir, to film the full-scale Queens and Manhattan segments of the picture. The four-week shoot climaxed with a three-night shoot at the twin towers of the recently-opened World Trade Center, where Guillermin and his team had to manage the 30,000 New Yorkers who turned up to watch and serve as extras in Kong's death scene. The crowds were so big that Trade Center officials became worried the complex's central plaza would collapse under the incredible weight. That didn't happen, but things did get out of hand on another night when an unruly crowd broke through the protective barriers and swarmed the full-sized Styrofoam model of Kong that had been placed in the center of the plaza to represent the fallen king. The rioters made off with hunks of Kong's hair, one of his fingers, and a basketball-sized eyeball before they were driven back.

- The unit then returned to MGM to film the presentation scene. The scene was originally scripted to take place in Shea Stadium, but for budget and logistical reasons was shot on the same set as the sacrifice scene, with the natives' wall redressed to resemble the gates of an arena. This sequence included 3,000 more extras and the debut of the full-scale mechanical Kong. Soon after, production wrapped once and for all.

The technical aspects of the production were also a challenge:

- Getting a performance from the miniature Kong required Guillermin to collaborate both with Rick Baker, who provided the creature's overall movement, and with Carlo Rambaldi and his team of cable operators, who had to work together with balletic precision to manipulate the mechanisms that generated Kong's facial expressions, and then co-ordinate the actions of both. Making things even more difficult was the fact that Rambaldi's operators spoke only Italian, which Guillermin did not. This required the director to convey his instructions through Rambaldi, whose English was iffy at best. The process was complex, time-consuming, and more than a little frustrating.

- Utilizing the big hands was also a collaborative process—this one between Guillermin and Eddie Surkin and his team of operators. Getting the hands to perform even the smallest gesture required a tremendous amount of coordination, practice, and patience. Together, this group managed to elicit surprisingly graceful and delicate movements from the crane-mounted, hydraulically-controlled duraluminum constructs so successfully that it was sometimes easy to forget that the hands were pieces of heavy machinery that weighed 1,650 pounds each. They were reminded of this on several occasions; once when one of the hands suddenly lost power and slammed to the ground, nearly injuring the stunt woman who was sitting in it; again when one

Kong's mechanical hand lifted by a crane in King Kong Lives

of the fingers caressing Jessica Lange brushed her with too much force and left the actress with a painfully pinched nerve in her neck; and yet again when a jokester on the operating team extended one of the hands' middle finger, which then froze in that position for several days until the mechanism could be repaired.

• Many of the film's visual effects shots employed the blue screen travelling-matte process. At the start of the process, an object (e.g. the miniature Kong) was photographed in front of a large blue backing. Utilizing a complex technical process, the color blue was then subtracted from the image, leaving the foreground object isolated against a clear background. A series of holdout mattes were then generated that allowed the image of the foreground object to be combined with a separately photographed background image (called a "plate") and so created a hybrid image that would allow the miniature Kong to appear in the same frame as Jessica Lange or to show real men falling into a painted ravine or to have real helicopters fire on Rick Baker as he stood atop a miniature version of the World Trade Center. Blue screen work required the crew to go to great lengths to ensure that the foreground images and plates were perfectly aligned. They were aided in this process by an innovative video assist developed by the film's optical effects assistant Barry Nolan.

The blue screen process could be physically grueling—the large cobalt backing screen needed a tremendous amount of illumination generated by a dozen or more large carbon arc lights. These powerful lamps required constant maintenance and generated so much heat that Baker reported losing up to five pounds a day in water weight because he sweat so much.

- Because of the immovable release date, Guillermin—working with film editor Ralph E. Winters, composer John Barry, and a team of sound editors and mixers—was required to cut, score, and mix large chunks of the picture while he was still filming the rest of it. This was far from the usual practice—Guillermin was literally finishing the first reels of the movie before the final reels had even been shot.

All of these challenges put Guillermin under tremendous, unrelenting pressure and this pressure frequently caused him to act out. The director already had a reputation for losing his temper and he lost it a lot during this production, to the point where following one particularly volcanic eruption at Federico De Laurentiis on the beach in Hawaii, Dino De Laurentiis actually considered firing Guillermin. De Laurentiis relented after Guillermin apologized to Federico and promised to keep his spleen in check.

Although there is no doubt that Guillermin had an irascible personality and that his irascibility was frequently exacerbated by his alcoholism, many people close to the director feel that Guillermin's ardent behavior was as much a product of his creative passion (intensified by his naturally passionate French nature) as it was his explosive anger. Interviews done with the director at the time of the production and after as well as the intense emotional investment on display in those behind-the-scenes photos bear out this hypothesis—Guillermin's goal was to make a great picture and he gave it his all to do so.

And what sort of movie did Guillermin's passion generate? In her *New Yorker* review of the film, Pauline Kael called *King Kong* '76, "... a marvelous *Classics Comics* movie" and it's an apt description. The 1933 *King Kong* was a primal myth—an archetypal, black-and-white fever dream of a film set in a contained, nightmarish landscape inspired by the Gothic woodcuts of Gustave Dore. In comparison, John Guillermin's version of the story is a colorful, widescreen epic—a massive romantic fantasy adventure told in the broad strokes and brilliant hues of a great graphic novel.

Guillermin's filmmaking in the first half of the movie is expert and self-assured and those qualities are on display from the very first shot: *King Kong* begins with an isolated image of the *Petrox Explorer*'s mast positioned against the night sky. As a cargo crate is swung through the frame by a crane, the camera tilts down to reveal the ship itself. A guard steps into the picture, which now becomes a close-up of the man. The image then tracks along with the guard as he patrols the pier. Next, the guard walks away from the lens and as he does the camera cranes up into a wide-angle shot of the pier as people and equipment move about preparing the ship for departure. This is an elaborate, intricate, and very deliberate shot that does a wonderful job of bringing the audience into the world of the film and getting the narrative off to an intriguing start. The scenes that follow are equally good. The action is well-staged, framed in potent wide-screen compositions *(Kong* cinematographer Richard H. Kline has stated that Guillermin had "a great eye") enhanced when required by meticulously choreographed camera movement and then edited together with extreme precision to generate maximum impact.

All of this builds to the film's most spectacular and effective sequence—the sacrifice scene. Beginning with a close-up of Dwan as the natives feed her a hypnotic potion to keep her from trying to escape, the angle widens as the helpless young woman is carried to the great wall. She is then made the focus of a ritual dance—a dazzlingly primal routine choreographed by Claude Thompson that features hundreds of natives cavorting by smoky torchlight in a marvelously photographed pageant that makes one wonder to what heights Guillermin could have soared had he ever chosen to helm a full-on movie musical. The natives then open the wall's gates, take Dwan through, and tie her to an altar on the other side. Following a brief cut-away to Jack, Fred, and the *Petrox Explorer* crew landing on the beach as they race to the rescue, the action shifts back to the wall as the natives blow into horns to summon Kong from the inner recesses of the island. We only get brief glimpses of the great ape as he pushes through the foliage and knocks down trees on his way to the wall. When he reaches the altar, Dwan looks up, and only then do we and she see Kong fully revealed for the first time as he pounds his chest and let loose with a mighty roar. Dwan screams as Kong lifts her off the altar, sniffs her scent, roars again, and then carries her off into the jungle.

Everything in the sacrifice scene works at the absolute highest level: Guillermin's expert direction; Richard H. Kline's atmospheric cinematography; John Barry's thrilling score; the various representations of Kong (in this case, Rick Baker in the suit and the mechanical hands) and the visual effects, which include several blue screen shots marrying Jessica Lange to the miniature Kong, as well as a perfect split-screen shot looking over the full scale wall at Baker standing before the altar. It is a sequence full of spectacle, mystery, and suspense that climaxes with the introduction of the film's title character in a way that sells this fantasy creature of myth and legend as an actual living, breathing animal. The entire success of the movie depends on its ability to convince the audience that Kong is real and this sequence accomplishes that to perfection.

The filmmaking in the second half of the movie isn't quite as solid as it is in the first, which is likely the result of the tight production schedule. The scene in which Kong attacks the rescue party and hurls most of its members into a deep chasm; the scene in which Kong fights the giant snake to save Dwan; and the New York presentation scene are all choppy and feel rushed. In addition, a number of the visual effects in this part of the movie lack the polish of those presented earlier in the film—most notably the mismatch between the big Kong and the miniature ape in the presentation scene and the rough quality of some of the blue screen shots in the New York segment—presumably because there just wasn't enough time to perfect them. Despite this uneven quality, Guillermin still delivers some terrific sequences including Kong smashing through the great wall and getting captured, Kong going berserk in the hold of the supertanker; his attack on the elevated train, and the firefight atop the World Trade Center that prompts Kong to leap from the roof of one tower to the roof of the other.

Stylistically, Guillermin takes a generally straightforward approach to telling his story, but at a number of points he peppers the film with offbeat bits of visual poetry that give the movie a wonderful mood and texture. These bits include:

- The primal moment when the landing party's boat breaks through the fog bank and we see Kong's island for the very first time.

- The spectacular shot in which the landing party is seen making its way along a jungle path as the camera zooms out slowly, eventually revealing that the explorers are trekking through Kauai's Waimea Canyon (a breathtaking piece of prehistoric volcanic landscape known as "the Grand Canyon of Hawaii")—imagery that expertly establishes the remote, isolated grandeur of the supposedly uninhabited island.

• The eccentric, wandering zoom shots peppered throughout the picture—shots in which the camera initially seems to drift aimlessly across the setting before finally zeroing in on some specific and inevitably important element. The first of these wandering zooms is employed in the scene in which the landing party notices the native village's pool of (what appears to be) oil.

• The extreme, floating close-up (shot with a 1,000 mm lens) of Kong's eyes and muzzle that introduces the great ape as he makes his way through the jungle on his way to the wall in the sacrifice scene—a impressionistic image that gives us a partial glimpse of Kong, teasing us in preparation for the full reveal to come.

• The haunting image of the overcome Kong's hand rising up out of the cloud of chloroform after he is captured.

• The moment when Kong withdraws and sinks into a deep depression after he releases Dwan in the hold of the supertanker.

• Kong roaring at the soldiers hiding in the shadows right after he arrives in the plaza of the World Trade Center. As scripted, this bit is just meant to show a threatened Kong warning his enemies to back off, but as Guillermin stages it in the film, Kong appears to know he is doomed and so his roar comes across as a final act of bravado from a creature who knows his end is near. As such, it is heartbreaking.

Trekking through the Waimea Canyon—

known as the Grand Canyon of Hawaii

- The eccentric, silent bit in which photographers hoping for a scoop climb up onto Kong's bloody chest as he lays dying in the Trade Center plaza and are then pulled off by a few of New York's finest.

- The penultimate shot of the film—in which the camera pulls up and away from the fallen giant as the crowd engulfs a weeping Dwan, perfectly encapsulating all of the spectacle, fantasy, and tragedy of the legend of King Kong.

Guillermin does solid work with the film's actors:

- Encouraged by his director, Jeff Bridges delivers a sincere, charismatic turn as Jack Prescott, the film's strait-laced human lead.

- With Guillermin's assent, Charles Grodin injects his performance as Fred Wilson, the movie's villain, with a generous dose of humor. Grodin's reasoning was that since Kong wasn't going to make his first appearance until almost an hour into the movie, he would keep the audience entertained with comedy until the great ape finally showed up. It was a controversial choice and some who worked on the film (including Barry Diller) felt Grodin went too far over the top. However, this author feels that Guillermin kept Grodin sufficiently in check and gave the actor a few sufficiently dark moments—especially the chilling bit in which Wilson dismisses the concerns of the *Petrox Explorer*'s Captain Ross for the safety of the search party with a cold-blooded "Don't worry about it"—that leave no doubt Wilson is a true villain. These bits make it easy for us to cheer when Kong finally stomps him into oblivion.

- Guillermin's initial direction to Jessica Lange was to think of Marilyn Monroe when performing Dwan. After a shaky start in which the fledgling actress sometimes appears to take this direction a bit too literally, Lange quickly comes into her own and under her director's tutelage gives a terrifically appealing performance as Kong's inamorata.

All three thespians reported having a good experience working with Guillermin. He also worked well with the supporting cast members and elicited solid performances from Rene Auberjonois as geologist Roy Bagley, John Randolph as Captain Ross, Jack O'Halloran as drill foreman Joe Perko, Julius Harris as driller Boan, and Ed Lauter as first mate Carnahan.

As good as the cast is, Guillermin's greatest performance-related achievement in the film is Kong. The director's decision to treat the giant ape as a principal cast member rather than a special effect paid off and the collaboration between Guillermin, Rick Baker, Carlo Rambaldi, and Rambaldi's team of operators resulted in a vivid characterization. The Kong of *King Kong* '76 has a distinct, palpable personality—he is a fierce, magnificent beast capable of rage, tenderness, jealousy, confusion, sadness, and love. And it is this personality that allowed Guillermin to successfully develop the heart of his tale.

Cooper and Schoedsack's *King Kong* was a surprisingly tragic monster movie but Guillermin's is a deliberately tragic love story. The relationship between Kong and Dwan is the focus of Lorenzo Semple, Jr.'s narrative. In the original movie Kong becomes infatuated with Ann Darrow (the character played by Fay Wray), but Ann is never anything but terrified by Kong—whenever she is in his presence she either screams or faints. In Semple's version, Dwan is initially terrified of Kong, but her feelings soon begin to change. When the frightened girl tries to run away from the giant ape, she trips and falls into a mud puddle. Initially furious at the attempted escape, Kong suddenly softens. He picks Dwan up, carries her to a waterfall, washes her off after, and then gently blows her dry with his breath. At this point, Dwan realizes Kong does not intend to hurt her. She is still eager to get away from him because of his awesome

Kong gently blows Dwan dry with his breath

potential for destruction and his implied sexual threat, but she no longer thinks he wants to kill her. After Kong risks his life to save her from the giant snake, Dwan is grateful and returns the favor when the captain of the supertanker taking Kong to America decides to drown the giant ape after he goes berserk in the vessel's hold. To prevent this, Dwan climbs out onto the grill covering the hold and threatens to jump in unless the captain lets Kong live—Dwan puts her life on the line for Kong in the same way he did for her and the supertanker captain finally relents. Kong continues to protect Dwan—first by catching her when she accidentally falls into the hold and later by breaking out of captivity during Petrox's New York extravaganza when he thinks she is being attacked by photographers. Dwan shows her appreciation atop the World Trade Center when she begs him to pick her up, knowing the helicopters won't fire on Kong if he is holding her. However, like a true hero, Kong pushes

Dwan away to keep her safe and so is gunned down. After Kong plunges one hundred-ten stories to the Trade Center plaza, he and Dwan share a final look as his life fades and she weeps genuine tears over his demise.

This is grand, operatic stuff—far more complex and layered than the relationship depicted in the 1933 film—and none of it would work if we didn't believe in the connection between Kong and Dwan. Fortunately, we do. And we do because Guillermin does. For this writer, Guillermin's greatest creative contribution to *King Kong* 1976 was that he took it seriously. The premise of the story is obviously a preposterous one and the notion of creating a deep and emotionally affecting relationship between a woman and a forty-foot-tall ape is even more outrageous. It would have been very easy for Guillermin to send up this material by treating it as a spoof or as camp, but he did not do so. (The movie has a reputation among some critics for being campy, but all one has to do is watch the film to see this is not the case. Yes, the picture has a sense of humor about itself, but it never treats itself—and especially not the relationship between Kong and Dwan—as a joke.) Guillermin knew he was making a fantasy and he knew the only way to make a fantasy work in a realistic medium such as cinema was to take it on its own terms without condescension or apology and that is what he did.

Guillermin enhanced the strong connection between his two main characters by introducing a number of marvelously lyrical elements:

- The full moon makes a running appearance in the movie. In the screenplay, the shining satellite serves as a visual link between Kong's twin-peaked mountain lair on Skull Island and the twin towers of the World Trade Center on Manhattan Island—Kong sees the glowing orb hanging in the night sky over his home and then later sees it floating above the Trade Center, which is what motivates him to climb to the top. Guillermin expanded the moon's role in the story, also using it as a symbol of the connection between Kong and Dwan. The shipwrecked actress is briefly entranced by the full moon in the scene in which she wanders around on the darkened bridge of the *Petrox Explorer* just before she is kidnapped. Later in the story, Kong is also entranced by it just before he begins romancing Dwan. At the end of the tale, both characters look at it together as they stand atop the World Trade Center, sharing a last peaceful moment together before the helicopters arrive to gun Kong down.

- In the script, the scene in which Kong blows Dwan dry with his powerful breath after her waterfall shower is pretty straightforward: it's meant to show that Kong cares about Dwan and to demonstrate something cool the giant ape can do. Guillermin adds an extremely sensual dimension to the scene by having Dwan writhe in apparent rapture as she is caressed by the great beast's exhalations.

- Kong's sexual attraction to Dwan is indicated in the screenplay but Guillermin enhances it in the film by focusing on the excited look on Kong's face during the sequence in which Kong peels away Dwan's garments. Guillermin further enhances the scene's sensuality by incorporating a brief glimpse of PG-level nudity (Dwan's, not Kong's). With its suggestions of rape and bestiality, this sexual element is one of the movie's most problematic when viewed today. It was less so at the time of the film's release because, as mentioned previously, in the mid-1970s it was generally accepted in critical and academic circles that Kong's relationship with the woman was a sexual one.

- Guillermin chronicles the end of Kong and Dwan's relationship in a dreamlike scene that occurs after the mortally wounded giant has plummeted from the top of the World Trade Center and crashed into the plaza below. As he lies dying, Kong turns and improbably sees Dwan — who just a moment ago was one hundred-ten stories above the ground — standing next to him. Have minutes passed or has it been hours? We can't tell — time suddenly feels as if it has been suspended. Both characters are isolated from one another in separate close-ups, with Dwan standing in front of one of the twin towers, its out-of-focus lights bathing her in an eerie green luminosity, and Kong framed against endless black. The two of them lock eyes as Kong's heartbeat is heard gradually slowing down on the soundtrack. Finally, Kong's heart stops and he dies. As Dwan sobs, we suddenly see and hear the crowd of thousands that has obviously been there all along. It's a slightly surreal sequence and its unreality only heightens the tragedy.

In a famous quote given to *Time* magazine in his enthusiastic (if inexact) English, Dino De Laurentiis described the emotional impact he hoped the film would have on viewers: "When Jaws die, nobody cry. But when Kong die, everybody cry." Thanks to John Guillermin's adept handling of the story's Beauty and her beast and the director's sensitive dramatization of their relationship, De Laurentiis got his wish. At the end of *King Kong* '76, Dwan is devastated by Kong's death. And so are we.

Finished at a final cost of $23 million dollars (making it, at the time, the most expensive movie ever made) *King Kong* opened in 1,200 theaters in the US and Canada on December 17, 1976. It received reviews ranging from mixed to raves and was a terrific box office success. Because there were expectations (many of them self-generated by Dino De Laurentiis and Paramount) that *King Kong* might gross more than *Jaws* (then the all-time highest grossing film with over $100 million in domestic earnings) and it did not, it is sometimes mistakenly identified as being as a financial flop. However, this is not correct. *Kong* '76 earned approximately $90 million dollars worldwide — a very impressive sum at the time. Thanks to a massive marketing and merchandising campaign it also became a pop culture phenomenon and retains a dedicated fan base to this day.

King Kong 1976 is not a perfect film. Far from it — it has numerous flaws, some quite significant. However, it also has many wonderful elements, some of which outdo the 1933 original. In total, it is an affectionate, respectful, and highly entertaining re-telling of a beloved tale that adds—primarily through its depiction of the title character as a hero and in its deepening of the relationship between Kong and his lady love—some important new facets to one of the great cinematic legends of the twentieth century. Dino De Laurentiis' production may not be a classic like its forerunner, but due in large part to the contributions of John Guillermin, it is—as it was once described by film critic and historian Richard Schickel—"a confidently conceived, exuberantly executed work of popular movie art."

CHAPTER 16

A GORGEOUS PANOPLY: DEATH ON THE NILE

SARAH STREET

During the years 1974–82 a distinctive formula was developed by British film producers John Brabourne and Richard B. Goodwin for adapting Agatha Christie's fiction for the screen. Four films were produced: *Murder on the Orient Express* (1974), *Death on the Nile* (1978), *The Mirror Crack'd* (1980) and *Evil Under the Sun* (1982). Each was based on a successful Christie novel and, with the exception of *The Mirror Crack'd*, involved the Belgian detective Hercule Poirot. The films were lavishly produced, featuring international star casts and showcasing remarkable locations shot by highly regarded British cinematographers. I have described elsewhere how this formula gained ascendancy, whereas previous attempts to adapt Christie for the screen failed to generate a consistent style that satisfied both critics and the public (Street, 2008). The earlier films demonstrated that although Christie's work was quite difficult to adapt, certain characteristics — the deployment of many well-known film stars and the use of exotic/spectacular locations — could be productive. It was these aspects that Brabourne and Goodwin developed, and in turn the cycle of films influenced subsequent successful television series involving Miss Marple and Hercule Poirot. From this perspective the films occupy an important place in establishing screen conventions that television drew upon when devising its own formulae that produced new stories, not penned by Christie but which highlighted iconic elements of what has become indicative of an imitative "Christie style." It was particularly suited to Christie's narrative games and a revival of ensemble performance, introducing a host of intertextual references since many of the stars were associated with the classic Hollywood studio system. This chapter will concentrate on *Death on the Nile*, the second film in the cycle that was directed by John Guillermin. I argue that while it is exemplary of the successful formula described above, it also demonstrates specific elements that mark it as distinctive, particularly in terms of direction, use of settings, costume design and cinematography. As such it emerges as a very important film in Guillermin's catalogue that permitted him to explore Egyptian locations and to work closely with key collaborators including distinguished British cinematographer Jack Cardiff and costume designer Anthony Powell.

Murder on the Orient Express, the first of Brabourne and Goodwin's Christie adaptations, established conventions that to some extent became the template for *Death on the Nile*, particularly in its approach to casting but then going forward as a distinctive contribution to the popular cycle. Before considering *Death on the Nile* in more detail, it is important to understand the qualities that had proved so successful in the screen adaptation of *Murder on the Orient Express*. This was an ambitious production that attracted top international stars, partly because of tax laws that were lenient on foreign actors working in the United Kingdom (Walker, 1985: 129). Many of the stars were in the later years of their careers, so ensemble performances were considered appropriate at a time when older actors were seldom given major roles. The film had an international flavour which suited its story of characters of different nationalities travelling by train eastwards across Europe. Although the film was registered as British, the director, Sidney Lumet, was American, as were cast members Lauren Bacall and Anthony Perkins; it was co-funded by Paramount and distributed in the USA, Canada and Japan. Other stars included Albert Finney (as Poirot), Sean Connery, Wendy Hiller, John Gielgud, Michael York, Jacqueline Bisset, Rachel Roberts, Ingrid Bergman and Vanessa Redgrave. This approach emphasised the stars' often-brief scenes which were designed to extend the sparseness of the novel's characterisation. Ingrid Bergman, for example, received an Academy Award for Best Supporting Actress for her performance as Miss Ohlsson, a Swedish missionary. When comparing the novel and film, the part was clearly embellished for Bergman so that she could invest it with distinctive, memorable qualities while at the same time introducing a comic element that is not exploited in the novel. In addition, Anthony Perkins' performance as McQueen plays very much on his edgy, neurotic persona established in *Psycho* (1960). As well as enjoying the story's intricate puzzle which is still entertaining even when one knows the outcome, audiences appreciated how the casting of well-known actors introduced suspicions about the characters as the film exploited the stars' screen personas for additional dramatic effect.

The huge box-office success of *Murder on the Orient Express* — the film was made for $1.4 million but accrued $35.7 million — encouraged producers Brabourne and Goodwin to adapt *Death on the Nile* (IMDB, 2018). Agatha Christie thought that her novel was suitable for dramatisation since she had adapted the story as a play titled *Murder on the Nile* (1944), but this did not feature Poirot. She sent a copy of the script to Brabourne who she knew was interested in making a film version of the novel (Aldridge, 2016: 140). After she died in 1976 Brabourne's screen adaptation was finally initiated. The tax advantages that were a contributing factor to the all-star cast for *Murder on the Orient Express* were no longer operating, which is reflected in the perhaps less-overtly "starry" cast for *Death on the Nile*. There were, however, some distinguished names including Bette Davis, David Niven, Mia Farrow, Maggie Smith and Peter Ustinov as Poirot. The location cinematography by Jack Cardiff provided a suitably spectacular background for the drama, and the screenplay was by well-known writer Anthony Shaffer. Some of the formulaic elements that had been evident in *Murder on the Orient Express* were further extended in *Death on the Nile*. These include enhancing the material's camp potential which is articulated primarily through the characters played by Maggie Smith as Mrs. Van Schuyler's (Bette Davis) companion Miss Bowers, and Angela Lansbury as Salome Otterbourne, a flamboyant romantic novelist. Although Albert Finney's portrayal of Poirot in *Murder on the Orient Express* was generally praised, not least by Agatha Christie, the casting of Peter Ustinov in *Death on the Nile* permitted a more expressive, avuncular characterisation. This drew on Ustinov's celebrated ability to speak many languages, and his well-known reputation as a cultured raconteur. Both Brabourne and Ustinov were keen to present a softer Poirot so that the characterization stood out as different from Finney's portrayal of the more self-contained, emotionally distant detective in *Murder on the Orient Express* (Aldridge, 2016: 142). *Death on the Nile* established Peter Ustinov as the screen's most convincing Hercule Poirot. He was to play the role in several subsequent films including *Evil Under the Sun* before David Suchet's perhaps more definitive television performance as the detective in *Agatha Christie's Poirot* (UK, ITV, 1989–2013).

The production of *Death on the Nile* was a complex operation, the cast and crew spending seven weeks filming on location in Egypt, mostly in a reconditioned paddle steamer but also in other sweltering locations, and then in a replica of the steamer that was built for the large set at Pinewood Studios in the UK. Director John Guillermin made the most of the authentic location and of the space within the steamer as the primary site for the drama. Christie's fiction often took place in confined settings, and the physical layout of the environment in which a murder took place, whether it be a train or boat, was often highly significant in the unravelling of the plot. This was especially the case with *Death on the Nile*. Aldridge argues that, " . . . it sometimes feels like the picture has been shot in a deliberately slow and old-fashioned style in order to make it fit with the period," as opposed to the style deployed in *Murder on the Orient Express* which " . . . had successfully centred on contrast, with cosy, nostalgic expectations set up on one hand by the *mise-en-scène*, only to be countered on the other by the harsh truth of the murder and the striking visual accompaniment" (2016: 143). But this reading fails to appreciate how Guillermin's choices were influenced by a cinematographic design that privileged space and place in a pictorial fashion associated with British cinema that can be dated back to the 1920s (Gledhill, 2003: 55-61) and which became particularly prevalent in the 1980s "heritage films" cycle. Films such as Merchant-Ivory's *Heat and Dust* (1983) and *A Room with a View* (1985) are similarly distinguished by period costumes, and their vividly depicted locales are an important part of their rich visual attractions. Although it might be argued that Guillermin allowed Anthony Shaffer's sharply-scripted dialogue to be uninterrupted by superfluous editing, there were other reasons to adopt a slower camera style than had been deployed in *Murder on the Orient Express*. One obvious point is that the steamer's interiors were far less confined than those of a train, offering a more varied number of spaces within which the characters interacted. Also, the Egyptian locale lent itself to exoticism as depicted by Jack Cardiff's colour cinematography, whereas the cold, icy terrain of the Orient Express invited a more restrained visual style. *Death on the Nile*'s set at Pinewood was very large to accommodate the replica paddle steamer in a water tank erected on the studio floor. Jon Finch, who played the character James Ferguson, recalled that the space was congenial to work in because it was very easy to move around and the full-size vessel acquired a real sense of authenticity for the actors *(Death on the Nile*, DVD).

The film's opening sequences provide a good example of the style Guillermin adopted. As well as showcasing pictorially-organised images this could be quite varied, conforming to the narrative's pace and the extent of dialogue. When introducing the characters and providing some context for the fateful trip on the Nile, he was to some extent replicating Christie's approach in the novel of presenting "the characters in order of their appearance" before they went to Egypt (Christie, 1937). The film opens with shots of an idyllic English village on a summer's day. These linger on the picturesque setting: green fields, blue sky, pretty cottages and garden flowers that convey the hues of pastoral stability. The motorcar that is then seen travelling down the country roads seems somewhat incongruous in comparison with a landscape that seems otherwise to belong to a bygone era. We learn that the car carries Linnet Ridgeway (Lois Chiles), a young woman who has just inherited her grandfather's fortune and the country mansion located in the area. The first scenes in its opulent interiors, again showcased for the camera as Linnet shows her friend Jacqueline de Bellefort (Mia Farrow; her character is referred to as "Jackie") around, establish the wealthy milieu the characters inhabit. With economic storytelling, we then learn of Jackie's request for Linnet to hire her fiancé Simon Doyle (Simon MacCorkindale) to manage the estate, their introduction and then the shock of a wedding photograph that shows that Simon married Linnet rather than Jackie. This sets up the story's central conflict as Simon and Linnet honeymoon in Egypt, stalked by an apparently vengeful Jackie on their travels.

This scenario permits the first, stunning scenes shot in Egypt. These linger on the momentous landscape, accompanied by strident music to match the monumental sight of the limestone pyramids beneath vivid blue skies. Low and high camera angles work towards accentuating this spectacle, and some shots have clearly been taken from halfway up a pyramid. Filming in a logistically challenging location such as Egypt appears to have inspired Guillermin and Jack Cardiff to make the most of the locale's potential for visual spectacle, since the novel lacks lengthy descriptions of the landscape. For example, our first sight of Simon and Linnet on their honeymoon is of them riding galloping horses across the dusty, barren terrain then climbing to the top of one of the Great Pyramids at Giza. The area appears to be completely absent of other tourists, which heightens the sense of them having a unique visit to the ancient site. But their exhilarating experience is interrupted by the sudden appearance of Jackie, who has also climbed to the top of the pyramid in a bizarre encounter that further establishes the lengths to which she will go to convey her hatred of the happy couple. The idea of the vast spaces of the locale concealing things is also evident when we see that the scene has been witnessed from afar by Hercule Poirot. In this way the breath-taking sight of the landscape momentarily gives way to the establishment of important plot and character points, a strategy used to great effect in a later sequence when the passengers of the steamer go ashore to visit the Karnak Temple Complex.

Before the steamer sets off on its journey on the Nile, departing from Aswan, the characters are presented to us in a very distinctive way in a hotel setting. We see Linnet and Simon dancing in the middle of a sumptuous hotel dance floor. The camera pans out, following a waiter balancing a drink on a tray as he walks to the area where other guests are sitting. There are no cuts as the camera glides with this movement and then goes past the characters who are soon to board the S.S. *Karnak*. The presentation of the ensemble cast in this way is highly effective, since the uninterrupted, smooth camera movement allows us to momentarily glance at them, taking in how they are dressed and posed. All of the characters are looking towards the dancing couple, as if crystallising their various grudges against Linnet in one sceptical glance. James Ferguson, the left-wing scholar/traveller, wears a tweed jacket and red tie, and his serious demeanour is further emphasised by his glasses. He slowly rolls a cigarette as he looks disapprovingly at the wealthy couple. Rosalie Otterbourne (Olivia Hussey) and her mother Salome are seen next, establishing a stark contrast between the women that is primarily expressed through their costume. Rosalie is wearing a pale beige evening gown with very little adornment whereas Salome's gown is inspired by a sumptuous Art Deco look as exemplified by the work of 1920s fashion designer Erté. Dark velvet is embellished with touches of green and red, and Salome is bejewelled in glittering necklaces and as a feature of her hat. Her costume expresses her flamboyant reputation as the author of risqué novels, lover of life and risk — the apparent opposite of her daughter. Next is wealthy American socialite Mrs. Van Schuyler and her companion, Miss Bowers, also attired completely differently with Bowers in a black tie and suit representative of the 1920s' mannish fashions and Mrs. Van Schuyler in a gold evening dress with dangling necklaces, long white gloves and looking intently through a monocle. Even though the drama is set in the mid-1930s, costume designer Anthony Powell was careful to vary the fashions worn by the characters so that these reflected their status and personalities. Mrs. Van Schuler is seen in fashions from just after the First World War since Powell wanted to work with verisimilitude to convey how older people often stick with wearing the fashions they wore when they were happiest or most successful. Salome Otterbourne was typically dressed in costumes from the 1920s to express her character of being outrageous, a novelist with an "extravagant imagination" and exaggerated costumes to match (Powell, *Death on the Nile*, DVD). This long duration shot continues as it completes its survey with Colonel Race (David Niven) before tilting upwards, so we can see the maid Louise (Jane Birkin) on a balcony above, a character we have seen earlier at Linnet's house. In this way the film's direction and costume design have complemented each other to sketch brief impressions of the characters with a light touch that nevertheless establishes key markers of personality before the *Karnak* sets sail down the Nile. The scene finishes with Simon and Linnet being joined on the

Anthony Powell won an Oscar for the glamorous costumes

dance floor by some of the other characters for a tango. Jackie appears to disrupt the gaiety, a significant event since the characters, including Poirot, witness her bitterness first hand.

The following days provide additional location footage and character interactions to establish an atmosphere of expectation before the cruise begins. As Poirot and Doyle walk from the market along the bank of the Nile, for example, the camera tracks their gentle perambulation from the front, allowing their conversation to be heard and slow movement followed as they talk of Jackie's vengeful behaviour. A shot of a spectacular sunset marks the end of the day. By this time the theme of Jackie's disturbing appearances has been well established, including an almost comically-timed scene the next day in which Simon and Linnet attempt to thwart her following them on the cruise. They pretend to go to the railway station in a horse and carriage. She follows but we then see that they turned back when out of her sight. Key to the effectiveness of the scene is it being tied to Poirot's viewpoint as we see him watching the ruse as he breakfasts on his balcony, again establishing a strategy of his careful looking and listening as the drama unfolds. When the steamer sets sail the atmosphere of anticipation is further communicated by the scene's rousing musical accompaniment, the camera zooming in as the *Karnak*'s horn blows followed by a contrasting shot from the perspective of the riverbank as the vessel sails into the distance. As it gets smaller and smaller, we are aware that a momentous journey has commenced where anything could happen.

The steamer provides Guillermin with the opportunity to contrast its role as a comfortable vessel for its well-off passengers who are used to opulent luxury hotels with the surrounding terrain. As already noted, the ancient sites they visit are backdrops for surprising, suspenseful events as the monuments' nooks and crannies appear to provide cover for the evil that is in their midst. As the *Karnak* steams ahead, the barren landscape on shore is presented as strange and uninhabitable. When Mrs. Van Schuyler sits comfortably on deck she sees a group of young boys running alongside the riverbank, shouting and waving excitedly at the vessel. She smiles at them, charmed by the spectacle but this mood suddenly switches as the boys turn around and pull down their trousers, laughing. Her expression changes from pleasure to disapproval; the incident is another reminder that the privileged lives of the passengers are isolated from the realities of their environment; they are Western tourists whose engagement with Egypt is both limited and selective. Shots of the steamer taken from the shore also work to isolate it as a floating hotel, a vessel that is vulnerable to the river's treacherous rapids and rocks. The film's opening and closing shots isolate the river as deep and unknowable: at the final credits the camera zooms away from the steamer and tilts downwards to show only the water. In this way Guillermin exploits the contrast between the *Karnak* as a container of familiar signifiers of human comfort and wealth, and the flowing river as both mysterious and eternal.

> John told me that one day he was sitting on the boat rail talking to Bette Davis who was whatever age by this time and had a reputation for being difficult, as did John, but he told me he always got along with Bette Davis very well. So he was perched on the guardrail wearing shorts as he always did, even in the wintertime (in California at least), and Bette Davis was sitting opposite him and she said, "You have very attractive knees, John."

In the Karnak Temple excursion sequence a combination of cinematographic responses to the awe-inspiring environment are deployed as well as varied editing strategies. High camera angles trace the tourists' journey, their figures appearing small against the huge monuments they are visiting. Their touristic gaze is followed as the camera selects pillars and statues for closer inspection while evoking a sense of mystery as the mood changes in tone to suspense. The characters look intently at their surroundings as they each appear from behind a pillar. They are surrounded by an ominous silence, as if something is about to happen. The camera movements convey the characters' exploration of the space, the absence of dialogue permitting concentration on the temple's awe-inspiring impact. A series of shorter-length, snapshot-like shots taken from different angles show a succession of images of the site. These have the effect of punctuating the leisurely pace to allow the following, contrasting shots to have the greatest impact. The silence is interrupted as we hear quick footsteps and a person breathing as if running briskly up a steep incline. A shaky, hand-held camera adopts the viewpoint of this unknown person as they rush upwards through a dark enclosed space towards the light. The previous stable camera style then resumes as we see Simon and Linnet walking below. But this is only momentary, as the hand-held movement returns to show the exterior sunlight at the top of the ruin being reached. This is followed by closer shots of Simon and Linnet at the base of a pillar, the camera tilting upwards to emphasize its great height. The next shot is vertiginous, taken from the top of the pillar looking downwards. It is particularly effective because it shows the exact opposite perspective from the previous shot. We then see a large stone rocking, about to fall on Simon and Jackie below. They rush out of its path as it falls, narrowly missing being crushed. The other characters rush to their assistance, and the silence is broken by dialogue and music. In a few minutes the scene thus changes dramatically in tone with its use of different camera angles and editing pace to set up the incident to achieve maximum suspense. Later in the film when Poirot is speculating on who might have attempted to kill Linnet in this way, we are shown the reverse shot of the hand-held camera to reveal that it was Linnet's American trustee, Andrew Pennington, who wants to prevent her from learning he has embezzled funds from her estate.

This is not however the end of Simon and Linnet's ordeal and once again Guillermin exploits the scenery for maximum dramatic effect. After recovering from the shock of nearly being crushed by the falling stone, they wander to the statues at the Temple of Abu Simbel. Their contemplative mood is disturbed as the wind picks up and the camera slowly zooms into the statues just before the sudden appearance of Jackie looming above them, shouting out the Temple's history as a rather maniacal guide. She is magnificent in her triumph, as if the environment has given her courage to re-launch her challenge. Once again, she appears to conspire against their happiness in yet another scene that establishes a strong motive for her wishing Linnet harm. At the same time and as typical of Agatha Christie's plots, we learn that the other characters each bear their own grudge against Linnet so that when she is murdered all, except Poirot and Colonel Race, had a motive. Poirot's later remark, "I feel the presence of evil all about me," is suggested very strongly here, as the Temple's mystical sense of place is contrasted with the plot's heightening of suspicions about the characters.

Jackie looms above the lovers

The spaces of the *Karnak* are used judiciously, often exploiting their close proximity to facilitate eavesdropping, the accidental overhearing of conversations or glimpsing of key interactions. This strategy is an integral aspect of Christie's novel which even reproduces a plan of the decks to show which cabins the passengers occupied as well as logistical details that are important in the unravelling of the plot (Christie, 1937: 168). Poirot's observations of the characters are staged in this way, particularly towards the end of the film when he presents various scenarios as to how each character could have committed the murders (there are three in all, the second and third related to the killing of Linnet). Information overheard through a thin wall, for example, allows Jackie to shoot Salome just before she can reveal to Poirot and Colonel Race that she saw her leave Louise's cabin. Jackie murdered Louise because she was blackmailing Simon after she had witnessed him leaving Linnet's cabin following her murder. The truth that Jackie and Simon had engineered the killing of Linnet is finally revealed — two people whose apparently cast-iron alibis are shown by Poirot to be part of their mercenary, deadly scheme.

Guillermin worked with the actors to effect performances that took advantage of their star personas. In this way the film nuanced the characters differently from the novel, for example Mrs. Van Schuyler who is accompanied on the cruise by her cousin as well as Miss Bowers. In the film there is no cousin and the role of Miss Bowers is styled to suit Maggie Smith who had starred in *The Prime of Miss Jean Brodie* (Ronald Neame, 1969). The dialogue scripted by Schaffer for Bette Davis as Mrs. Van Schuyler is consistent with her reputation for delivering definitive statements using her very distinctive voice. When Linnet introduces herself on deck, Mrs. Van Schuyler makes several categorical statements, rather than asking or simply answering questions. She says that rules are made to be broken, "... at least mine are, by me," before informing Linnet how the pearls she is wearing are formed. The encounter has established in a few minutes the essence of the Van Schuyler persona — a woman who is used to being right and having her way, while also indicating her admiration for other people's jewellery which causes her to later steal Linnet's necklace. Miss Bowers is however presented as her sparring partner, their relationship thriving on what appears to be mutual disrespect. We learn that Bowers dislikes hot climates, but Mrs. Van Schuyler insists on going to Egypt, and the pair are frequently rude to each other. But there is a sense of enjoyment in their interactions, and in the second half of the film a more serious side to Bowers is revealed as we learn that her father was ruined by the Ridgeways and that she was a professional nurse. She is called to nurse Jackie after she has shot, or we think we have seen her shoot, Simon in the leg. Her sensitivity is clear, and it is pleasing to see Maggie Smith developing Miss Bowers beyond camp caricature. Jane Birkin plays the maid Louise. Her role is a very small one but crucial in terms of the plot. Birkin's performance gives the role an essence of impending tragedy as we see Linnet refuse to give her the money she needs so she can marry. She is murdered later when she attempts to blackmail Jackie. Birkin was perhaps a strange choice for this role, but her exotic demeanour (an English actress known for roles in French films and association with Serge Gainsbourg) contributes to the lasting impression of the effectiveness of her brief scenes.

Mia Farrow's performance as Jackie draws upon her complex screen persona established with *Rosemary's Baby* (Roman Polanski, 1968) and as Daisy Buchanan in *The Great Gatsby* (Jack Clayton, 1974). In these roles she demonstrated her capacity to play enigmatic women who may have allowed corruption or evil to enter their world. In *Death on the Nile* Jackie is capable of quixotic behaviour, making a spectacle of herself as she "performs" the part of the jilted lover whose best friend has stolen her fiancé. The tragedy behind her ingenious collaboration with Simon to acquire Linnet's fortune is only made clear to us in Poirot's final scenario of how the murders occurred. This forces us to reconsider

Jackie's intrusions as those of a woman in control of executing a persuasive masquerade of bitterness. Her scenes with Poirot also acquire greater significance in retrospect since his stern warnings to her against allowing evil to enter her heart turn out to be even more prescient. The exaggeration of her motive to wish Linnet harm while presenting herself as emotionally unstable is even more calculated when we learn that this was a key element in the plan to then eliminate herself as a suspect because of an apparent cast-iron alibi. Farrow's performance is highly convincing, especially in moments when Jackie appears to be enjoying the disruptive impact she is having on Linnet and the other passengers. As Jackie suddenly emerges at the Temple of Abu Simbel she appears to be elated by the environment, as if possessed by a mystical strength in her brazen stalking of Simon and Linnet.

The casting of Peter Ustinov as Poirot has already been discussed, but it is important to note that his role is made even more effective because of his pairing in solving the crimes with Colonel Race. David Niven's performance gravitates towards his character being a dependable sounding board for Poirot's suspicions. Race is solid, sensible and trustworthy. Apart from Poirot he is the only character who is above suspicion. The role accords with Niven's gentlemanly persona as an ex-Army officer who saves Poirot's life when he is threatened by a snake that has been let loose in his cabin. The significance of their friendship is signalled directorially near the beginning of the film, in a scene directly following the long duration shot when the characters are introduced at the hotel. Poirot is surprised to encounter his old friend Colonel Race and they briefly discuss previous cases and how they happen to both be taking the steamer up the Nile. It is as if we are being told here that these men are different from the other characters, that Race will be a reliable confidante when Poirot can trust nobody else.

The stars in the cast featured as a major attraction in the film's British poster, with Ustinov in the centre with the *Karnak* steamer and

Sphinx behind him. The US poster designed by Richard Amsel used the triangular shape of a pyramid with the nine stars' faces as a border and Tutankhamen holding a dagger in the centre. This design was intended to capitalize on the American exhibition of treasures from the tomb of Tutankhamen. In this way the film was promoted as an "event movie" giving viewers a vicarious experience of Egypt from the perspective of wealthy tourists on the *Karnak*. The film's premiere in September 1978 in New York City was timed to coincide with the build-up to the opening of a travelling exhibition showing artefacts from the tomb of Tutankhamen held at the Metropolitan Museum of Art. The treasures had never been transported to America before, so the film was poised to capitalize on the intense interest in Egyptian history and a popular craze in celebration of "King Tut." The mystique surrounding archaeologist Howard Carter's Egyptian excavations and rumours of a curse following the disturbance of Tutankhamen's tomb in 1922 fuelled public interest as the film's release coincided with the exhibition. Although there was no explicit connection between Tutankhamen and *Death on the Nile*, the film's marketing exploited long-standing traditions of Egyptomania in America and Europe. It also took advantage of the renewed popularity of Christie's novels following her death.

Death on the Nile made a profit, nearly doubling its budget. It cost $8 million and made $14.5 million at the box-office (IMDB, 2018). Although this was not nearly as huge a profit as with *Murder on the Orient Express,* the film was particularly successful in Japan and was purchased by several U.S. television networks (Walker, 1985: 131). It has since been shown frequently on British television and has enjoyed sustained popularity with Christie fans as interest in her work intensified in the wake of the numerous Poirot and Marple series broadcast on television. As a British-registered film it is associated with international genres that were popular at the box-office such as the James Bond franchise, adventure and fantasy films (Harper and Smith, 2012: 212-3). *Death on the Nile*'s production team represented well-established independents John Brabourne, who was responsible for selecting Christie's novel for screen adaptation, finalising Schaffer's script, selecting the cast and crew, and Richard B. Goodwin, the production manager who supervised shooting in Egypt. Reviews were mixed and inevitable comparisons with *Murder on the Orient Express* tended to influence opinion (Aldridge, 2016: 143). The scene-stealing performance by Angela Lansbury attracted considerable praise, as did Peter Ustinov's casting, Jack Cardiff's cinematography and Anthony Powell's costumes, but some reviewers found the film too long and drawn out. This perhaps relates to the decision to show Poirot's speculative scenarios one-by-one towards the end of the film concerning how the various characters could have committed the murders. As noted earlier, the film's pace was otherwise very carefully measured to communicate notions of space and place that are integral to the plot, character development and locale. As Gordon Gow, writing in *Films and Filming* noted, "The pictorial quality of *Death on the Nile* is superior to that of most thrillers, and does much to hold the attention through those moments when one grows conscious of the movie's somewhat reckless length" (1978: 39).

The film won several key awards. Anthony Powell won an Academy Award and a BAFTA for Best Costume Design; Peter Ustinov won the *Evening Standard*'s Best Actor award and a BAFTA, and Guillermin received the *Evening Standard*'s award for Best Film. Angela Lansbury won a U.S. National Board of Review award for Best Supporting Actress. Guillermin worked well with his key collaborators in the large-scale production. It appears that he allowed expertise to flourish, particularly in the case of theatre and film costume designer Anthony Powell. He had very clear ideas about how the characters should be dressed, visiting Bette Davis when he was in America preparing costumes for the production. Powell persuaded her that her face would be shown to best advantage if she wore large black hats, and the wigs she wore presented a tightly curled, close hairstyle that again emphasized her imposing visage. He also emphasized her slim ankles and small feet, having a pair of python skin shoes made specially for her in London (Powell, *Death on the Nile*, DVD). Powell's designs for the costumes show the precision of these sartorial choices, including fabrics to be used and descriptions such as "tarnished gold tassels round bottom of jacket" for one of Salome Otterbourne's flamboyant outfits. Powell indeed created an opulent spectacle to match this larger-than-life character. The matching black silk pyjamas and dressing gown worn by Maggie Smith in the scene when she is called in to look after Jackie is another apposite costume. The black is complemented by the ensemble's red border with ivory semi-circles. Although hardly a uniform, the nightwear is suitably formal to indicate the change in persona, as Miss Bowers' professionalism is called upon in an emergency. The cinematographic style adopted by Guillermin and Jack Cardiff allowed the details of costumes to be seen, and the film is overall a very precise example of how colour, textures and fabrics combine to produce the impression of a high-quality production.

Death on the Nile's contribution to the popular cycle of Christie adaptations is considerable. It established an even more opulent visual style than was evident in *Murder on the Orient Express*, and it was a key influence on *Evil Under the Sun* (Guy Hamilton, 1982), the last adaptation produced by Brabourne and Goodwin, that was filmed in Majorca rather than the north Devon setting of the novel, and with plush hotel interiors filmed in London. Combined with judicious use of a stunning location, the film exaggerates the camp elements that had become established in *Death on the Nile*, particularly Maggie Smith's performance as Daphne and Diana Rigg's as Arlene. The screenplay again highlights the rivalries between the characters, relishing the source novel's scope for wit, misunderstanding and irony. *Death on the Nile* had firmly put in place these elements as key to the rich visual and narrative pleasures offered by the films. Brabourne and Goodwin did not, however, make Christie adaptations after *Evil Under the Sun*, perhaps because while *The Mirror Crack'd* doubled its budget at the box-office, the last film in the series did not make a profit. Michael Winner later directed *Appointment with Death* (1987) but this was a poor imitation of the style that had been showcased with *Death on the Nile*. This was better exploited by television producers who later reprised the "heritage crime" formula with great success in long-running series involving Poirot (UK, ITV, 1989–2013) and Miss Marple (UK, BBC, 1984–92 and ITV, 2004-13). Angela Lansbury went on to play Miss Marple in *The Mirror Crack'd* (Guy Hamilton, 1980), the film that followed *Death on the Nile*, a role that contributed to her casting as the mystery novelist Jessica Fletcher in *Murder, She Wrote*, a popular U.S. television series (1984–96).

John Guillermin's long career demonstrated that he could work successfully in a variety of popular genres including action-adventure, disaster and costume drama. *Death on the Nile* is exemplary of an ambitious spirit that rose to the challenge of filming in difficult, if monumental, locations, and used Pinewood's facilities astutely to execute the thriller's audacious, multi-character plot. Writing in 2018, history would appear to be repeating itself since Kenneth Branagh has announced that his lavish, multi-star film, *Murder on the Orient Express* (2017), which has been a global box-office success, will be followed by a new screen version of *Death on the Nile*. Whether or not Branagh uses Guillermin's film as an inspirational template remains to be seen, but he would do well to study the approaches described in this chapter which ensured that the film produced in 1978 has remained on screens ever since and that its legacy has been significant for British film and television history.

EPILOGUE

LIFE AFTER DIRECTING 1998 TO 2015

WHEN I MOVED TO CALIFORNIA to live with John, I discovered he owned not one copy of any of his many films. He did not like any of his work, with one exception. He would say repeatedly, "I only made one good film, *Rapture*, and only half a dozen people have seen it" — the latter claim being nearer to truth than falsity. He was, though, proud of the entertainment his films had afforded to "millions of people all over the world."

Once we were living together in John's Malibu home, I began buying copies of his films and building a library of them. In 1999, films were only available in VHS tape format and only one or two of his British films were on tape, along with some of the bigger films he had made after moving to America with his first wife and family in the mid- to late Sixties. Friends of mine in the UK would record John's early black and white films when they were shown on British television, and we watched them on a multi-region VHS player.

Later when DVDs took hold, more of his films were released, including many of his early, powerful black and white British films. The majority of his thirty-four feature films are available, some through small companies such as Renown in the UK, or the BFI (British Film Institute) Collection, as well as everything that is available for purchase or rental being listed on Amazon.

Mary and John at the marina after sailing in Santa Monica Bay

When a film arrived, we would sit together to watch this film he hadn't seen since it was made, maybe had never seen in the theatrical version. As it ran, John would comment, "I don't remember a single shot" — all his memories and stories were of the crew, actors and producers — the people without whom the film couldn't have been made. The only other comment he would make, sitting quietly till the end of the film, was, "Not bad," or, "Better than I remembered," in a tone of grudging appreciation.

The only film he wouldn't watch through was *Towering Inferno* — he had had a hard time making this film, both from the demands of such a large-scale project and the power struggles with the producer and, frustratingly for John, director of the action sequences, Irwin Allen, and he was left with a bad feeling about it. I believe that his distaste was partly because he was best known for this popular disaster movie and not known at all for the work for which he wished he had been recognized, his personal masterpiece, *Rapture*.

On my first visit to California, a few months after we had met, I came to visit John in Malibu on a vacation he nicknamed "The Nine

Day Wonder." He called Fox Studios and arranged a private screening of *Rapture*. As we entered the large screening room, he directed me to sit on the opposite side of the theater, where I felt, being in the first throes of love, rather lonely. Now I can appreciate how apprehensive he must have felt, viewing the film he thought of as his finest achievement after a gap of thirty-four years. He was moved and silent afterwards. I cried, as I always have, during the many times I have viewed this beautiful film.

In 2010, I read in the *Los Angeles Times* that Nick Redman of the Music Department at 20th Century Fox was launching Twilight Time, releasing limited editions of vintage Fox films. I tracked down Redman's contact information, and John took things from there — the only time I saw him actively pursue something to do with his long career. Redman told John he was already negotiating with Fox about *Rapture,* and in 2011, *Rapture* was one of eleven films released by Twilight Time that year. John was gratified by the beautiful Blu-ray print and the praise his work received in online movie review sites, with the general consensus that the film was a little-known gem and forgotten masterpiece.

In early 2012 John was interviewed by Redman for the Heritage documentary series produced by BAFTA on British directors — a project created to record important British directors before they died. That John agreed to do this, when he was not in the best of health, is something for which I am very grateful, as I can spend seventy-five minutes in the company of the man I loved so deeply as he tells his amusing and thoughtful memories.

By the time he died just six weeks short of his ninetieth birthday in September 2015, John had come to appreciate his own large body of work. His feelings of disappointment and regret about his career had slowly lightened and altered, though he was still deeply proud of *Rapture* as the crowning artistic achievement of his life and forever grateful to the great producer, Darryl Zanuck, who "never interfered" or came on set, and gave John his one solitary experience of seeing a project through from conception to completion in sole charge of his own artistic vision.

APPENDIX A

FILMS THAT NEVER GOT MADE AND OTHER COMPLAINTS

JOHN OFTEN TOLD STORIES about his hopes and disappointments around films he had hoped to make. These missed opportunities lived on in him and were part of his story about his career. John and I had met ten years after he stopped directing, or, as he would say, "I didn't give up directing, directing gave me up." He often told the story of Richard Zanuck axing his own father's favored project, *Last Days in Berlin* and

What a film Tai-Pan *would have been!*

he regretted not having the chance to direct Sean Connery as the lead in Tai-Pan, a film adaptation that didn't happen based on the book of that name by James Clavell. The two photos of the Art Director's designs for the sets featured here are part of six John had somehow held onto. Below the photo of John with Zanuck, Williams and Christian Ferry, his oldest friend, he wrote, "Alas, he lives in Paris and I'm not up to the trip." In fact, we did make it across the Atlantic together just once during our sixteen years in California; to see Christian Ferry and his wife in Paris when it was clear Christian was dying of cancer. Difficult or not, John was a true friend to those he admired and respected.

Never made

Sketches for Tai-Pan, *Jim Clavell's best seller —*
Sean Connery was going to play Tai-Pan *—film never made*

After Richard Zanuck took over Fox from his father, Darryl Zanuck, he ordered John to come to LA and announced, "We're not making the *Last Days of Berlin*. War films are over."

John was taken aback and said, "You're laughing! They all said that about *The Longest Day!* It was a smash. What are you going to make?"

"Myra Breckinridge."

"Myra Breckinridge! That's a piece of porn. You're making a terrible mistake, Dick."

John wrote below this photo: David Wolper the asshole who refused to take an option on Richard Portis' True Grit

I'M TELLING ELMO WILLIAMS, WHO RUNS FOX FOR DARRYL IN LONDON'S WARDOUR STREET, THAT HE'S A FRUSTRATED DIRECTOR, AND NOT TO FUCK ME UP WITH HIS USELESS SUGGESTIONS ON HOW TO DIRECT "'RAP[TURE.' T HE MAN ON THE RIGHT IS CHRISTIAN FERRY WHO WAS DARRYL'S RIGHT-HAND MAN ON "THE LONGEST DAY" AND IS MY CLOSEST FRIEND TODAY. ALAS, HE LIVES IN PARIS AND I'M NOT UP TO THE TRIP. DARRYL, OF COURSE, IS ON THE LEFT, WITH CIGAR.

I'm telling Elmo Williams, who runs Fox for Darryl in London's Wardour Street, that he's a frustrated director and not to fuck me up with his useless suggestions on how to direct "Rapture." The man on the right is Christian Ferry who was Darryl's right-hand man on "The Longest Day" and is my closest friend. Alas, he lives in Paris and I'm not up to the trip. Darryl, of course, is on the left, with cigar.

APPENDIX B

FROM CRAZY TO SANE: OR AM I?

The marriage section from Mary Guillermin's one-woman play

MARY: By my mid-forties when I met John, it was some years since I'd been crazy. The happy times were no longer manic, and the long depressions were a flat grey rather than black. A few months after John and I met, I arranged an appointment with a National Health Service psychiatrist. I wanted my new relationship to work, so I was considering taking medication. The psychiatrist asked me:

PSYCHIATRIST: Do other people find you overbearing, or too loud, Mary? Do you often interrupt people while they are talking?

MARY: All the questions were about whether I could tell how I came across to other people when I was manic. At the end of the assessment, he pronounced:

PSYCHIATRIST: I have never assessed anyone with as much self-awareness of their behavior as you have, Mary. I think you will be okay without medication.

MARY: So, on to a look back at life with my husband. After my first solo show free class, I was standing outside the Whitefire Theater talking to classmates, and I saw the card for the solo show about Marilyn, Marilyn Monroe. Off I launched.

"My husband was a film director and he did the second *King Kong* with Jessica Lange, and she hadn't acted before, so she asked him:

JESSICA: John, how do I act when I'm discovered floating on the raft in the ocean?

JOHN GUILLERMIN: Just pretend to be Marilyn Monroe, Jessica.

MARY: As I drove away, I thought, a little queasily, "Was I name-dropping?" Actually, I loved John to bits and five years after his death, I still look for any opportunity to talk about him. But let's name drop.

John Guillermin! Yeah, most of you don't recognize the name, right? Okay, how about this?

Death on the Nile?

Towering Inferno!! You might have heard of that one.

Of course, John didn't like being best known for his personally most-hated film (but that's another story). He must have spun in his grave like a wood drill to read all those obituaries headlining, "Director of *Towering Inferno* Dies at 89."

Talking of name-dropping, it's May 1998. I'm standing starry-eyed in John's Malibu kitchen on my first trip to California after us meeting in London. He is so handsome.

Lined!!! What do you expect at 73? But gorgeous!

And listen to him, he's talking about his buddy Steve McQueen, and NO, can you believe it? Freddy Astaire!

I'm in Malibu, California with someone who was friends with Fred Astaire. This man surely isn't going to find me overwhelming. And he didn't.

I had met John at a dinner party when he was over in London talking to an Italian producer about one of his scripts. We saw each other across the room — and that was it! Love at first sight. When I plucked up my courage to tell my mother that I was in love with someone four years older than her, she said,

JEAN: Oh, darling, I'm so glad. I could see you were right for each other.

MARY: Once I was home, John missed me and FedExed me a pile of romantic greeting cards every few days. Then at age 73 he rented out his house and came to live near me in Essex for a year, hoping he could win me. Within a few months, after much agonizing, I left my life with my friends and went to live with John in the countryside.

John knew from the beginning how devotional I was and how much I loved the Divine Mother. But he loved to revel in his atheism. He would say proudly:

JOHN GUILLERMIN: I chucked the catechism in the wastebasket at the age of sixteen. And I never looked back.

MARY: His other frequent saying:

JOHN GUILLERMIN: I like to call god "dog."

MARY: He didn't care that I was uncomfortable with him saying that. Sometimes I used to think, why on earth does the Mother want me to be with this man who doesn't believe in any God, swears frequently and loudly, drinks too much and shouts at me? Then one day, we were standing at our back door in Essex when:

JOHN GUILLERMIN: Look at that night sky, Mary, isn't it magnificent? The stars stretch out into infinity. Infinity! Can you imagine that? The universe is so unimaginably huge.

MARY: Okay, I thought, that works. I'll take the Universe as his Higher Power.

Fast forward. We'd been married a few years. I used to pray, Please God, give me at least ten years. Once we reached ten years together, I saw every year as a bonus. We ended up with seventeen years together.

Our whole marriage, he'd frequently say to me:

JOHN GUILLERMIN: Promise me you won't let me die in hospital.

MARY: I can't really promise that, darling, but I'll do my very best.

In the night preceding his unexpected death, he had fallen over and I couldn't lift him. After trying for ages, I called the paramedics against his wishes. The two men lifted him and sat him down in his chair. They tried to take his blood pressure.

JOHN GUILLERMIN: Stop! You're too rough, you're hurting me.

MARY: A paramedic turned to me and said,

PARAMEDIC: Is he behaving just the same as usual?

MARY: He's behaving exactly as usual. Being his usual stubborn self.

So, they left John alone without taking his blood pressure. If they had, he probably would have been carted off to hospital, and died there. A little later he started breathing with difficulty.

John, I think you've got pneumonia again. Please, let me call the paramedics.

JOHN GUILLERMIN: NO!

MARY: John, more elderly people die of pneumonia than anything else. Do you want to die?!

JOHN GUILLERMIN: No, I don't want to die, but I don't want to die in hospital.

MARY: He sounded bad: I called the paramedics. As we waited for them to come, he said:

JOHN GUILLERMIN: Mary, will you come and hold my hand. I'm frightened.

MARY: I sat next to him and held his hand. That was our goodbye, although I didn't know it at the time. As the paramedics carried John out to the ambulance he was dying, his arms moving and jerking like an agitated cockerel's wings. It was disturbing, but I'm grateful I saw with my own eyes that my tough old husband really did die in his own home, even if he was too tough to die peacefully in his bed.

John's love has stayed with me after his death. When he was alive and sick, he was, let's say, challenging. After he died, I enjoyed my deep love and the emotional health that his steadfast love for me had brought into my life. My exuberance is now channeled into my creativity; my depressions have left me. I have felt John's presence many times since his death, and as a friend once said poetically about our love:

KATRINA: Mary, you are alive and dance with death. John is dead and dances with life.

APPENDIX C

LOVE POEMS FROM JOHN TO MARY

I'm 88
Not Yet In My Crate
And I Have A Wonderful Wife.
I'm 88
She's My Only Date
She Keeps Me Clinging To Life.
I'm 88
And It's Not Too Late
To Spend My Last Days Without Strife —
To Greet Once More
The World Like Before
To Make Amends
To See My Friends
Take My Wife Out To Eat
Talk To People We Meet
Go To See The New Shows —
<u>And</u> (Pause) <u>Ignore-All-The-Lows</u> . . .

5/9/14
Love,
John

2/16/07

HAPPIEST BIRTHDAY

my love
on the eve of our move
to our country mini-estate
in the heart of the Topanga
hills.
  I wish you all the
happiness in the coming
year, my darling, as you
create our new home,
develop your career, meet
and make new friends and
fully enjoy all the good things
life has to offer — including
my everlasting love!
    Luv you,
    John

P.S. The fifties are the best
    years of your life —
    from one who knows!

Whatever you think

would make

your birthday sensational —

that's what I'm wishing

for you — a nice
dinner at the
French restaurant in
Santa Monica (forgotten its
name)?

2/16/07

HAPPIEST BIRTHDAY

*my love
on the eve of our move
to our country mini-estate
in the heart of the Topanga hills.*

*I wish you all the
happiness in the coming
year, my darling, as you
create our new home,
develop your career, meet
and make new friends and
fully enjoy all the good things
life has to offer — including
my ever-lasting love!
Luv yer, John*

*P.S. The fifties are the best
years of your life —
from one who knows!*

Whatever you think
Would make
Your birthday sensational
That's what I'm wishing for you —

*a nice
dinner at the French restaurant in
Santa Monica (forgotten its name)?*

For My ^*gorgeous* Wife
On Our Anniversary

You're the most beautiful flower
I ever picked!

(absolutely true)

Happy Anniversary
With^*all my* Love

My dearest
darlin'

Since I've known you — the greatest
ten years of my long life,

Your John x x x x x x x

[Nov 5, 2009]

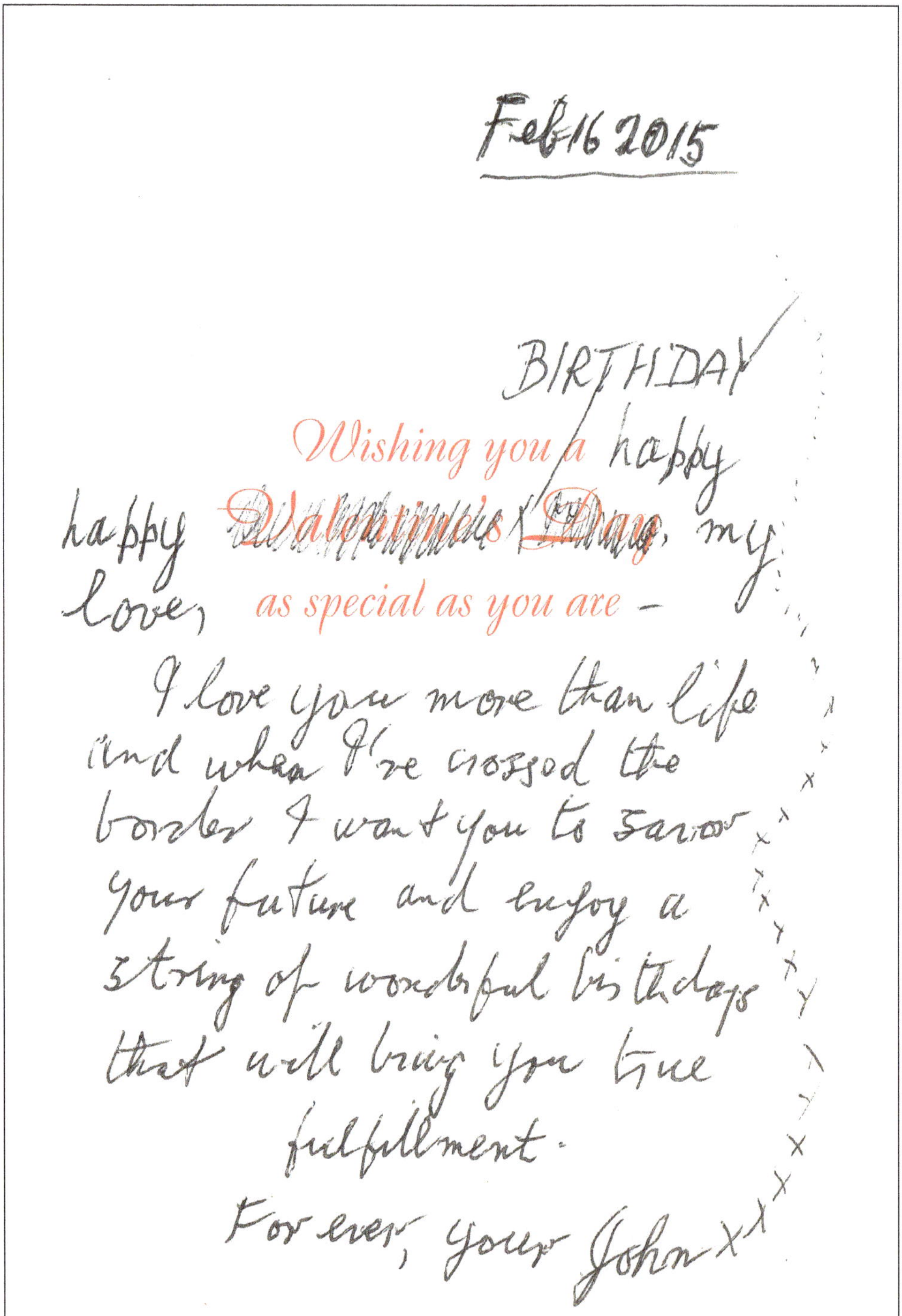

Feb 16 2015

BIRTHDAY
Wishing you a happy
happy ~~Valentine's Day~~, my
love, *as special as you are —*

I love you more than life
and when I've crossed the
border I want you to savor
your future and enjoy a
string of wonderful birthdays
that will bring you true
fulfillment.
For ever, your John xx

Feb 16, 2015

Wishing you a ^ happy, happy Birthday, my love

~~Valentines Day~~

as special as you are

*I love you more than life
itself and when I've crossed the
border I want you to savor
your future and enjoy a
string of wonderful birthdays
that will bring you true
fulfillment*

For ever, your John x x x x x x x x x x x

NOTES

Chapter 4: Irascible Iconoclast

1. *In the Arena,* Harper Collins, 1995, p. 464
2. ibid.
3. Thomson, Secker & Warburg, 1975, p. 224.
4. Charlton Heston, *The Actor's Life: Journals,* 1956–1976, Penguin Books, 1980, p. 370.
5. Gullermin was apparently irked that Lean never gave him credit for this. If this were the case, one wonders if *The Bridge at Remagen* (1969) can be seen as Guillermin's revenge, a sort of mock-heroic take on Lean's *The Bridge on the River Kwai* for a more iconoclastic decade. It is another story about a bridge over which neither the Allies nor their enemies can agree on whether it should be preserved or destroyed. Like Lean's film, it includes a completely redundant feminine presence and has a curiously anti-climactic ending, where the bridge is not blown up but will collapse of its own accord after the pummelling it has received. "Madness, madness," was the verdict at the end of Lean's film; "It's a farce" is the conclusion of Guillermin's. One producer who worked with both directors at different times was Richard Goodwin. When asked to comment on the widely publicised feud between Lean and his leading lady, Judy Davis, during the making of *A Passage to India* (1984), Goodwin said, "It was minor compared to a director like John Guillermin." (Quoted in Kevin Brownlow's *David Lean,* Faber, 1996, p. 674). Goodwin was the producer on *Death on the Nile* (1978).

6. Interview in *An Autobiography of British Cinema*, edited by Brian McFarlane, Methuen, 1997, p. 565.
7. Gill Plain, *John Mills and British Cinema*, Edinburgh University Press, 2006, p. 156.
8. Allen Eyles, *Films and Filming*, October 1964, p. 30
9. Brian McFarlane (editor), *Encyclopaedia of British Cinema, 4th edition*, Manchester University Press, 2010, p. 315.
10. *Time Out Film Guide 2009*, p. 744.
11. Raymond Durgnat, *A Mirror for England*, Faber and Faber, 1970, p. 42.
12. Quoted in *British Crime Cinema*, edited by Steve Chibnall and Robert Murphy, Routledge, 1999, p. 104.
13. Durgnat, p. 175.
14. Alexander Walker, *Peter Sellers: The Authorised Biography*, Coronet, 1982, p. 121.
15. ibid.

Chapter 9: Filming *Rapture*

16. I am very grateful to Mary Guillermin for her patience and encouragement, and for allowing me access to John Guillermin's heavily annotated shooting script for *Rapture*.
17. Anonymous, "Lives Remembered: John Guillermin," *Express*, 2 October 2015. Available at: https://www.express.co.uk/life-style/life/609544/John-Guillermin-obituary-lives-remembered [accessed 30/08/2020].
18. Kevin Lyons, "John Guillermin (1925-2015)," *BFI*, 2 October 2015. Available at: https://www2.bfi.org.uk/news-opinion/news-bfi/features/john-guillermin-1925-2015 [accessed 31/08/2020].
19. Ibid.
20. Ibid.
21. Quoted in Lyons, 2015.
22. Mike Sutton, *Rapture* (Eureka Classics DVD, 2014), p. 11.

23. Ibid.
24. Stanley Mann, *Rapture*, 3rd Draft Screenplay, 3 May 1964.
25. Roland Denning, 'The Arri 35II: The Camera that Defined a Generation', *Red Shark*, 2020. Available at: https://www.redsharknews.com/production/item/5208-the-arri-35ii-the-camera-that-defined-a-generation-of-film-directors [accessed 30/08/2020].
26. Ibid.
27. Ibid.
28. John Boorman, *Adventures of a Suburban Boy* (London: Faber and Faber, 2004), p. 19.
29. Jim Owens and Gerald Millerson, *The Video Production Handbook* (Oxford: Focal Press, 2012) p. 362.
30. On an aside note, I would also argue that the long, graceful tracking shots of Agnes and Joseph running on the beach before they consummate their relationship are as exhilarating an image of youthful freedom and vitality as the final shots of Tarkovsky's film, where two characters also run along a beach.
31. Anonymous, "Film: Darkness in Brittany," *Time*, vol. 86, No. 9, 27 August 1965. Available at: http://content.time.com/time/magazine/article/0,9171,828378,00.html [accessed 31/08/2020].
32. Lyons, 2015. https://www2.bfi.org.uk/news-opinion/news-bfi/features/john-guillermin-1925-2015

BIBLIOGRAPHY

Chapter 8. Girl on the Edge: *Rapture*

Anon (1965), "On location with *Rapture*," *Films and Filming*, February, pp. 53–55.

Butler, Jeff (1967), Letter to *Films and Filming*, December, p. 50.

Durgnat, Raymond (1971), *A Mirror for England: British Movies from Austerity to Affluence* (New York: Praeger).

Johnston, Trevor (2014), "Girl to the front," *Sight and Sound*, September, pp. 110–111.

Kafka, Franz, (2009), translated by Crick, Joyce, "Letter to his Father" [1919], in *The Metamorphosis and Other Stories* (Oxford: Oxford University Press), pp. 100–140.

Möller, Olaf (2014), "Olaf's World" *Film Comment*, January/February, pp. 20–21.

Redman, Nick and Kirgo, Julie (2014), DVD commentary for *Rapture*, Eureka Entertainment.

Chapter 16. A Gorgeous Panoply: *Death on the Nile*

Aldridge, Mark, *Agatha Christie on Screen* (London: Palgrave Macmillan, 2016).

Christie, Agatha, *Death on the Nile* (London: Collins, 1937; paperback edition, Harper Collins, 2014).

Death on the Nile DVD, Studio Canal Films, OPTD4070. This includes a documentary made by EMI when the film was being shot and an interview with Anthony Powell.

Gledhill, Christine, *Reframing British Cinema, 1918–1928: Between Restraint and Passion* (London, British Film Institute, 2003).

Gow, Gordon, review of *Death on the Nile* in *Films and Filming*, 25:1, Oct 1978, p. 39.

Harper, Sue and Smith, Justin, *British Film Culture in the 1970s: The Boundaries of Pleasure* (Edinburgh: Edinburgh University Press, 2012).

IMDB (Internet Movie Data Base), box-office figures for *Murder on the Orient Express* and *Death on the Nile*, consulted August 2018: imdb.com

Street, Sarah, "Heritage Crime: The Case of Agatha Christie" in Shail, Robert, *Seventies British Cinema* (London: British Film Institute/Palgrave Macmillan, 2008), pp. 105–116.

Walker, Alexander, *National Heroes: British Cinema in the Seventies and Eighties* (London: Harrap, 1985).

ACKNOWLEDGMENTS

First and foremost, I want to thank Neil Sinyard, Emeritus Professor of the film department he founded at Hull University and a contributor to this book. Neil came to my attention when I was searching for a potential publisher of a book about John's work, in his capacity as co-editor of a series called *British Film Makers*. This series of twenty-four volumes about twenty-seven men of the world of films, had, along with the rest of the publishing world, ignored my late husband's major contribution to cinema and film history. Since our initial contact, Neil has been a constant source of encouragement and support over the more than four years it has taken to bring this project to fruition. The other contributors from the academic world — Brian Hoyle, Sarah Street and Melanie Williams — were brought into our mutual endeavor by Neil's efforts. I thank you all for adding your expertise to our enterprise.

My thanks also go to Kate Lees of Adelphi Studios, who is a contributor, along with Vic Pratt of the BFI, and Jo Botting, also of the BFI, who had intended to be a contributor, but life got in the way. Jo's special interest lay in *Thunderstorm;* I hope she approves of my brief take on it. Kate and Jo met with me several times for lunch at the BFI South Bank when I was visiting family in London, and they were both vital for breathing life into the project.

The above-mentioned contributors are all aware of the power and originality of John's cinematic contribution to British cinema in the early part of his career, spanning the years 1950 to '65. I am very grateful for your reevaluations of his work.

Olaf Möller, an international film critic, also provided early encouragement, and I quote from a 2016 email: "I was also thinking about how to get a book on John going, but if you have a go at it, then do it! As long as someone who loves John's work does it, I'm happy." Thank you, Olaf, for your belief in and enthusiasm about my husband's work.

Ray Morton, a prolific writer on the history and appeal of the mythical *King Kong,* soon joined our group. Ray, a psychotherapist in Los Angeles with whom I have a mutual therapist friend, organized a 40th anniversary showing of *King Kong* at the retro Aero Theater, in Santa Monica, California. It was thrilling to see *Kong* on the big screen and feel how enthralled the audience members were.

A later addition to our band of contributors was Brett Hart, a director who tells his own story of first encountering John's work. Again, I am grateful for your admiration of John, one of the several people who have told me face to face that their desire to make a career in films came upon them as they watched *Towering Inferno* or *King Kong* as a young child.

Thank you to all of you for helping to keep me going through the long haul when the prospect of a completed book seemed a long way off.

I also thank Julie Kirgo and the late Nick Redman, of Twilight Time, who brought *Rapture* out of obscurity and who were excited about this project. John derived so much benefit in the last years of his life from your belief in his talent. Julie considers *Towering Inferno* to be the best of the disaster movies of the Seventies.

Last but not least, I want to thank the lovely ladies of Precocity Press, who have brought our collection of essays to a beautiful completion. I wouldn't have this exquisitely-presented book without the labors of Susan Shankin, the owner, who conjured the beautiful layout and Susan Peters, the editor, who worked with me in a harmonious, collaborative way as we demonstrated the power of women working together.

BIOGRAPHIES

MARY GUILLERMIN was married to John for the last sixteen years of his life. She is the Director of Communications and a Senior Practitioner at the Pellin Institute, which offers training in Contribution Training & Gestalt (pellininstitute.com). She is a Licensed Marriage & Family Therapist in California, and a writer and solo show artist. She performed her first one-woman show, *From Crazy to Sane: A Tale of Feminine Mysticism, Magic & Madness* at Solofest 2020, the largest solo show festival on the West Coast, just before theaters closed due to the pandemic. In her show she highlights some key aspects of her marriage to John. She is also an accomplished collage artist.

BRETT A. HART (HartandSoul.net) is an Emmy-winning writer, producer, director, and owner of Hart & Soul Entertainment. Before he made his way to Hollywood as a high school student, Brett caught the attention of director Richard Franklin *(Psycho II, Cloak & Dagger)*. Mr. Franklin took the young aspiring director under his wing, which launched Brett's journey into film, spanning decades in both commercial television and features.

As creative director of one of the most innovative advertising agencies in the Midwest, Brett has received many awards including an Emmy and multiple Telly Awards. He went on to garner more accolades for his short films, most importantly *Dead End,* which was screened at the DGA as part of the TX Filmmakers Showcase. This led to his debut feature film, *Bone Dry*, starring Lance Henriksen and Luke Goss. After leaving Austin, Texas where he wrapped his PBS series *Ain't It Cool With Harry Knowles* (sponsored by IMAX), Brett now resides in Hollywood, where he is developing several television series in addition to his next feature film with his wife, singer/composer/writer/producer, Bonnie E. Hart.

Dr. Brian Hoyle is a Senior Lecturer at the University of Dundee. He has written extensively on British, European, and American cinema. In addition to numerous articles and book chapters on subjects ranging from Derek Jarman, to Joseph H. Lewis, to William Walton's film scores, he is the author of *The Cinema of John Boorman* (Scarecrow Press, 2012) and the co-editor of *British Art Cinema: Creativity, Experimentation, and Innovation* (Manchester University Press, 2019).

Kate Lees (adelphifilms.com) is the owner of Adelphi Films, which was a major producer and distributor of British films throughout the 1940s and '50s. Adelphi was established by Arthur Dent, Kate's grandfather, and produced and distributed numerous feature films. It gave many stars of the day their first appearance on the big screen, including Peter Sellers, Diana Dors, Petula Clark, Prunella Scales, Ronnie Corbett and many more. The company retains rights and ownership of the collection. The material is stored and preserved by the BFI in the National Archive. There is a wonderful document archive of stills, posters, original signed contracts, production costs and other memorabilia.

Olaf Möller is a critic based in Cologne. He had long-running columns in *Film Comment* and *Cinema Scope* magazines; in addition, he co-wrote and co-edited several books. He is currently also a senior programmer at the International Film Festival Rotterdam and holds the position of Professor for Film History and Theory at Aalto University (Helsinki).

RAY MORTON (raymorton.com) is a writer and film historian and the author of seven books including *King Kong: The History of a Movie Icon; Close Encounters of the Third Kind: The Making of Steven Spielberg's Classic Film; Amadeus: Music on Film; A Hard Day's Night: Music on Film; A Quick Guide to Screenwriting; A Quick Guide to Television Writing;* and *A Quick Guide to Film Directing.* A graduate of New York University, Morton has also co-written several produced teleplays, been a staff writer and story consultant for several television series, works as a screenplay consultant, writes articles for numerous publications, and is a columnist for *Script Magazine* (www.scriptmag.com).

VIC PRATT is a film archivist, writer, historian, and Blu-ray/DVD producer for the British Film Institute (BFI). He has written on film and television history for a range of books, magazines and video releases, as well as introducing screenings and film seasons at BFI Southbank. His book *The Bodies Beneath: The Flipside of British Film and Television,* co-authored with William Fowler, was published by Strange Attractor Press in 2019.

NEIL SINYARD is Emeritus Professor of Film Studies at the University of Hull, UK (a Department which he founded) and Visiting Professor of Film at the University of Lincoln, UK. He has published numerous books and articles on the cinema, including monographs on directors such as Billy Wilder, William Wyler, Fred Zinnemann, Alfred Hitchcock, Steven Spielberg, Richard Lester, Jack Clayton, Woody Allen and Nicolas Roeg, as well as books on silent movies, film comedy, film adaptations of literature, and representations of childhood on film. He has contributed essays, commentaries and interviews to over sixty DVD and Blu-ray releases. He helped to program and write the notes for numerous film seasons at the National Film Theatre in London and for the Irish Film Institute in Dublin; and was also for a while the Deputy Film Critic of the *Sunday Telegraph*. He is currently the Literary Editor of the *Graham Greene Newsletter* (published quarterly) and a regular lecturer at the annual Graham Greene Festival in Berkhamsted; a consultant and contributor to the *Oxford Dictionary of National Biography;* and a co-editor of the series on British Film Makers for Manchester University Press. His most recent book, *George Stevens: The Films of a Hollywood Giant,* was published by McFarland & Company in 2019.

SARAH STREET is Professor of Film at the University of Bristol, UK. She has published extensively on British cinema with books including *British National Cinema* (1997) and *Transatlantic Crossings: British Feature Films in the USA* (2002). For several years she has been researching the impact of color film technologies, aesthetics and culture. Her several publications on colour films include *Colour Films in Britain: The Negotiation of Innovation, 1900–55* (2012), winner of the British Association of Film, Television and Screen Studies prize for Best Monograph. Her latest books are *Deborah Kerr* (2018) and *Chromatic Modernity: Color, Cinema, and Media of the 1920s* (2019, co-authored with Joshua Yumibe). Her latest project is as Principal Investigator on *STUDIOTEC: Film Studios: Infrastructure, Culture, Innovation in Britain, France, Germany and Italy, 1930–60,* a European Research Council-funded Advanced Grant.

MELANIE WILLIAMS is Professor of Film and Television Studies at the University of East Anglia, UK. She has written extensively on British cinema and her books include *Transformation and Tradition in 1960s British Cinema; Female Stars of British Cinema; David Lean; Ealing Revisited;* and *British Women's Cinema*.

For more information & to stay in touch: JohnGuillermin.com
Visit: Facebook.com/JohnGuillerminBook
Contact: Mary Guillermin through Facebook Messenger